APPROACHES TO HOMER

APPROACHES TO HOMER
ANCIENT & MODERN

Editor

Robert J. Rabel

Contributors

Jonathan S. Burgess, Donald Lateiner,
Elizabeth Minchin, James V. Morrison, Rick M. Newton,
Robert J. Rabel, Hanna M. Roisman, Ruth Scodel,
William C. Scott, Donna F. Wilson

The Classical Press of Wales

First published in 2005 by
The Classical Press of Wales
15 Rosehill Terrace, Swansea SA1 6JN
Tel: +44 (0)1792 458397
Fax: +44 (0)1792 464067
www.classicalpressofwales.co.uk

Distributor in the United States of America:
The David Brown Book Co.
PO Box 511, Oakville, CT 06779
Tel: +1 (860) 945–9329
Fax: +1 (860) 945–9468

ISBN 1–905125–04–6

A catalogue record for this book is available from the British Library

Typeset by Andrew Buckley, Clunton, Shropshire
Printed and bound in the UK by Gomer Press, Llandysul, Ceredigion, Wales

―――――――――

The Classical Press of Wales, an independent venture, was founded in 1993, initially to support the work of classicists and ancient historians in Wales and their collaborators from further afield. More recently it has published work initiated by scholars internationally. While retaining a special loyalty to Wales and the Celtic countries, the Press welcomes scholarly contributions from all parts of the world.

The symbol of the Press is the Red Kite. This bird, once widespread in Britain, was reduced by 1905 to some five individuals confined to a small area known as 'The Desert of Wales' – the upper Tywi valley. Geneticists report that the stock was saved from terminal inbreeding by the arrival of one stray female bird from Germany. After much careful protection, the Red Kite now thrives – in Wales and beyond.

CONTENTS

INTRODUCTION

Robert J. Rabel

The choice of a title for this book of essays on the *Iliad* and the *Odyssey* requires some explanation. The title, it should be said, is not intended to mark a mutually exclusive dichotomy between ancient and modern approaches to the Homeric poems. Of course, it is certainly possible to point out many advances made in Homeric scholarship since the publication of F.A. Wolf's *Prolegomena ad Homerum* in 1795, an event usually taken to inaugurate the modern era of scholarship on Homer. However, much of what is most *modern* in the way the Homeric poems are currently being studied is at the same time also in an important sense quite *ancient*. As a result, the efficacy and truth of any kind of simple evolutionary model for the development of Homeric scholarship, tracing a movement from an ancient and imperfect to a modern and purely scientific understanding of the *Iliad* and *Odyssey*, need to be called into question.

In what still remains one of the best surveys available on the history of Homeric scholarship, Adam Parry proposed just such a model. Parry uses the terms *ancient* and *modern* to mark different historical stages in an evolutionary march toward a more perfect understanding of the *Iliad* and *Odyssey*, gained in the nineteenth and twentieth centuries. In Parry's view, the ancients simply lacked the kind of historical sense that characterizes the modern period, and they suffered under the additional handicap of possessing the *Iliad* and the *Odyssey* as too much a part of themselves to be able to look at the poems with the necessary and proper degree of objectivity. Thus Parry speaks of a distinctly 'scientific' approach to the study of the *Iliad* and *Odyssey* beginning with Wolf's work (A. Parry 1971, xi–xiv).[1] (Indeed, Wolf seems to have understood his approach to Homer in exactly these terms, seeing his work as a reaction against ancient ways of understanding Homer [Graziosi 2002, 13].) As Parry tells the story, Wolf ushered in the development of the so-called 'Higher Criticism' of the Homeric poems in the nineteenth century, a movement led primarily by German scholars like Lachmann, Hermann, and Wilamowitz, the latter of whom Parry in a nice phrase characterizes as 'one of the most influential of the discerping critics' (ibid., xvii). In the nineteenth century and afterwards, scholars known collectively as Analysts saw the Homeric poems as in one way or another combinations of originally separate poems or accretions added later on to an original text (A. Parry, ibid., xvi–xvii). On the other hand, the Unitarians argued for unity of authorship, believing that the Homeric poems were too perfect in structure and content to be the compositions of a series of poets and editors (ibid., xviii). Following his account of the Analysts and Unitarians, Parry takes up the contribution to scholarship of his father Milman Parry. In addition to the work of the Analysts and Unitarians, Milman Parry found background upon which to draw in recent linguistic study that demonstrated the dependence of Homeric language on the verse form in which it was composed. Out of these three major influences, according to Adam Parry, Milman Parry developed the oral-formulaic theory of Homeric composition (A. Parry 1971, xxi), which has proved to be an indisputably fruitful modern approach to the *Iliad* and *Odyssey*. Several essays in this volume adopt some variant of the approach to Homeric poetry that Milman Parry inaugurated.

Nonetheless, the question as to whether modern approaches to Homer possess the initial advantage over ancient approaches of being more 'scientific' obviously depends upon how one chooses to define the term 'scientific'. If scientific facts are facts 'detached from the circumstances of their fabrication, which come to be used and accepted without qualification' (Kennedy 2002, 15) or 'statements with no modality and no trace of authorship',[2] modalities being defined here as 'qualifying phrases or other perspectival markers of temporal or local reference' (Kennedy 2002, 15), then modern approaches to the Homeric poems seem to lose the special advantage over the ancients of being scientific. For just such perspectival markers characterize modern as well as ancient approaches to the *Iliad* and the *Odyssey*. Adam Parry's account of Homeric scholarship, for all its importance and acute insight, mistakenly, I think, analyzes modern Homeric scholarship as if it were work taking place in scholarly laboratories dedicated to the discovery of objective facts about the poems, facts divorced from the immediate circumstances of their discovery and existing in their own right apart from the conditions of their representation. But such does not seem to be the case. Though the introduction to a collection of essays on Homer does not seem the place to pursue the point in the detail it deserves, I suggest that 'unscientific' modalities bearing traces of perspectival markers and temporal references are to be found in Homeric scholarship of any age, modern as well as ancient, and that particularly glaring examples can be gleaned from even a cursory examination of the 'war' between the Analysts and Unitarians early in the twentieth century, which Adam Parry places in the age of scientific criticism. This was a scholarly war in many respects mimicking the First World War, waged in that period on the battlefields of Europe.

E.R. Dodds opens up a broad historical perspective from which to view the controversy between the Analysts and Unitarians. Dodds points out that the fields of literary criticism, religious studies, and philosophy were simultaneously undergoing rapid changes in the early decades of the twentieth century, as many began to find fault with much of the thought characteristic of the more robust, self-confident intellectual life of the nineteenth century. Unitarian thought is at least partly a reaction against the analyst tradition of the preceding hundred years. So far Dodds' analysis resembles Adam Parry's. At the same time, however, Dodds notes – though only in passing – that social and political issues may have played a part in determining the intensity of the controversy. For in some quarters, Dodds says, resentment against the Germans arose as a result of the First World War and, he adds, the arrogance of some of the exponents of analysis was felt to be typical of the German mind (1954, 8–9). To take several specific examples of the kind of hostility Dodds describes, in the pages of *The Classical Journal*, an American publication at that time largely under the control of the arch-Unitarian John A. Scott (at least insofar as Homeric scholarship was concerned), salvos still reverberate from academic missiles fired across the Atlantic at German philology in general and the Analysts' approach to the Homeric poems in particular. Without addressing the Germans by name, Scott's review of Walter Leaf's *Homer and History* quotes with favor Leaf's protest against 'the extinction of intellectual interest in the flood of barbarous materialism which has been let loose upon Europe' (Scott 1915–16, 509–10). B.W. Mitchell's analysis of the nature of German *Kultur* is more direct and, I think, would have found favor with Scott and other Unitarians. (The more cool-headed Unitarian Samuel Eliot Bassett, himself also a frequent contributor to the pages of *The Classical Journal*, would remain a notable exception.) Mitchell defines *Kultur* as,

> the integration of individual and national energies for national and dynastic aggrandizement, relentlessly and unscrupulously employing to this end all the resources of contemporary knowledge, both theoretical and practical, and postulating the exclusive and discriminatory favor of a God conceived as a magnified reflection of national characteristics.

'A people with this attitude', Mitchell continues, 'inevitably...becomes the victim of its own psychology' (1918–19, 418). Mitchell's point is expressed in even blunter language in an unsigned editorial in the same volume of the *Classical Journal*, which quotes with favor a remark of Arthur Quiller-Couch: 'As I see it, the more you beat Fritz by becoming like him, the more he has won'. 'More and more are we coming to hate the word [*Kultur*]', the editorial concludes, 'and in the not distant future we will have none of it, in the German sense of the term' (*Classical Journal* 1918/19, 3–4). While the Unitarian approach to Homer obviously goes back to the Greeks, the special brand of Unitarian thought that came into being in the early decades of the twentieth century – at least in America – seems in some large measure to have been an attempt to prove that Unitarians were different from 'Fritz'.

The objection might be raised that the above definition of the 'scientific' is far too stringent and needs to be amended so as to impart a more constructivist sense to the term, which would acknowledge that particular historical and perspectival conditions at least partly determine the nature and outcome even of scientific research. In that case, however, the boundaries between scientific work and the interpretive activity of textual research would be dissolved, as Kennedy has pointed out (2002, 16). Modern approaches to the Homeric poems would then still appear to be no more scientific than any of a variety of ancient approaches.

The last several decades of Homeric scholarship have been characterized by the fresh application to the *Iliad* and *Odyssey* of work derived from a number of academic disciplines, harnessed to serve the interests of traditional philology. As R.B. Rutherford explains the complexities of the current scenario,

> Readers in a post-war, post-modernist, post-imperialist age naturally find themselves interested in different aspects of the Homeric poems and the world that they portray from those which preoccupied Arnold or Jebb or Wilamowitz. In the last fifty or so years anthropology, psychology, comparative religion, feminism, narratology, have all provided fresh and provocative ideas which have enriched or modified earlier certainties.[3]

What needs to be emphasized, however, is that many of these quite modern ways of looking at Homer are also in many respects returns to ancient ways of looking at Homer. In the words of Jasper Griffin, much of value can be garnered in the study of the Homeric poems when one approaches the texts 'in a manner not wholly different from the way in which the Greeks themselves approached them' (1980, xiv). Many of the essays in this volume conform to such a methodological approach. In summarizing them, I emphasize the ways in which the various topics covered adopt approaches to the Homeric poems that resemble those prevalent in antiquity. I hope that in the process I have not acted presumptuously nor done too much violence to the authors' original intentions. The summaries and the views expressed in them are my own.

In 'Demodokos' "*Iliad*" and Homer's', Donna F. Wilson examines in detail the semantics of Homeric μῆτις, taking a lead from the ancient scholiasts, who offered a plausible explanation for Demodocus' song about a quarrel between Achilles and Odysseus in Book 8 of the *Odyssey*. Ancient commentators locate the quarrel between the two heroes in events taking place after the death of Hector and concerning a dispute as to whether Troy would be taken by means of physical force (βίη) or mental prowess (μῆτις). While modern scholarship has consistently equated the mental prowess (μῆτις) at issue with a power of cunning and deceit operating through disguise, the language of the ancient scholiasts bears witness to an ambiguity over whether Homeric μῆτις is in fact σύνεσις (intelligence) or δόλος (cunning). Beginning from the scholiasts' observation, Wilson examines the semantics of Homeric μῆτις in detail. She argues that although μῆτις refers to intelligence, and specifically to intelligent self-restraint, in both Homeric epics, the meanings and functions of μῆτις are not identical in the two poems. Whereas the *Odyssey* is concerned to conflate μῆτις and δόλος, making mental prowess the equivalent of cunning, the *Iliad* distinguishes between the two. (In fact, the conflation of μῆτις and δόλος almost invariably produces negative results in the *Iliad*.) Wilson is not concerned to suggest a diachronic development in which μῆτις originally designated intelligence (σύνεσις) and was later conflated with cunning (δόλος) in the *Odyssey*. Rather, Homeric epic seems to evince two quite different traditional definitions of μῆτις and, as a result, two distinct understandings of the strength-intelligence polarity. Moreover, as Wilson argues, the proper definition of heroic μῆτις and, hence, of the opposition between μῆτις and physical force (βίη) formed a locus of inter-textual polemic between two competing poetic traditions.

In different ways and to different extents, the articles by William C. Scott, Elizabeth Minchin, James V. Morrison, and Donald Lateiner are concerned with questions of psychology and thus take up a concern with Homeric psychology prevalent in antiquity – especially among the Stoics.[4] In 'The patterning of the similes in Book 2 of the *Iliad*', Scott studies the similes of Book 2 in order to examine the force of the tradition on both poet and audience. He shows that it is of major importance to the interpretation of the similes to acknowledge that the audience had a firm knowledge of the alternatives that the poet considered and thereby could evaluate what he was accepting, modifying, and suppressing in supporting his narrative with a simile. In analyzing the processes of composition employed by the poet, Scott acknowledges the importance of Gestalt psychology and frame semantics in enriching our understanding of the interpretation of Homeric similes, but he expresses a preference for the theory of scripts developed by Schank and Abelson as offering a more precise parallel to both the interpretation and creation of the Homeric simile. In drawing on the knowledge of simile families shared with his audience, the poet exercises artistic choice within the traditional devices and language of early Greek narrative in order to tell his own story as well as possible. The creative processes that produced the final formation of each simile can never be adequately defined, yet the talent, poetic brilliance, and remarkable abilities of later poets should not be denied to Homer, as though he were mindlessly dependent on modes of expression which were prevalent in his own time.

In 'Homer on autobiographical memory: the case of Nestor', Elizabeth Minchin assesses the ancient understanding of the workings of memory in Homer in comparison with modern studies of memory and its functions in everyday life. She concentrates upon a case-study that illustrates particular aspects of memory in Homer: namely, the elderly Nestor and his habit of reminiscence. Modern psychology has shown that people retain in memory recollections of events in which they played a part, especially those in which they played a leading role. These recollections are gathered together into a life-history, which is edited and adjusted at will, so that it conforms to and supplements a person's self-image. As people age, they tend more and more to reminisce about the past. Individuals draw upon a life-history, in particular upon the events of their second and third decades, the period of 'landmark' events in their lives. These memories appear to be particularly vivid, partly because they were critical events that occurred in the formative years, partly because the individual reminiscing was the protagonist in these narratives, and partly because the events are rehearsed so often. The poet's account of Nestor is consistent with these modern findings. Indeed, one respect in which the poet may be tested is in his use of the so-called 'nostalgic wish', which Nestor expresses when he introduces memories from his youth and early adulthood, but which he does not use when he refers to events of subsequent decades.

In 'Similes for Odysseus and Penelope: mortality, divinity, identity', James V. Morrison examines comparisons applied to Odysseus and Penelope in Books 19–23 of the *Odyssey*. One aspect of the exploration concerns whether similes describe physical appearances or inner psychological states. Homer's use of similes is then related to the Odyssean themes of mortality, divinity, and identity. While Odyseus is often described as god-like, it is possible to see certain similes as a corrective to this view of heroes. A second function of similes is to offer insight regarding Penelope, the most enigmatic of Odyssean characters. While the external audience is privy to Telemachus' and Odysseus' plot against the suitors, for an inordinately long time they do not learn definitively what Penelope is thinking or planning. The similes, however, allow us – even without knowing exactly what Penelope is thinking – to know what she is feeling.

While Homer reveals character in a variety of ways, inner psychological states may be subtly revealed by means of similes.

'Telemakhos' one sneeze and Penelope's two laughs (*Odyssey* 17. 541–50, 18. 158–68)' continues Donald Lateiner's work in the application to the Homeric poems of research in the field of physiological psychology, which cuts across three millennia of Homeric textual and contextual criticism. (Somatic semiosis, he tells us elsewhere, has been studied not only in the modern world but also by the ancients, including Plato, Aristotle, Cicero, Dionysios of Halikarnassos, Quintilian, and the Homeric commentator Eustathios [Lateiner 1995, 6].) Lateiner discusses the one sneeze that appears in the Homer poems, a sneeze of Telemakhos (*Od.* 17.541 ff.). He argues that the time and place of this uncontrollable act and his mother's instant and aggressive reading of this spasmodic 'accident' as an omen conform to widespread ancient divinatory practice and interpretation. It is a nonverbal κληδών (omen), one of many divine signs that crowd the crisis of the plot of the *Odyssey*. Penelope's immediately consequent first laugh marks a shift from female victimhood to active resolve. She soon laughs again, her last laugh, as she explains to a maid her table-turning plan for wealth-extraction from the dull-witted suitors. Humans' seizing on seemingly arbitrary or apparently coincidental events as divine signs activates them in Homeric narrative (and elsewhere even in non-fictional texts). A catalogue of ancient sneezes and sneeze-interpretation (ptarmoscopy) is also provided.

In 'Old men and chirping cicadas in the *Teichoskopia*', Hanna M. Roisman presents a reading of the *Teichoskopia* in *Iliad* 3 that follows in the Aristarchean tradition of 'interpreting Homer from Homer'.[5] She argues that Homer crafts the scene to present a double view of the old men, one positive and one negative. On the one hand, Priam and his companions on the wall of Troy are presented as foolish, garrulous, and ineffectual. On the other hand, the old men are depicted as more reliable and cautious than the young, more stable of mind, and able to give thought to consequences by being able to base their judgments on prior experience. The dual perspective given to the old men on the wall brings together their wisdom and their powerlessness and thus embodies the tragedy of the human condition.

Jonathan S. Burgess' 'The death of Achilles by rhapsodes' uses the methods of modern Neoanalysis to demonstrate the presence within the *Iliad* of non-Homeric material about the death and funeral of Achilles. He shows, first, that reflections in the poem of myths about Achilles are more organized than has previously been suspected and then proceeds to argue that the patterning of Homeric allusion is comparable to techniques of rhapsodic performance. The similarity, he argues, is more than coincidental and is indicative of the influence of performance on Homeric narrative. Moreover, reference to the techniques of performance explains much about narrative strategy in the *Iliad* and also suggests something about the historical context of the poem's genesis within a performance culture. The *Iliad* was not simply a poem that happened to be performed, he argues; rather, its very composition resulted from performance.

The essays of Rick M. Newton, Ruth Scodel, and Robert J. Rabel approach the *Odyssey* from a narratological perspective, a modern approach to Homer that was pioneered in antiquity by Plato in the *Republic* and by Aristotle in the *Poetics*. According to Plato, all literature is properly analyzed as one or another form of narrative (*Rep.* 392d). Aristotle, for his part, seems to have taken the first steps in the critical narratological project of distinguishing between the author and the narrator of a work of literature (de Jong 2004, 8), a fundamental principle of narratology that was not fully recognized by modern scholars until the mid-1950s (Stanzel 1984, 81). In 'The Ciconians, revisited (Homer, *Odyssey* 9.39–66)', Newton analyzes the competing voices and points of view through which the Ciconian episode is narrated and in terms of which it must be interpreted and understood by both the internal audience of Phaeacians and the external audience of the poem. On the one hand, the external audience is invited by the narrative of the *Odyssey* to balance Odysseus' allegation that Zeus willed the disastrous attack against the Ciconians with Zeus' own claim in Book 1 that the gods are not responsible for undue mortal suffering. The external audience is thereby compelled to consider the possibility that Odysseus is to be included among those mortals who blame Zeus for sufferings they themselves could have prevented. The internal audience of Phaeacians, on the other hand, who have not heard the opening book of the poem and must rely solely on Odysseus' personal narrative, remain completely unaware of any possible discrepancy between the hero's and the god's differing points of view. The *Ciconeia*, he concludes, is 'narratively paradigmatic' for the external audience of the poem – though not for the Phaeacians – in that it establishes the hero's propensity for mistakenly attributing to the gods sufferings he actually brings upon himself.

In 'Odysseus' ethnographic digressions', Ruth Scodel reviews the peculiarities of the introductions to some of Odysseus' adventures (Cyclopes, Aeolus, Laestrygonians, Cimmerians). Much scholarship has looked for the sources of the material in travelers' tales, folklore, and earlier epic. Although critics have certainly noticed the narrative peculiarities of these passages, their complexities have not received the attention they deserve from a narratological perspective. These introductions are not relevant to the adventures, exceed what Odysseus could plausibly have learned, and use a strongly authoritative style. Scodel argues that these passages represent a 'proto-ethnographic' subgenre that bestows special authority on autopsy.

In 'The art of creative listening in the *Odyssey*', Robert J. Rabel argues that in the prologue of the *Odyssey* the poet is concerned to acknowledge the important role that listening played in his own creative work as a poet. Using evidence garnered from the prooemium and from the poem itself, Rabel argues that we can derive a conception of the good poet as a skilled listener, who both attends to others and – perhaps of equal importance – overhears *himself* in the process of composition. Likewise, within the poem, Odysseus, the poet's self-reflexive counterpart, flourishes as both hero and storyteller at least partly because of an aptitude for creative listening. And finally, the poet invites the poem's external audience to reflect on the importance of their being good listeners also.

The recent breakdown of the barriers separating ancient from modern approaches to the Homeric poems finds an apt analogue in the study and interpretation of Plato and perhaps signals a significant movement in Classics in general. Julia Annas has argued that in the study of Platonic ethics something is to be gained when we look at ancient methods of interpreting Plato – in particular, when we consider the work of the so-called 'Middle Platonists'. In the writings of these early interpreters of Plato, we may find something *old*, Annas argues, in the sense that the works of ancient interpreters are worthy objects of historical study. At the same time we may also find something *new*. For while modern scholarship would never accord to Plato the kind of reverential respect and authority granted him by the ancients, ancient interpreters offer insightful ways of looking at Plato that, while having had little influence on the last two hundred years or so of Platonic criticism, offer much from which modern scholars can and should profit. The Middle Platonists offer a non-developmental or Unitarian approach to the study of Plato that cuts against the grain of the distinctly modern developmental model that divides the Platonic dialogues into early, middle, and late stages (Annas 1998, 1–2).

In the writings of early critics and interpreters of Homer, we in similar fashion find something *old* in the sense that the views of the ancients regarding the Homeric poems are increasingly being investigated as worthy objects of historical study and are being represented in new editions, translations of texts, and works of secondary literature.[6] At the same time, however, we also find something *new*. Of course, just as in the study of Platonic ethics, scholars no longer accord the *Iliad* and *Odyssey* the kind of reverential status later reserved for the Bible in the ancient

Mediterranean region – and in many quarters today. No modern scholar would think of tracing back to Homer virtually *all* accomplishments in the fields of rhetoric, historical methodology, and political discourse, as is done, for example, in Pseudo-Plutarch's *Essay on the Life and Poetry of Homer* (Keaney and Lamberton, 1996). Nonetheless, the fact remains that much of what is most modern in the study of Homer is not so distinctly modern after all.

The essays collected in this volume (with the exception of William C. Scott's) were all delivered at the ninety-ninth meeting of the Classical Association of the Middle West and South in Lexington, Kentucky in April of 2003. Beyond being characterized – more or less – by a certain 'unity of place' the essays, it is to be hoped, display a certain 'unity of time' as well. For they illustrate a modern movement that characterizes much recent Homeric criticism: a willingness to reach back across the entire span of Homeric reception in order to shed light on many aspects of the *Iliad* and the *Odyssey*.

Notes

[1] Latacz 1996, 5 ff., like Parry, notes that 'Homer's works have been analyzed with scientific methods in modern times for roughly two hundred years'. Latacz, however, places special emphasis in his account on the 'many dead ends' and the 'wasted energy' that characterize Homeric research over the course of these centuries.

[2] Latour and Woolgar 1986, 82, quoted in Kennedy 2002, 15.

[3] Rutherford 1998, 1.

[4] For example, in Galen's *De Placitis Hippocratis et Platonis*, a particularly rich source of direct quotations of the early Stoics, there are thirty-five direct quotations attributed to Chrysippus regarding Homeric psychology: see Blumberg 2004.

[5] The principle is preserved in a D-scholium at *Iliad* 5.385.

[6] See, for example, Keaney and Lamberton 1996 and Lamberton and Keaney 1992. Graziosi has recently argued against the tendency to disregard ancient conceptions of the poet Homer and his poems (Graziosi 2002).

Bibliography

Annas, J.
   1998   *Platonic Ethics, Old and New*, Ithaca.
Blumberg, L.
   2004   *Chrysippean Quotations from Galen's* De Placitis Hippocratis et Platonis, M.A. thesis, University of Kentucky, Lexington.
de Jong, I.J.F.
   2004   *Narrators and Focalizers: The presentation of the story in the* Iliad, 2nd edn, London.

Dodds, E.R.
    1954   'Homer', in M. Platnauer (ed.) *Fifty Years of Classical Scholarship,* Oxford.
Graziosi, B.
    2002   *Inventing Homer: The early reception of epic,* Cambridge.
Griffin, J.
    1980   *Homer on Life and Death,* Oxford.

Keaney, J.J. and Lamberton, R. (eds.)
    1996   *[Plutarch] Essay on the Life and Poetry of Homer,* Atlanta.
Kennedy, D.F.
    2002   *Rethinking Reality: Lucretius and the textualization of nature,* Ann Arbor.
Lamberton, R. and Keaney, J.J. (eds.)
    1992   *Homer's Ancient Readers: The hermeneutics of Greek epic's earliest exegetes,* Princeton.
Latacz, J.
    1996   *Homer: His art and his world,* trans. J.P. Holoka, Ann Arbor.
Lateiner, D.
    1995   *Sardonic Smile: Nonverbal behavior in Homeric epic,* Ann Arbor.
Latour, B. and Woolgar, S.
    1986   *Laboratory Life: The construction of scientific facts,* 2nd edn, Princeton.
Mitchell, B.W.
    1918–19   'The early centuries of *Kultur*', *Classical Journal* 14, 418–32.
Parry, A.
    1971   'Introduction', in *The Making of Homeric Verse: The collected papers of Milman Parry,* New York and Oxford.
Rutherford, R.B.
    1998   'Introduction', in I. McAuslan and P. Walcot (eds.) *Homer,* Oxford.
Scott, J.A.
    1915–16   Review of Walter Leaf, 'Homer and History', *Classical Journal* 11, 509–10.
Stanzel, F.K.
    1984   *A Theory of Narrative,* Cambridge.

1

DEMODOKOS' '*ILIAD*' AND HOMER'S

Donna F. Wilson

The *Iliad* and *Odyssey* present perhaps the most celebrated instances of the ancient Greek inclination to structure reality in terms of polarities. It has, accordingly, been an axiom of Homeric interpretation that the *Iliad* presents its hero as an exemplar of heroic might, or βίη, and the *Odyssey* its hero as a man of cunning intelligence, or μῆτις. Notwithstanding, the poet sets the two epic heroes and their primary modes of operation in *direct* competition only in Demodokos' song about a quarrel between Odysseus and Achilleus (*Od.* 8.73–82).[1] Previous scholarship has shown that the poet deploys Demodokos' first song, about the quarrel, taken together with his second and third songs about the love of Ares and Aphrodite and the wooden horse respectively, to exalt intelligence, μῆτις, over might, βίη. As we shall see, the bard's songs also advance an Odyssean project of conflating intelligence, μῆτις, and guile, δόλος – a conflation the *Iliad* implicitly resists. In fact, the difference in the semantics of μῆτις and resulting constructions of the μῆτις-βίη polarity in the *Iliad* and *Odyssey* is sufficiently marked that it leads me to posit the nature of the opposition as a locus of intertextual polemic. Put another way, each canonical epic deploys a substantively different concept of μῆτις in a poetic competition to define the μῆτις-βίη polarity. At stake is each poem's project of presenting and praising its hero as successfully mediating the μῆτις-βίη opposition while, at the same time, depicting the hero of the other epic as operating successfully in only one of the two heroic modes. As a result, in addition to their primary modes of operation, the Iliadic Achilleus and the Odyssean Odysseus can also be seen to exercise μῆτις and βίη respectively; yet the traditional differences between the two heroes are not deconstructed radically. Further, Demodokos' first song can be seen to exploit an 'older' Iliadic epic model, featuring extreme polarization of μῆτις and βίη, in order to privilege the *Odyssey*'s 'newer and more sophisticated' synthesis of the two modes of operation.

In this paper, I examine the Homeric semantics of μῆτις, not only in relation to terminology with which it is associated, but also in relation to the strength-intelligence polarity in which it is embedded and to the intertextual project in which it is implicated. In conclusion, I explore briefly comparanda from Near Eastern and Indo-European traditions for the Iliadic semantics of μῆτις and the corresponding polarity. To begin, however, we turn to Demodokos' song about a quarrel between the best of the Achaians, which foregrounds both the semantics of μῆτις and a purported intratextual contest between μῆτις and βίη.

Demodokos' *'Iliad'*

Demodokos performs his first song for Alkinoös, king of the Phaiakes, and his guests, following a banquet in the palace hall. The narrator summarizes the contents for the Homeric audience:

> Μοῦσ' ἄρ' ἀοιδὸν ἀνῆκεν ἀειδέμεναι κλέα ἀνδρῶν,
> οἴμης, τῆς τότ' ἄρα κλέος οὐρανὸν εὐρὺν ἵκανε,
> 75 νεῖκος Ὀδυσσῆος καὶ Πηλεΐδεω Ἀχιλῆος,
> ὥς ποτε δηρίσαντο θεῶν ἐν δαιτὶ θαλείῃ
> ἐκπάγλοις ἐπέεσσιν, ἄναξ δ' ἀνδρῶν Ἀγαμέμνων
> χαῖρε νόῳ, ὅ τ' ἄριστοι Ἀχαιῶν δηριόωντο.
> ὣς γάρ οἱ χρείων μυθήσατο Φοῖβος Ἀπόλλων
> 80 Πυθοῖ ἐν ἠγαθέῃ, ὅθ' ὑπέρβη λάϊνον οὐδὸν
> χρησόμενος. τότε γάρ ῥα κυλίνδετο πήματος ἀρχὴ
> Τρωσί τε καὶ Δαναοῖσι Διὸς μεγάλου διὰ βουλάς.

> The Muse stirred the singer to sing the famous deeds of men
> from the song whose fame then reached the wide heaven,
> 75 the quarrel between Odysseus and Peleus' son, Achilleus,
> how these once contended at the gods' generous festival,
> with terrible words, so that the lord of men, Agamemnon,
> was happy in his mind that the best of the Achaians were quarreling;
> for so Phoibos Apollo had spoken, prophecying to him
> 80 in sacred Pytho, when he had stepped across the stone threshold
> to consult; for then the beginning of woe rolled on, for
> Trojans and Danaans, through the plan of great Zeus.[2]

> (*Od.* 8.73–82)

Whether or not the details of this quarrel were familiar to Homer's audiences – a question I take up below, Demodokos' first song presents us with an allusion to an otherwise unattested epic song about a quarrel between Achilleus and Odysseus. Some of the elements bear thematic resemblance to Homer's *Iliad*. The poet, inspired by the Muse, sings the epic fame, κλέα ἀνδρῶν, of heroes in the Trojan War.[3] He begins with a quarrel, νεῖκος, between two heroes whom he identifies as best of

2

the Achaians, ἄριστοι Ἀχαιῶν. Achilleus appears as 'son of Peleus' and Agamemnon as 'lord of men'. Apollo and the plan of Zeus are implicated in the quarrel, which is in turn the beginning of woes for the Achaians and Trojans. Given its striking evocation of Iliadic themes, Demodokos' first song has generated controversy at least since the time of Aristarchus. Does it allude obliquely to Homer's *Iliad*? to an alternate *Iliad*, a casualty of Panhellenic selection? to a phantom epic the poet created from a cloud? And as important, what is Demodokos' '*Iliad*' doing in our *Odyssey*?

The idea that Demodokos' song is a pastiche based on the proem to our *Iliad* has been shown to be untenable.[4] Even if one accepted the literary methods of source criticism implied in that theory, the differences between the two texts are decisive. Neoanalyst critics have posited that the story derives from the *Cypria*, where Achilleus is reported to have quarreled with Agamemnon over being invited last to a banquet on Tenedos.[5] The only reason to connect Odysseus with the quarrel from the epic cycle is a fragment from Sophocles' *Syndeipnoi* (fr. 66, Pearson), in which Odysseus gets involved and an altercation with Achilleus ensues. But, as Jenny Clay points out, the real quarrel on Tenedos is between Achilleus and Agamemnon, and not between Achilleus and Odysseus.[6]

Ancient commentators offer a more plausible account of the matter. They surmised that the dispute Demodokos alludes to took place toward the end of the Trojan War, after the death of Hektor, with which Homer's *Iliad* ends. At issue was whether Troy would be taken by means of strength or intelligence (Scholia H.Q.V. at 8.75 and B.E. at 8.77). On this view, Demodokos' '*Iliad*' sets the two heroes and their primary modes of operation in direct conflict in one epic song.

Gregory Nagy and Jenny Clay, in independent and influential analyses of this passage, both accept the scholiasts' explanation as the most feasible, as do I. They arrive, however, at divergent interpretations of Demodokos' first song. Nagy argues that what we see in Demodokos' song amounts to an Iliadic overture.[7] It draws on a repertory of traditional material, common to our *Iliad* and *Odyssey*, which includes a standard motif involving rival heroes who reify the opposition between μῆτις and βίη. He concludes that Demodokos' song alludes to an extant Iliadic tradition, but not to Homer's *Iliad*.

> Like our *Iliad*, the *Iliad* that Demodokos could have sung would feature the *mênis* 'anger' of Achilles and Apollo. Unlike our *Iliad*, however, this Iliadic tradition would feature Odysseus, not Agamemnon, as the prime offender of Achilles. Unlike our *Iliad*, this *Iliad* would have the chief resentment of Achilles center on the slighting of his *biē* 'might'. An *Iliad* composed by Demodokos would have been a poem with a structure more simple and more

broad, with an Achilles who is even perhaps more crude than the ultimately refined hero that we see emerging at the end of our *Iliad*. I have little doubt that such an *Iliad* was indeed in the process of evolving when it was heard in the *Odyssey* tradition which evolved into our *Odyssey*.[8]

Clay contends that it is contrary to the *Odyssey*'s strategy to deploy a caricature of Achilleus.[9] She thus concentrates on Demodokos' song as expressing the contrast between μῆτις and βίη, embodied in the two heroes and carried out in a rivalry between the two poetic traditions. She demonstrates that Demodokos' first song complements his last, the song about the wooden horse (*Od.* 8.499–520): the issue raised in the quarrel is thus decided in the event of the wooden horse, and μῆτις wins the day. She departs from Nagy in her view that, although Demodokos' *Iliad* is composed of an amalgam of familiar material, it comprises an *Iliad* that never existed. Accordingly, the purpose of Demodokos' '*Iliad*' is to display the poet's freedom to transform traditional themes into something new, and, additionally, to imply not that Agamemnon misunderstood the oracle, but that the *Iliad* got the wrong quarrel.

Heubeck, West and Hainsworth, in their commentary on Demodokos' first song, propose that it exalts Odysseus as an opponent of Achilleus, which he is not in the *Iliad*.[10] Moreover, they say, this elevation is significant for critical interpretation, for:

> Achilles was the last and greatest of those heroes who solved their problems by excess of violence; Odysseus represents a newer idea…probably congenial to many in the Homeric audience, the cool opportunist, valiant but prudent, and not ashamed to stoop to conquer.[11]

Put another way, Achilleus and, by extension, Iliadic heroism win conflicts and contests for supremacy (ἔρις) by an older and cruder strategy of brute force, or βίη, and that in excess. In contrast, Odysseus and, by extension, Odyssean heroism win such conflicts and contests by a newer and mentally more sophisticated strategy of cunning, or μῆτις. Their analysis illustrates a reflex in Homeric scholarship to interpret the relation between the *Iliad* and the *Odyssey* in evolutionary terms. This reflex is arguably conditioned, at least in part, by the *Odyssey*'s own apparently successful strategy of intertextual allusion, in which it deploys its narrative of post-Trojan War events to (mis)represent itself as also post-Iliadic – chronologically, theologically, and socially. Demodokos' first song, for instance, positions the singers' internal and external audiences as looking back at Trojan War epic as an artifact, a thing of the past, even as Odysseus' return is yet unfolding.[12] That tactical positioning is not necessarily indicative of the actual historical relation between the two epic traditions as they were being textualized.

If we accept the proposition that Demodokos' first and third songs, taken together, set μῆτις and βίη in direct confrontation and assert the superiority of μῆτις, we should ask whether the semantics of μῆτις and, hence, construction of the μῆτις-βίη polarity in Demodokos' *'Iliad'* correspond to that presented in Homer's *Iliad*. Since publication of Marcel Detienne's and Jean-Pierre Vernant's seminal *Cunning Intelligence in Greek Culture and Society*, the view has prevailed that μῆτις was used and understood consistently in Greek myth and literature, from Homer to Oppian, to mean a power of cunning and deceit, operating through disguise.[13] On this view, μῆτις was associated throughout with a coherent semantic field including guile (δόλος), deceit (ἀπάτη), and many-faceted (ποικίλος). It was used regularly, Detienne and Vernant contend, to describe situations governed by use of cunning intelligence, deceit, and guile, rather than force. Indeed, μῆτις emerges in their discussion as something of a trump card, for it enables one to reverse unfavorable circumstances and triumph over stronger adversaries.[14]

The scholiasts, however, commenting on Demodokos' song, hint at ambiguity over the meaning of the mental prowess at issue in the contest between Achilleus and Odysseus. They express the opposing modes of operation as 'courage' vs. 'intelligence' or 'understanding' (ἀνδρεία vs. σύνεσις), 'might' vs. 'guile' (βίη vs. δόλος), or 'the physical' vs. 'the mental' (τὰ σωματικά vs. τὰ ψυχικά). In other words, the scholiasts do not associate μῆτις necessarily with trickery. Moreover, as we shall see, the word μῆτις is associated in Homer not only with terms for guile and deceit, but also with a semantic field including counsel (βουλή), prudent (ἐπίφρων), thought (νόος), and, indirectly, with justice (δίκη).

The semantics of μῆτις in Homer

Both Homeric epics associate μῆτις with terms for prudence and good counsel, with no discernible connotation of deceit or cunning. Moreover, both poems depict the opposition between μῆτις and βίη as a contest between brute (natural) force and patient self-restraint.

In Homer's *Iliad*, μῆτις and βίη are brought most directly into confrontation in the story of Antilochos and the chariot race in the funeral games. Although the narrative brings μῆτις and δόλος into the same orbit, it does so not to equate but to distinguish them. Prior to the contest, Nestor counsels Antilochos how a driver endowed with μῆτις may win a chariot race against an opponent who possesses faster horses and, hence, superior βίη:

> τῶν δ' ἵπποι μὲν ἔασιν ἀφάρτεροι, οὐδὲ μὲν αὐτοὶ
> πλείονα ἴσασιν σέθεν αὐτοῦ μητίσασθαι.

ἀλλ' ἄγε δὴ σὺ φίλος μῆτιν ἐμβάλλεο θυμῷ
παντοίην, ἵνα μή σε παρεκπροφύγῃσιν ἄεθλα.
315 μῆτι τοι δρυτόμος μέγ' ἀμείνων ἠὲ βίηφι·
μῆτι δ' αὖτε κυβερνήτης ἐνὶ οἴνοπι πόντῳ
νῆα θοὴν ἰθύνει ἐρεχθομένην ἀνέμοισι·
μῆτι δ' ἡνίοχος περιγίγνεται ἡνιόχοιο.

The horses of these men are faster, but they themselves do not
understand any more than you of the science of racing.
Remember then, dear son, to have your mind full of every
kind of μῆτις, so that the prizes may not elude you.
315 The woodcutter is far better for μῆτις than he is for βίη.
It is by μῆτις that the sea captain holds his rapid ship
on its course, though torn by winds, over the wine-blue water.
By μῆτις charioteer outpasses charioteer.   (*Il.* 23.311–18)

As Christopher Faraone and Emily Teeter point out, none of Nestor's *exempla* hint of trickery or deceit; they suggest instead a kind of intelligence or skillfulness humans draw on when facing brute forces of nature.[15] Detienne and Vernant assert that a strategy of μῆτις, *qua* cunning intelligence, enabled Antilochos to triumph over Menelaos, who drove faster horses. In sum, Nestor had counseled Antilochos to restrain his horses and keep them steady, to watch the post and the leader, and to take advantage of any recklessness on the part of the competitor driving the faster horses, for 'trusting in his βίη, he may be careless and create an opportunity for you'. It is clear, however, that what Antilochos does is not what Nestor meant. Instead, the young man himself drove recklessly, urging his horses on at full tilt to compete in speed with Menelaos' team. As a result, he won not by restraining himself and taking advantage of the leader's carelessness, as his father had advised (23.322), but by taking advantage of Menelaos' carefulness and self-restraint (23.433–7). In fact, when challenged to swear that he did not use δόλος, Antilochos cannot. He instead admits lightweight μῆτις (24.590) and disarmingly pleads his youth. On this view, Homer's *Iliad* presents Antilochos not as an exemplar of μῆτις, but as having mistakenly confused μῆτις and δόλος, with near-disastrous results. As we shall see, conflating μῆτις and δόλος produces almost invariably negative results in the *Iliad* and wildly successful ones in the *Odyssey*.

Direct confrontation of μῆτις and βίη, which assists us in discerning the *Iliad*'s definition of μῆτις, appears in still other scenes in the *Iliad*. Achilleus, for example, tells the embassy that the Achaians will have to find a better μῆτις to save their ships in the life-and-death contest with Hektor, mightiest of the Trojan warriors:

ἀλλ' ὑμεῖς μὲν ἰόντες ἀριστήεσσιν Ἀχαιῶν
ἀγγελίην ἀπόφασθε· τὸ γὰρ γέρας ἐστὶ γερόντων·
ὄφρ' ἄλλην φράζωνται ἐνὶ φρεσὶ μῆτιν ἀμείνω,
ἥ κέ σφιν νῆάς τε σαῷ καὶ λαὸν Ἀχαιῶν
425 νηυσὶν ἔπι γλαφυρῆς, ἐπεὶ οὔ σφισιν ἥδέ γ' ἑτοίμη
ἣν νῦν ἐφράσσαντο ἐμεῦ ἀπομηνίσαντος·

Go back, therefore, to the great men of the Achaians,
and take them this message, since such is the privilege of the princes:
that they think out in their minds some other μῆτις that is better,
which might rescue their ships, and the people of the Achaians
425 who man the hollow ships, since this one will not work for them
which they thought of by reason of my anger.   (*Il.* 9.421–6)

Whether Achilleus is referring to the wall the Greeks had hastily put up or
to the embassy itself, the *Iliad* describes both as μῆτις and ascribes both to
Nestor, whose counsel had always been best:

τοῖς ὁ γέρων πάμπρωτος ὑφαίνειν ἤρχετο μῆτιν
Νέστωρ, οὗ καὶ πρόσθεν ἀρίστη φαίνετο βουλή·

The old man first of all began to weave a μῆτις for them,
Nestor, whose βουλή had in time past seemed best.
                                        (*Il.* 9.93–4 = 7.324–5)

Μῆτις is thus associated with prudent counsel as a means of winning over
brute force. On the *Iliad*'s view, Nestor's μῆτις is no match for Achilleus'
βίη in combating the (βίη of the) Trojans, nor, as it turns out, is it any
match for Achilleus' own skills of perception and speech. Neither construction of the wall nor dispatching of the embassy is conceived of as a δόλος.
It is significant, however, that Odysseus attempts to turn the embassy into
a δόλος by disguising the true nature and intent of Agamemnon's gifts.
When Nestor's μῆτις is thus strategically transformed into a δόλος through
dissembling, Achilleus exposes it as such and renders it an abject failure.
Patroklos' entry into battle in Achilleus' armor presents the *Iliad*'s internal
and external audiences with the poem's most striking instance of Nestor's
βουλή, *qua* δόλος, at its destructive worst.

   Another important conjunction of μῆτις and βίη occurs in the quarrel
between Agamemnon and Achilleus, when Achilleus decides to take
Agamemnon's life (*Il.* 1.188–205). Athene, goddess of μῆτις par excellence,
restrains Achilleus, who is about to decide the contest by means of his
superior physical strength:

ἦλθον ἐγὼ παύσουσα τὸ σὸν μένος, αἴ κε πίθηαι,
οὐρανόθεν· πρὸ δέ μ' ἧκε θεὰ λευκώλενος Ἥρη
ἄμφω ὁμῶς θυμῷ φιλέουσά τε κηδομένη τε·

210 ἀλλ' ἄγε λῆγ' ἔριδος, μηδὲ ξίφος ἕλκεο χειρί·
ἀλλ' ἤτοι ἔπεσιν μὲν ὀνείδισον ὡς ἔσεταί περ·
ὧδε γὰρ ἐξερέω, τὸ δὲ καὶ τετελεσμένον ἔσται·
καί ποτέ τοι τρὶς τόσσα παρέσσεται ἀγλαὰ δῶρα
ὕβριος εἵνεκα τῆσδε· σὺ δ' ἴσχεο, πείθεο δ' ἡμῖν.

I have come down to stay your anger – but will you obey me? –
from the sky; and the goddess of the white arms Hera sent me,
who loves both of you equally in her heart and cares for you.
210 Come then, do not take your sword in your hand, keep clear of
    fighting,
though indeed with words you may abuse him, and it will be that way.
And this also will I tell you and it will be a thing accomplished.
Some day three times over such shining gifts shall be given you
By reason of this ὕβρις. Restrain yourself
then, and obey us.   (*Il.* 1. 207–14)

Athene offers Achilleus a way to prevail over Agamemnon without
resorting to βίη: exercising self-restraint and taking gifts. It is justifiable, in
view of the two alternatives presented for deciding the contest – slicing off
Agamemnon's head or waiting for gifts – to interpret Athene's strategy as
μῆτις (but with no hint of δόλος).[16]

On the analogy of Athene's strategy of winning through restraint and
taking gifts, we may analyse accepting ransom or other forms of material
compensation as embodying the μῆτις-βίη theme, even where neither
term appears. In a contest on the battlefield, a warrior may consolidate his
victory either by killing his victim and stripping the spoils or by taking
him alive and returning him to his family in exchange for ransom. The
first is a strategy of pure βίη; the second combines βίη – needed to prevail
over an enemy warrior in the first place – with μῆτις *qua* material exchange
(but not δόλος). On this view, the *Iliad* sets itself up to figure Achilleus'
accepting Priam's ransom as an act that corresponds to μῆτις. Put another
way, in the *Iliad*'s construction of μῆτις and βίη, accepting ransom for
Hektor's corpse demonstrates that Achilleus is not intransigent in his βίη;
he also exhibits the qualities of a judicious mind and a heart subject to his
own power of restraint.

Finally, when Nestor supposedly recalls for Patroklos the parting words
of his father, Menoitios, he says that Achilles is greater in βίη, but since
Patroklos is older, he should speak 'judiciously' and give Achilleus good
advice:

τέκνον ἐμόν, γενεῇ μὲν ὑπέρτερός ἐστιν Ἀχιλλεύς,
πρεσβύτερος δὲ σύ ἐσσι· βίη δ' ὅ γε πολλὸν ἀμείνων.
ἀλλ' εὖ οἱ φάσθαι πυκινὸν ἔπος ἠδ' ὑποθέσθαι
καί οἱ σημαίνειν·

My child, by right of blood Achilleus is higher than you are,
but you are the elder. Yet in βίη he is far the greater.
You must speak judicious words to him, and give him good counsel,
and point his way.   (*Il.* 11.786–9)

Nestor's, or Menoitios', exhortation does not deny judicious speech to
Achilleus or βίη to Patroklos; it only serves as a reminder that Patroklos
is no match for Achilleus in βίη (a lesson soon to be lost on Patroklos).
Moreover, it sets up wise counsel as the complement, or opposite, of
physical strength, implicitly aligning prudence with μῆτις. If we accept
that, we may conclude that one crucial function of Iliadic μῆτις is
restraining and guiding βίη so that it is beneficial and not destructive
(a point to which we shall return).[17] This is true whether the opposing
qualities are distributed between two heroes or are exercised, and hence
mediated, by a single hero.

In addition to the representative examples I have just cited, Homer's
Iliad in general associates μῆτις with neutral terms for thought and counsel:
νόος at 10.226, 15.509, 7.447, 14.61–3, and βουλή at 7.324, 9.93, 10.19.
The *Odyssey*, too, aligns μῆτις in several instances with thoughtfulness,
prudence, and even justice, with no hint of cunning or deceit. Athene-
Mentor, for instance, advises Telemachos that his father's μῆτις has not
given out in him; he is, thus, not to be 'thoughtless', ἀνοήμων, or a coward,
in contrast to the suitors (already established as embodying βίη), who are
neither 'thoughtful', νοήμονες, nor 'just', δίκαιοι (*Od.* 2.278–84).

Penelope, when she proposes appealing to Laertes' μῆτις as a strategy for
combating the suitors, imagines that Laertes will appeal to the people to
stop the suitors' violence (*Od.* 4.739–41). Her father-in-law's μῆτις would
thus involve reasoning with the people and perhaps even an appeal to
justice. Penelope refers to her own νόος and ἐπίφρων μῆτις (*Od.* 19.306)
when she instructs her maids to prepare a bath for Odysseus-beggar so that
he does not go to the banquet dirty and unkempt.[18] A similar association
of μῆτις with prudence and, additionally, with truthfulness appears in
Athene-Mentor's description of Nestor:

> ἀλλ' ἄγε νῦν ἰθὺς κίε Νέστορος ἱπποδάμοιο·
> εἴδομεν ἥν τινα μῆτιν ἐνὶ στήθεσσι κέκευθε.
> λίσσεσθαι δέ μιν αὐτόν, ὅπως νημερτέα εἴπῃ·
> 20 ψεῦδος δ' οὐκ ἐρέει· μάλα γὰρ πεπνυμένος ἐστί.

> So come now, go straight up to Nestor, breaker of horses,
> For we know what μῆτις is hidden in his breast,
> You yourself must entreat him to speak the whole truth to you.
> 20 He will not tell you any falsehood; he is too thoughtful.
>   (*Od.* 3.17–20)

9

Erwin Cook has presented compelling evidence for the alignment of μῆτις and self-restraint in the *Odyssey*.[19] He demonstrates that Odysseus' survival, and hence his return, depend not only on his use of technology, disguise, and deceit, but on restraining himself from using natural strength or his sword when circumstances (e.g. meeting Circe or Nausikaa) render them at best futile and at worst self-destructive. Whether or not the restraint is directly referred to as μῆτις, it is structurally defined as such because it is set in opposition to the use of force. Μῆτις is associated with 'thought', νόος, and 'counsel' or 'plan', βουλή, elsewhere in the *Odyssey*, though the plan referred to is frequently Odysseus' entry into his household by a strategy of deceit (see, for example, *Od*. 13.299–301 and 386). This brings us, then, to the close association of μῆτις and δόλος in the *Odyssey*.

To repeat a point made earlier, Jenny Clay demonstrates that the scholiasts' interpretation allows us to connect Demodokos' first song closely to the third, about the wooden horse. Their interpretation in fact allows us to connect all three songs in *Odyssey* 8 and, as a result, to define the μῆτις at issue in Demodokos' '*Iliad*' as δόλος, 'deceit'. When Odysseus requests a song about the wooden horse – the μῆτις by which the *Odyssey* figures Troy was taken – he refers to it as a δόλος 'trick', neatly and explicitly conflating the two terms:[20]

> ἀλλ' ἄγε δὴ μετάβηθι καὶ ἵππου κόσμον ἄεισον
> δουρατέου, τὸν Ἐπειὸς ἐποίησεν σὺν Ἀθήνῃ,
> ὅν ποτ' ἐς ἀκρόπολιν δόλον ἤγαγε δῖος Ὀδυσσεὺς
> 495 ἀνδρῶν ἐμπλήσας, οἳ Ἴλιον ἐξαλάπαξαν.

> Come to another part of the story, sing us
> the wooden horse, which Epeios made with Athene helping,
> the δόλος great Odysseus filled once with men and brought it
> 495 to the upper city, and it was these men who sacked Ilion.

> (*Od*. 8.492–5)

Demodokos furthers the identification of μῆτις and δόλος by describing as a δόλος the web with which Hephaestus – master of technology and, hence, a figure of μῆτις – captured Ares and Aphrodite:

> αὐτὰρ ἐπεὶ δὴ τεῦξε δόλον κεχολωμένος Ἄρει,
> βῆ ῥ' ἴμεν ἐς θάλαμον, ὅθι οἱ φίλα δέμνια κεῖτο·
> ἀμφὶ δ' ἄρ' ἑρμῖσιν χέε δέσματα κύκλῳ ἀπάντῃ,
> πολλὰ δὲ καὶ καθύπερθε μελαθρόφιν ἐξεκέχυντο,
> 280 ἠΰτ' ἀράχνια λεπτά· τά γ' οὔ κέ τις οὐδὲ ἴδοιτο,
> οὐδὲ θεῶν μακάρων· περὶ γὰρ δολόεντα τέτυκτο.

> Now when, in his anger against Ares, he had made this δόλος
> he went to his chamber where his own dear bed lay,
> and spun his fastenings around the posts from every direction,

while many more were suspended overhead, from the roof beams,
280   thin, like spider webs, which not even one of the blessed
gods could see. For he fashioned it to be a δόλος.
(*Od.* 8.276–82)

I am suggesting not just that Odyssean μῆτις is understood to mean
trickery or deceit, though it occasionally is, but that in several passages
crucial to construction of the μῆτις-βίη opposition, the *Odyssey* overtly and
programmatically asserts the equation of μῆτις with δόλος. This conflation,
as the opposition to βίη, is set forth most notably in the wonderful word
play when the Cyclopes respond to Polyphemos' cries:

ἦ μή τίς σ' αὐτὸν κτείνει δόλῳ ἠὲ βίηφι;
    τοὺς δ' αὖτ' ἐξ ἄντρου προσέφη κρατερὸς Πολύφημος·
ὦ φίλοι, Οὖτίς με κτείνει δόλῳ οὐδὲ βίηφιν.

Surely none can be killing you by δόλος or βίη?
    Then from inside the cave strong Polyphemos answered:
Good friends, Nobody (Οὖτίς) is killing me by δόλος or βίη.
(*Od.* 9.406–8)

Odysseus the narrator thus figures the μῆτις that 'Nobody' wields in the
contest between μῆτις and βίη explicitly as δόλος. To cite other examples
of this strategy: Odysseus describes his device of using Polyphemos' sheep
to convey himself and his companions safely out of the cave as μῆτις and
δόλοι (*Od.* 9.422);[21] Penelope refers to her trick of weaving and unweaving
the shroud – a tactic to combat the suitors' βίη – as a δόλος, and laments
that since the suitors have caught on, she can't find another μῆτις (*Od.*
19.137 and 158). Similarly, Nestor remembers the Trojan War as waged
with all kinds of δόλοι and adds that no one could compare to Odysseus
in μῆτις because of his surpassing δόλοι:

εἰνάετες γάρ σφιν κακὰ ῥάπτομεν ἀμφιέποντες
παντοίοισι δόλοισι, μόγις δ' ἐτέλεσσε Κρονίων.
120   ἔνθ' οὔ τίς ποτε μῆτιν ὁμοιωθήμεναι ἄντην
ἤθελ', ἐπεὶ μάλα πολλὸν ἐνίκα δῖος Ὀδυσσεὺς
παντοίοισι δόλοισι,

For nine long years we plotted their ruin, trying
all kinds of δόλοι, but scarcely did the son of Kronos bring it to pass.
During all this time there was no one who could compare with your
    father
in μῆτις, since goodly Odysseus far excelled
in all manner of δόλοι.   (*Od.* 3.118–22)

Odyssean examples of μῆτις understood in context to mean something
like cunning intelligence can, of course, be multiplied (for example,

Od. 13.297–9, 303 and 386, and 20.20–1). Nonetheless, the *Odyssey's* conflation of μῆτις and δόλος in opposition to βίη is so pronounced as to suggest that, even if the equation of the two is traditional, it is combatting a distinction between μῆτις and δόλος that is, or may be, equally traditional. Indeed, as we have already seen, the *Odyssey* itself preserves a traditional meaning of μῆτις that is unencumbered with cunning, trickery, or deceit. Moreover, if the effect of Demodokos' three songs is to exploit an 'Iliadic' alignment of Achilleus with βίη and to define μῆτις in the rivalry between poetic traditions as δόλος, the strategy would appear to be aimed at denying Achilleus the quality of heroic μῆτις. But in what world would such a strategy not be superfluous, even inane? If not in Demodokos' '*Iliad*', perhaps in Homer's.

The Homeric μῆτις-βίη polarity

Βίη is the uncontested term of the homeric polarity. Βίη in Homer refers regularly to natural strength, might, or the force used to overpower an adversary, especially in a contest for supremacy. It is figured consistently as a desirable heroic resource that accrues benefits for the hero who possesses it and for his community. The hero whose βίη is diminished potentially incurs a corresponding decrease in status or value to his community (compare, for example, *Il.* 3.45 and 431, or 7.157 and 4.314; see also *Od.* 14.468). Βίη appears as periphrasis for a person whose might comprises their thematic identity, such as βίη Ἡρακληείη, literally 'Heraklean might' (*Il.* 11.690). In this positive sense, βίη may be paired with 'strength', κάρτος (*Od.* 6.197 and 13.143).

At the same time, βίη is potentially transgressive and, thus, ambiguous: it always threatens to edge over into brute force or rapacity without restraint. Agamemnon, for instance, is said to have taken Briseis away from Achilleus by βίη (*Il.* 1.428–30). As such, βίη may be paired with ὕβρις 'wanton disregard for another's honor (τιμή)' (*Od.* 15.329 = 17.565) or, again, with κάρτος 'strength' (*Od.* 18.139).[22] In the *Odyssey*, yielding to one's own βίη produces ἀτάσθαλα, the deeds of criminal folly that Odysseus-the-beggar claims to have committed,

> καὶ γὰρ ἐγώ ποτ' ἔμελλον ἐν ἀνδράσιν ὄλβιος εἶναι,
> πολλὰ δ' ἀτάσθαλ' ἔρεξα βίη καὶ κάρτεϊ εἴκων
>
> For I myself once promised to be a man of prosperity,
> but, giving way to violence and strength, did many reckless deeds
>
> (*Od.* 18.138–9)

which the suitors are at that very moment devising,

οἵ᾿ ὁρόω μνηστῆρας ἀτάσθαλα μηχανόωντας,
κτήματα κείροντας καὶ ἀτιμάζοντας ἄκοιτιν
145 ἀνδρός, ὃν οὐκέτι φημὶ φίλων καὶ πατρίδος αἴης
δηρὸν ἀπέσσεσθαι· μάλα δὲ σχεδόν. ἀλλά σε δαίμων
οἴκαδ᾿ ὑπεξαγάγοι, μηδ᾿ ἀντιάσειας ἐκείνῳ,
ὁππότε νοστήσειε φίλην ἐς πατρίδα γαῖαν·
οὐ γὰρ ἀναιμωτί γε διακρινέεσθαι ὀΐω
150 μνηστῆρας καὶ κεῖνον, ἐπεί κε μέλαθρον ὑπέλθῃ.

Even so, now, I see the suitors, their reckless devisings,
how they show no respect to the wife, and despoil the possessions
145 of a man who, I think, will not for long be far from
his country and friends. He is very close by. But I hope your destiny
takes you home, out of his way. I hope you never will face him,
at the time he comes back to the beloved land of his fathers.
For I believe that, once he enters his halls, there will be
150 a reckoning, not without blood, between that man and the suitors.
(*Od.* 18.143–50)

and for which Odysseus' crew (*Od.* 1.7) and Aigisthos (*Od.* 1.32–43; in *Od.* 1.300, 3.198, and 308 associated with the epithet δολόμητις) are likewise punished. Similarly, in Homer's *Iliad*, those assemblies in which humans pass crooked decrees and drive justice, δίκη, from their midst are characterized by βίη and, as a result, are punished by Zeus:[23]

385 ὅτε λαβρότατον χέει ὕδωρ
Ζεύς, ὅτε δή ῥ᾿ ἄνδρεσσι κοτεσσάμενος χαλεπήνῃ,
οἳ βίῃ εἰν ἀγορῇ σκολιὰς κρίνωσι θέμιστας,
ἐκ δὲ δίκην ἐλάσωσι θεῶν ὄπιν οὐκ ἀλέγοντες·

385 when Zeus sends down the most violent waters
in deep rage against mortals after they stir him to anger
because in violent assembly they pass decrees that are crooked,
and drive righteousness from among them and care nothing for what
the gods think. (*Il.* 16.385–8)

In both Homeric epics, this ambiguous βίη is expressed especially as improper feasting. The suitors' rapacious consumption of Odysseus' cattle, for example, is referred to as βίη:

115 δήεις δ᾿ ἐν πήματα οἴκῳ,
ἄνδρας ὑπερφιάλους, οἵ τοι βίοτον κατέδουσι
μνώμενοι ἀντιθέην ἄλοχον καὶ ἕδνα διδόντες.
ἀλλ᾿ ἦ τοι κείνων γε βίας ἀποτείσεαι ἐλθών·

115 and [you will] find troubles in your household,
insolent men, who are eating away your livelihood

13

and courting your godlike wife and offering gifts to win her.
You may punish the violences of these men, when you come home.

(*Od.* 11.115–18)

As I have argued elsewhere, ambiguous βίη is associated implicitly with omophagic cannibalism, the most disturbing expression of improper feasting in Greek culture:[24] Polyphemos' savage consumption of members of Odysseus' crew (*Od.* 9.272–98); Zeus' allegation that Hera's anger could be cured only by eating Priam and the rest of the Trojans raw (*Il.* 4.30–6); Achilleus' own wish that he could hack Hektor's meat away and eat it raw (*Il.* 22.345–54); and Hekabe's wish that she could sink her teeth into Achilleus' liver (*Il.* 24.212–14). As such, it involves a negation of culture that dissolves human bonds, political and familial alike. Ambiguous βίη is accordingly thematically associated with lions, implicitly in the lion simile used of Polyphemos (*Od.* 9.292) and explicitly in Apollo's complaint about Achilleus' treatment of Hektor's corpse:[25]

ἀλλ' ὀλοῷ Ἀχιλῆϊ θεοὶ βούλεσθ' ἐπαρήγειν,
40   ᾧ οὔτ' ἄρ φρένες εἰσὶν ἐναίσιμοι οὔτε νόημα
γναμπτὸν ἐνὶ στήθεσσι, λέων δ' ὣς ἄγρια οἶδεν,
ὅς τ' ἐπεὶ ἄρ μεγάλῃ τε βίῃ καὶ ἀγήνορι θυμῷ
εἴξας εἶσ' ἐπὶ μῆλα βροτῶν ἵνα δαῖτα λάβῃσιν·

No, you gods; your desire is to help this cursed Achilleus
40   within whose breast there are no feelings of justice, nor can
his mind be bent, but he is savage, like a lion
who, when he has given way to his own great βίη and his haughty
spirit, goes among the flocks of men, to devour them.

(*Il.* 24.39–43)

In sum, Homeric βίη evinces both positive and negative aspects. In its more deleterious expressions, it is associated with failure to restrain the exercise of one's natural powers or appetites, with improper feasting and courtship, with deeds of criminal folly, and with wanton disregard for justice, for non-violent settlements, or for intelligent reasoning. It thus threatens a negation of the bonds and commensal feasting by which human communities order themselves and keep chaos at bay.

On the basis of the foregoing, we might expect both epics to figure the antipode of βίη at least as intelligence or thought, the exercise of self-restraint, displacement of violence, and acting in accordance with justice – as indeed proves to be the case.[26] The *Odyssey*, in addition, and in contrast to the *Iliad*, conjoins μῆτις *qua* prudence and justice with μῆτις *qua* trickery and deceit as a compounded polar opposite to βίη. I am not suggesting a diachronic development in which μῆτις 'originally' meant intelligence and was only later 'conflated' with δόλος, but only that Homeric epic evinces the existence – I would go so far as to say the co-existence – of two quite distinct traditional definitions of μῆτις and, hence, of the μῆτις-βίη opposition.

It is a rather straightforward matter to make the case that the Odyssean Odysseus reifies Odyssean μῆτις, but that he also has the capacity, and finally, in the slaughter of the suitors, the opportunity to exercise heroic βίη that equals or surpasses any acts of brute force in the *Iliad*. It is more difficult to establish that the Iliadic Achilleus, who embodies heroic βίη, is represented as also exercising μῆτις, especially since even the *Iliad* does not apply the term itself to him explicitly. Indeed, by the Odyssean definition of μῆτις, which prevailing scholarship has accepted as Homer's, Achilleus is effectively excluded from that mode of operation. But, as we have seen, the *Iliad* explicitly distinguishes between μῆτις and δόλος, defining μῆτις in such a way that Achilleus' self-restraint and material exchanges are clearly brought into its compass. The lion simile Apollo deploys against Achilleus (*Il.* 24.42) when he adamantly refused to accept Priam's ransom aligns him irredeemably with βίη; the lion simile the poet uses of Achilleus when he takes the ransom (*Il.* 24.572) argues eloquently for his heroic μῆτις.[27]

As Detienne and Vernant observed, the Odyssean association of μῆτις and δόλος prevailed in Greek poetics and society. But the Iliadic definition of the μῆτις-βίη polarity – a tradition, as we have seen, also preserved in the *Odyssey* – is not unparalleled as a Greek cultural theme. Athene's bridling of Pegasus, dismissed rather too quickly by Detienne and Vernant as an example of a μῆτις-βίη or culture-nature opposition, comes immediately to mind.[28] Moreover, in a recent article, Christopher Faraone and Emily Teeter mount a compelling argument that *Metis* in Hesiod is not a figure of amoral cunning or a threat to established order, but is on the contrary 'author of justice', τέκταινα δικαίων, who provides Zeus with moral guidance after he ingests her.[29] Faraone and Teeter draw on a comparison with Egyptian Maat to demonstrate that the presence of Metis, and hence μῆτις, as an internal advisor, is associated with legitimation of Zeus' monarchic rule. Specifically, Metis/μῆτις restrains Zeus' βίη – not to expunge it, but to render it constructive and subservient to justice and order. I quote their conclusions, which are complementary to my own in respect of μῆτις in the *Iliad*:

> It would seem, therefore, that in the *Theogony* and in fragment 343 Hesiod is thinking of another kind of *mêtis*, a non-Odyssean kind, which distinguishes Zeus' current reign from those that have preceded it, for he avoids both the violence and hybris of Ouranus' kingship and the deceit and 'crookedness' of Kronos... Metis is understood to sit permanently in the σπλάγχνα of Zeus

15

– the site of his violent emotions – from which she seems to exercise some kind of moral authority over his decisions, presumably by curbing these same emotions. Thus as a result of Zeus' very different kind of ingestion, he is able to establish a kind of just rule of which his father and grandfather were incapable.[30]

This is precisely the role Patroklos was supposed to fill for Achilleus (compare *Il.* 11.786–9 above), and which Achilleus in the end fulfills for himself. Were we to imagine Achilleus as restraining his violence and doing 'what is right' because μῆτις dwells within him, he would be a legitimate Hesiodic (or Egyptian) king. As it is, in Homer's *Iliad*, he is best of the Achaians.

If we accept Faraone's and Teeter's conclusion, it becomes more clear that the poets of the *Odyssey* could not assume a self-evident association between μῆτις and δόλος in Archaic Greek culture and society. Archaic epic poetry preserved traditional and competing meanings of μῆτις and, hence, competing constructions of the μῆτις-βίη opposition. A world in which Achilleus might lay claim to heroic μῆτις could be found not only in Iliadic traditions, specifically in the one that emerged as Panhellenic, but also in Hesiod.

Moreover, inquiry into Indo-European myth and poetics presents comparanda that seem genuinely relevant to the Iliadic construction of the μῆτις-βίη opposition. In the Indic epic Mahabharata, the divine twins Nakula and Sahadeva each present distinct qualities and play a distinct role. Nakula is a handsome warrior and breaker of horses, who has eyes of fire and the shoulders of a lion. Sahadeva, his opposite, is intelligent and patient, a hero associated with the domestic sphere and cattle, but not with deceit or disguise. Stig Wikander proposed that the functional polarity of the twins is Indo-European and dates back to the earliest strata of Indo-European mythology. A like opposition emerges in Welsh, Celtic, and Germanic twins. We are thus justified in conjecturing that Homer's *Iliad* could draw on inherited IE mythic patterns in formulating its μῆτις-βίη polarity.

Demodokos' '*Iliad*' and Homer's

If indeed Demodokos' '*Iliad*' brought both heroes, reifying opposing qualities of μῆτις and βίη, into confrontation in one epic poem, it is likely that the only direction in which its Odysseus and Achilleus could have developed would be extreme polarization. Demodokos' Achilleus would, on this view, be a hero exercising unmitigated brute force but incapable of μῆτις; Odysseus perhaps an unremediated deceiver and dissembler, with no 'great deeds in battle', ἀριστεία, to his credit. Erwin Cook has demonstrated that Odyssean heroism is not, however, characterized by the triumph of μῆτις, but by successful integration of μῆτις and βίη in the hero Odysseus, and, further, that it is this integration of strength and intelligence that qualifies him uniquely to rule in a benevolent monarchy in Ithaka.[31] Thus, in Demodokos' *'Iliad'*, Achilleus and Iliadic heroism fall short precisely because Achilleus controls only one term of the μῆτις-βίη opposition (as would Odysseus). Consequently, Demodokos' *'Iliad'* may be seen to advance an Odyssean project. If the Odysseus in Demodokos' alternative *'Iliad'* also fails to integrate μῆτις and βίη, it does no real disservice insofar as the *Odyssey* dismisses 'Iliadic' tradition as already obviated by Odyssean epic song.

But Demodokos' *'Iliad'* is not Homer's. Indeed, the efforts of the *Iliad* and *Odyssey* to define μῆτις and the μῆτις-βίη polarity to accommodate their respective heroes demonstrates that μῆτις was not a unified concept. The Homeric epics preserve different inherited semantics of μῆτις. But to what end? Surely not to expunge the difference between the two heroes and their primary modes of operation, but that each epic tradition may figure its own hero as mediating the defining polarity of heroic epic and hence as best of the Achaians. It does not matter for this point whether Demodokos' *'Iliad'* was an extant Iliadic tradition or not. But in view of evidence marshaled by James Marks that the *Odyssey* alludes to competing versions of itself for the purpose of deauthorizing them, it is not unthinkable that it would refer to a competing version of Iliadic tradition in order to authorize it.[32]

Acknowledgements

This paper, in various permutations, was read for the Classics faculty and graduate students at Bryn Mawr College (2003), at CAMWS (2003), and at the annual meeting of the American Philological Association (2004). I am indebted to my colleagues in the audiences and on the panels for their constructive comments.

Notes

[1] For convenience, I adopt the convention of referring to the written texts that have come down to us as the *Iliad* and *Odyssey*, and to the poet, as exponent of the Panhellenic tradition of oral poetry, as Homer or 'the poet'.

[2] My translations are based on those of Lattimore 1951/1965, with adjustments.

[3] Pucci 1986, 215–18, makes a convincing case that '[t]he expression κλέα ἀνδρῶν defines heroic Iliadic poetry, not the sort of poetry the *Odyssey* is'.

[4] Nagy 1979, 15–65.

[5] For example Kullmann 1960, 100 and 272. Aristotle, *Rhetoric* 2.24.6 alludes to

a quarrel between Achilleus and Agamemnon cited in Proclus; he claims it was over Achilleus' having been dishonored.

[6] Clay 1997, 99.

[7] For detailed discussion, see Nagy 1979, 15–65.

[8] Nagy 1979, 65.

[9] For detailed discussion, see Clay 1997, 96–112 and 241–6.

[10] Heubeck, West and Hainsworth 1998, ad loc.

[11] Heubeck, West and Hainsworth 1998, 351.

[12] See Pucci 1987, 220–7 and Clay 1997, 246.

[13] Detienne and Vernant 1978, 21–3.

[14] Detienne and Vernant 1978, 13.

[15] Faraone and Teeter 2004, 203. Nestor mentions in 1.322 that a man who knows κέρδεα, tricks or how to get the advantage, can win with inferior horses. Those words are apart from the encomium on μῆτις and, in any case, no trickiness is integral to Nestor's driving instructions.

[16] Athene makes one more significant appearance to assist Achilleus in deciding a contest: she disguises herself as Deïphobos in order to force Hektor to turn and fight Achilleus (*Il.* 22.227–31). Although this appearance seems to contradict the *Iliad*'s pattern of dissociating μῆτις from δόλος, the difficulty may be more apparent than real. The narrator says specifically that the goddess led Hektor on with κερδοσύνη 'trickery' (*Il.* 22.247), and Hektor that Athene has ἐξαπάτησεν 'deceived' him (*Il.* 22.299). Thus in this ambiguous case, the poet is still invested in not overtly associating the term μῆτις with deceit.

[17] For a similar pairing of terms, but to different effect, compare *Il.* 15.106.

[18] The term ἐπίφρων μῆτις evokes a Hesiodic description of Athena, who has ἐπίφρονα βουλήν (*Theog.* 896), almost always refering to a positive virtue. On this, see Faraone and Teeter, 2004, 180–1.

[19] Cook 1995, especially chapters 3 and 4.

[20] The following discussion of the Odyssean conflation of μῆτις and δόλος is heavily indebted to Cook 1999 on active and passive heroism in the *Odyssey*, which anticipates and complements my own argument.

[21] Odysseus deploys technology, of which the Cyclopes are completely innocent, to best the larger and stronger Polyphemos; but there is no reason to align μῆτις with the technology and δόλος with the trickery, since the contest is clearly set up as Odyssean μῆτις versus βίη.

[22] For this definition of *hybris*, see Fisher 1992, 1–6 and 150–84.

[23] It is tempting to think of punishment by violent waters as flood, which is frequently a sign of order reverting to primal chaos.

[24] Wilson, 2002b.

[25] For detailed discussion, see Wilson 2002b.

[26] For self-restraint as endurance or suffering, an expression of a passive aspect of the hero, see Cook 1999 and below.

[27] For discussion, see Wilson 2002a, chapter 5.

[28] For discussion, see Detienne and Vernant 1978, 187–206.

[29] Faraone and Teeter 2004.

[30] Faraone and Teeter 2004.

[31] Cook 1995 and 1999. I refer the reader also to Cook 1999, 153, where he

identifies μῆτις and βίη as active heroic qualities, and suffering/endurance as a passive one: 'Hero and trickster are distinct in Homer in that the active hero is defined by *biê*, the trickster by his use of *mêtis* to practice deception (*doloi*). Iliadic tradition asserts the superiority of its hero to that of the *Odyssey* by privileging force over the cunning intelligence that characterizes Odysseus. Odyssean tradition responds to Iliadic heroism by aligning *mêtis* with the trickster's *doloi* and the active exercise of *biê* with the persona of the Iliadic warrior.'

[32] Marks 2003.

Bibliography

Clay, J.S.
1997   *The Wrath of Athena: Gods and men in the* Odyssey, Lanham, M.D., and London.
Cook, E.F.
1995   *The* Odyssey *in Athens*, Ithaca and London.
1999   'Active' and 'passive' heroics in the *Odyssey*', *Classical World* 93.2, 149–67.
Detienne, M. and Vernant, J.-P.
1978   *Cunning Intelligence in Greek Culture and Society*, Sussex and Atlantic Highlands, N.J.
Dunkle, R.
1987   'Nestor, Odysseus, and the *Metis-Bie* antithesis: the funeral games, *Iliad* 23', *Classical World* 81.1, 1–17.
Faraone, C. and Teeter, E.
2004   'Egyptian Maat and Hesiodic Metis', *Mnemosyne* 57.2, 177–208.
Fisher, N.
1992   *Hybris: A study of honour and shame in ancient Greece*, Warminster, Wiltshire.
Heubeck, A., West, S. and Hainsworth, J.B.
1998   *A Commentary on Homer's* Odyssey, vol. I, Oxford and New York.
Kullmann, W.
1960   *Die Quellen der* Ilias, *Hermes Einzelschriften* 14, Wiesbaden.
Lattimore, R.
1951   *The* Iliad *of Homer*, translation with introduction, Chicago.
1965   *The* Odyssey *of Homer*, translation with introduction, New York.
Marks, J.
2003   'Alternative *Odyssey*s: The case of Thoas and Odysseus', *TAPhA* 133.2, 209–26.
Nagy, G.
1979   *The Best of the Achaeans*, Baltimore and London.
Pearson, A.D. (ed.)
1917   *The Fragments of Sophocles* I–III, Cambridge.
Pucci, P.
1987   *Odysseus Polutropos. Intertextual readings in the* Odyssey *and the* Iliad, Ithaca and London.

Ward, D.
   1970   'The separate functions of the Indo-European divine twins', in J. Puhvel (ed.) *Myth and Law among the Indo-Europeans*, XX, 193–202.
Wikander, S.
   1957   'Nakula and Sahadeva', *OSXX* 6, 66–96.
Wilson, D.
   2002a. *Ransom, Revenge, and Heroic Identity in the* Iliad, Cambridge.
   2002b. 'Lion Kings: heroes in the epic mirror', *Colby Quarterly* 35.2, 231–54.

THE PATTERNING OF THE SIMILES IN BOOK 2 OF THE *ILIAD*

William C. Scott

Book 2 of Homer's *Iliad* contains twenty similes, a large number.[1] There are other books which contain more; book 11 is the winner with thirty-two. And because of book 2's length there are other narrative sections where similes are more densely concentrated: again the first part of book 11 (1–596) offers the most intense use of similes in a continuous narrative. But book 2 is a better testing ground of the poet's choices in designing similes since Homer employs a large number of them in a wide variety of forms. This book not only contains a collection of different simile subjects and a mix of highly traditional similes with some that are uniquely structured (e.g. 144 and 209 vs. 478), but it also presents the greatest cluster of similes in the Homeric poems (455–483) and four rare juxtaposed similes (144 + 147, 468 + 469, 478–81, and 780 + 781).[2]

A series of extended similes, based on various subjects, concentrates on the book's major character, the army. The subjects are taken from familiar topics – wind, fire, birds, gods, and insects, and tradition firmly underlies the placement of each simile.[3] Yet there are signs that Homer significantly adapts traditional features of his similes to enhance the individual story: for example, the catalogue of Greek ships is introduced by a dense grouping of seven similes (five of which come from the traditional families) including three sets of unusual double similes.

The examination of the similes of book 2 will show the force of the tradition on both poet and audience. It is of major importance to the interpretation of the similes to acknowledge that the audience had a firm knowledge of the alternatives which the poet considered and thereby could evaluate what he was accepting, modifying, and suppressing in supporting his narrative with a simile. There was a virtual simile outline in their minds built from memories of previous performances that can be recaptured – to a degree – by identifying the elements which are repeatedly attached to the individual simile families.[4]

To form a correct assessment of the similes' poetic function in book 2 it is important to evaluate in detail the traditional language as well as the particular structure and placement of each simile. The questions to be addressed in such an examination are:

• is Homer seeking to maintain a focus when there is such a variety of topics?

• how does the choice to place the simile contribute to meaning?

• how do similes in one section of narrative relate to one another and to those in other sections?

• how does Homer use traditional epic diction in forming effective similes?

• what is the difference in meaning between short and extended similes?

• is there any value in omitting an anticipated or possible simile?

Book 2 of the *Iliad* falls easily into two narrative units: (1) efforts to organize the army and (2) its final marshalling and marching to meet the Trojans. The division between these sections is clearly signalled in lines 441–52 when Agamemnon orders his heralds to summon the Greeks for battle; leaders encourage their men and Athena marches with the army to rouse its spirit. This division of the book is supported by the different poetic strategies in each part. The first section presents the frenzied attempts of the Greek leaders to establish a direction for the army, while in the Catalogue the army appears as a unit of impressive and unified power. The organization implicit in, and imposed by, the catalogue form itself presents the army for the first time in the epic as a potent fighting unit; the names of men and the numbers of ships are listed as components of corporate strength, and individual lives and fates are mentioned only briefly. After the Greek catalogue the narrative continues to move toward battle as the Trojan heroes and troops are also listed.

While the narrative of book 2 develops from the army at rest to the army marching for its first battle in the *Iliad*, the theme of the book is the leadership of that army. In neither book 1 nor 2 does Agamemnon mold his army into a strong fighting unit.[5] Of course, the Greek army is big – the length and scope of the Catalogue exhibit the massive force which the Greeks possess at Troy;[6] but this force must be organized to move effectively toward a single goal if the war is to be won. Through the device of misinforming the troops about his dream Agamemnon misreads the spirit of the army and causes extreme disorganization.[7]

In order to understand the functioning of the similes in supporting this theme it is necessary to examine each simile closely as the product of the poet's choice. There is good evidence that the inherited language of early Greek narrative suggested a limited number of subjects at certain common junctures; on some occasions the poet chose to follow these prompts, often he made some modifications, and at times he passed over the option of using a simile at all. On each occasion his aim was to make the choice that allowed him to tell his story most effectively for an audience who also knew the traditional subjects and could appreciate the poet's art.

The similes of book 2

2.87

> ἠΰτε ἔθνεα εἶσι μελισσάων ἀδινάων,
> πέτρης ἐκ γλαφυρῆς αἰεὶ νέον ἐρχομενάων·
> βοτρυδὸν δὲ πέτονται ἐπ' ἄνθεσιν εἰαρινοῖσιν·
> αἱ μέν τ' ἔνθα ἅλις πεποτήαται, αἱ δέ τε ἔνθα

> just as the swarms of thronging bees
> flow ever anew from a hollow rock;
> in clusters they fly to the springtime flowers –
> some flitting here and some there[8]

This simile, describing the army gathering for the assembly, has insects as its subject. In the other two bee/wasp similes (12.167 and 16.259) the insects are stirred up to attack their provokers or else to defend themselves;[9] appropriately in each passage the narrative describes the fierce spirit of warriors. At 2.87, however, the army is only marching to a meeting where they will sit down and listen to their leaders; the poet has fitted an insect simile to this calmer context by removing any threat from these bees. They leave their homes only to seek the flowers of spring; they fly in different directions and gather in clusters wherever there is a flower. The crucial idea of an organized and spirited self-defense, so central to the other two similes, is deleted.

There are few parallel descriptions of groups that gather but do not go to war immediately; usually armies are mustered to attack each other or at least to advance to battle. In such scenes the similes center on lions, wind and waves, fire, and rushing rivers.[10] At 16.156 the simile of blood-thirsty wolves stresses the gory aspects of their attack on a stag – even though the Myrmidons are only arming themselves. Perhaps the closest parallel to the movement of troops not directly involved in battle occurs in the Epipolesis where Agamemnon encounters the two Ajaxes and their followers readying themselves for war:

> ὡς δ' ὅτ' ἀπὸ σκοπιῆς εἶδεν νέφος αἰπόλος ἀνὴρ
> ἐρχόμενον κατὰ πόντον ὑπὸ Ζεφύροιο ἰωῆς·

τῷ δέ τ' ἄνευθεν ἐόντι μελάντερον ἠΰτε πίσσα
φαίνετ' ἰὸν κατὰ πόντον, ἄγει δέ τε λαίλαπα πολλήν·

as when from a cliff a goatherd sees a cloud
coming across the sea driven by the blast of the west wind;
as it moves over the sea, it seems blacker than pitch
to him even though he is far away, and it brings a great whirlwind.
Seeing it he shudders and drives his flock into a cave   (4.275)

In this case men in armor are on the move and war is imminent; the simile emphasizes the goatherd's fear as he sees danger threatening his flock.

By choosing insects for the first of many similes describing the army in book 2, the poet prepares his audience, well aware of the traditional possibilities for insect similes, to focus on the fighting spirit of the Greeks. Yet at the same time when he rigorously deletes the available warlike elements to create a spring scene of untroubled bees, he counts on that same audience realizing that he has eliminated the warlike potential of the simile in order to present the most unwarlike army in the *Iliad*. The disorder and uncertainty in its movements are made clear in their random clustering (88–9) and their lack of direction (90).[11]

2.144, 147, and 209

κινήθη δ' ἀγορὴ φὴ κύματα μακρὰ θαλάσσης,
πόντου Ἰκαρίοιο, τὰ μέν τ' Εὖρός τε Νότος τε
ὤρορ' ἐπαΐξας πατρὸς Διὸς ἐκ νεφελάων.
ὡς δ' ὅτε κινήσῃ Ζέφυρος βαθὺ λήϊον ἐλθών,
λάβρος ἐπαιγίζων, ἐπί τ' ἠμύει ἀσταχύεσσιν

like the long waves of the deep,
the Icarian sea, which the East Wind and the South
rouse rushing from the clouds of father Zeus,
and just as the West Wind comes to a deep field of corn,
blowing briskly, and sets the ears to bobbing.

ὡς ὅτε κῦμα πολυφλοίσβοιο θαλάσσης
αἰγιαλῷ μεγάλῳ βρέμεται, σμαραγεῖ δέ τε πόντος

just as when a wave of the sounding sea
thunders on the long beach and the sea roars…

The unplanned and chaotic rush of the army to the ships and back again to the assembly is described by three wind and wave similes, two of which are juxtaposed and closely parallel in structure.[12] Because the subjects of winds and waves are complementary components of the same simile family and often accompany the charge and attack of a warrior or of the whole army, it is possible to identify degrees of intensity. The clearest example of the destructive potential developed in this simile family is:

> ὡς ὅτε κῦμα θοῇ ἐν νηῒ πέσῃσι
> λάβρον ὑπαὶ νεφέων ἀνεμοτρεφές· ἡ δέ τε πᾶσα
> ἄχνῃ ὑπεκρύφθη, ἀνέμοιο δὲ δεινὸς ἀήτης
> ἱστίῳ ἐμβρέμεται, τρομέουσι δέ τε φρένα ναῦται
> δειδιότες· τυτθὸν γὰρ ὑπὲκ θανάτοιο φέρονται

> as a fast moving wave
> swollen by the wind from beneath the clouds
> falls upon a swift ship; the whole ship is hidden by the foam,
> the terrible blast of the wind roars in the sail,
> and the sailors tremble in fear – for only barely do they escape death
> (15.624).

13.795 also expresses nature's power even though it does not specifically mention the threat of sinking the ship or destroying the men:

> ἀργαλέων ἀνέμων ἀτάλαντοι ἀέλλῃ,
> ἥ ῥά θ' ὑπὸ βροντῆς πατρὸς Διὸς εἶσι πέδονδε,
> θεσπεσίῳ δ' ὁμάδῳ ἁλὶ μίσγεται, ἐν δέ τε πολλὰ
> κύματα παφλάζοντα πολυφλοίσβοιο θαλάσσης,
> κυρτὰ φαληριόωντα, πρὸ μέν τ' ἄλλ', αὐτὰρ ἐπ' ἄλλα…

> like the blast of harsh winds
> that rush over the plain driven by the thunder of father Zeus
> and stir up the sea with a gigantic roar; many waves
> of the loud-sounding sea boil up,
> arching high and white – some before and some following after…

By comparison the three wind and wave similes in book 2 present an image of nature offering little threat or danger. At 2.144 waves on the sea are mentioned briefly in a phrase: then the second line locates the scene and names the winds which clash; the final line gives the source of the winds. For the most part proper names displace the direct description of the winds' powerful action. But the phrasing also softens the scene: the winds rushing down from the 'clouds of father Zeus' seem less dramatic than the winds which come to the plain 'driven by the thunder of father Zeus' (13.796).

The second simile describes a wind blowing through a cornfield. For comparison there is a simile of winds blowing through a forest at 16.765:

> ὡς δ' Εὗρός τε Νότος τ' ἐριδαίνετον ἀλλήλοιιν
> οὔρεος ἐν βήσσῃς βαθέην πελεμιζέμεν ὕλην,
> φηγόν τε μελίην τε τανύφλοιόν τε κράνειαν,
> αἵ τε πρὸς ἀλλήλας ἔβαλον τανυήκεας ὄζους
> ἠχῇ θεσπεσίῃ, πάταγος δέ τε ἀγνυμενάων

the East and South Winds battle one another
in shaking the deep woods in the ravines of a mountain,
beech, ash, and smooth-barked cornel.
These whip their sharp-pointed branches against one another
with an unbelievable noise and there is a crashing of shattered limbs.

This storm is a major event; the winds are strong enough to break branches. In contrast the bobbing ears in the cornfield recall an everyday scene on the farm which should only arouse delight in the hearer.

Each of the two similes in book 2 (144 and 147) is drawn from one of the most traditional subjects, but the poet diminishes the dangerous potential of the winds by omitting those parts of the simile family which menace or destroy. It is further significant that these two similes are joined with no intervening line, and the full unit is framed by the same phrase in the narrative: 'The council was moved' (144 and 149). Juxtaposed similes are found elsewhere at 2.478–81 and 14.394.[13] In each case the tone of the joined similes is complementary and the extending elements present the same level of violence and power. At 2.144 and 147 the poet has not only rejected the most powerful and threatening scenes available within the wind simile family but by the device of juxtaposing two separate scenes he underlines the moderate and unwarlike qualities of the army.[14]

At 2.209 the poet describes the noise of the army returning to the meeting place. The previously mentioned simile at 16.765 also presents the noise of a destructive windstorm. In book 2 the waves thunder on a broad beach and the sea roars; this is a scene which could well attract picnickers and hikers – not much threat compared to the violent whirlwind which is present elsewhere in the simile repertoire.[15] 13.795 presents the strengthened form drawn from this simile family.[16]

Yet, the poet has not chosen the mildest descriptions of wind and waves for book 2. There is no calmer picture of winds than that of the fog hanging over the mountain tops when the winds are asleep (5.522), and no more placid country scenes than the wind blowing the chaff around the winnowers (5.499) or the gusts which raise clouds of dust on dry country roads (13.334). The second half of the book will present the army's full power and at the moment the possibilities inherent in this simile family keep that power alive – though in a simile that the audience would realize expressed only medium strength. Most of the similes in book 2 present only middling or weak support to the actions of the army by a like diminution of the strongest traditional features within the simile family. It does not seem possible to identify a 'base' form for the simile families; rather the memories of both poet and audience recall a range of descriptions from the most powerful to the weakest and evaluate the individual simile by placing it within that range.

2.394

> Ἀργεῖοι δὲ μέγ᾽ ἴαχον ὡς ὅτε κῦμα
> ἀκτῇ ἐφ᾽ ὑψηλῇ, ὅτε κινήσῃ Νότος ἐλθών,
> προβλῆτι σκοπέλῳ· τὸν δ᾽ οὔ ποτε κύματα λείπει
> παντοίων ἀνέμων, ὅτ᾽ ἂν ἔνθ᾽ ἢ ἔνθα γένωνται.

> the Argives cried aloud just as a wave
> against a high cliff when the South Wind drives it
> against a jutting crag that the waves driven by every wind
> from this side or that never leave once they rise.

The Greeks shout their approval of Agamemnon's order to fight and then return to their camps. This simile is curious because it seems to have two focuses in the narrative, neither of which is directly supported within the simile. The simile is introduced by the phrase 'The Argives cried aloud...', but rejoins the narrative with the troops being scattered among the ships. In the simile there is no word for sound, and the only support for the scattering of the Greeks is the winds which blow 'from this side and that'.

The emphasis within the simile seems to be on steadfastness. The rock itself is a 'high, jutting crag that the waves never leave'; in support of this reading, there is a parallel passage in which both narrative and simile use the image of the crag to underline the steadfast resistance of a group:

> ἠΰτε πέτρη
> ἠλίβατος μεγάλη, πολιῆς ἁλὸς ἐγγὺς ἐοῦσα,
> ἥ τε μένει λιγέων ἀνέμων λαιψηρὰ κέλευθα
> κύματά τε τροφόεντα, τά τε προσερεύγεται αὐτήν·
> ὣς Δαναοὶ Τρῶας μένον ἔμπεδον οὐδὲ φέβοντο

> like a towering, huge crag, nearby the grey sea,
> which endures the swift blowing of the whistling winds
> and the swelling waves which break against it;
> thus fixed did the Greeks await the Trojans and did not flee.[17]
> (15.618)

In book 2, however, steadfastness does not seem relevant – especially since the assembly is in the process of scattering, each man to his own ship.

Even with this change in narrative situation, the simile in book 2 is not as strongly phrased as that in book 15. In book 2 the headland is high; in book 15 the crag is towering.[18] In book 2 only one wave breaks against the headland, which is daily subject to waves from this direction or that; in book 15 the winds are shrill and the waves are swollen. The crag simile in book 2 is formed by choices that diminish the force that such a simile can express and is set in a narrative which it is only tangentially prepared to support.

The clustering of similes, 2.455–483

The marshalling of the Greek army for its grand presentation in the Catalogue is a major moment. Never again will the power of the largest expeditionary force in Greek legend be made so explicit with the names of heroes from all parts of the Greek world joined in one panoramic display, nor will interesting details defining the various contingents be presented in one passage. This display of the Greek forces provides a moment of order from which the maelstrom of the *Iliad* will be generated; only at the ending of the *Iliad* in book 23 will the characters of the Greek heroic world be regathered.

The Catalogue is introduced with appropriate weight by the unique prelude of seven similes in twenty-nine lines:

455: a fire burns in the distance
459: flocks of birds fly here and there on the plain
468: the numbers of troops are like leaves or flowers in spring
469: flies swarm around milk pails in springtime
474: goatherds separate goats in the pasture
478: Agamemnon's appearance is like Zeus, Ares, and Poseidon
480: a bull stands out in the herd

Simply stated, there is no short passage of Homeric narrative that is as densely packed with similes. The effect of these similes is even greater because none of the seven is short.

2.455

> ἠΰτε πῦρ ἀΐδηλον ἐπιφλέγει ἄσπετον ὕλην
> οὔρεος ἐν κορυφῇς, ἕκαθεν δέ τε φαίνεται αὐγή

> just as a destructive fire burns an immense forest
> on the peaks of a mountain and from afar the glare is seen

The repertoire of fire similes contains two basic types: one fire is frightening in its ability to destroy; the other is beautiful and bright, an object of wonder. The destructive fire is nowhere better exemplified than at 17.737 where it describes the Trojans assaulting the two Ajaxes:

> ἠΰτε πῦρ, τό τ' ἐπεσσύμενον πόλιν ἀνδρῶν
> ὄρμενον ἐξαίφνης φλεγέθει, μινύθουσι δὲ οἶκοι
> ἐν σέλαϊ μεγάλῳ. τὸ δ' ἐπιβρέμει ἲς ἀνέμοιο...

> like a fire which suddenly rises and rushes
> against a city of men and burns it, and houses fall
> in the giant glare. The force of the wind sets it roaring...

But there is also the more lyrical fire that describes the gleam from the divine arms of Achilles:

> ὡς δ' ὅτ' ἂν ἐκ πόντοιο σέλας ναύτῃσι φανήῃ
> καιομένοιο πυρός, τό τε καίεται ὑψόθ' ὄρεσφι
> σταθμῷ ἐν οἰοπόλῳ· τοὺς δ' οὐκ ἐθέλοντας ἄελλαι
> πόντον ἐπ' ἰχθυόεντα φίλων ἀπάνευθε φέρουσιν

> just as when the gleam of a burning fire appears over the sea
> to sailors – a fire which burns high up in the mountains
> in a lonely farmstead. The winds carry them all unwilling
> far from their friends over the fish-filled sea   (19.375).

In this simile the gleam of a distant fire is so far away that the sailors are more concerned over friends left behind than any threat of storm damage.[19]

Fire is so common a comparison for the activity of warriors, alone or in groups, that there are many similes of fires describing the strong attack or impassioned spirit of various fighters. The simile in book 2 is a mixture; even though the fire is presented as ἀΐδηλον ('destructive'), the threat is diminished when compared with a simile describing the fighting of Agamemnon:

> ὡς δ' ὅτε πῦρ ἀΐδηλον ἐν ἀξύλῳ ἐμπέσῃ ὕλῃ,
> πάντῃ τ' εἰλυφόων ἄνεμος φέρει, οἱ δέ τε θάμνοι
> πρόρριζοι πίπτουσιν ἐπειγόμενοι πυρὸς ὁρμῇ

> as when a destructive fire falls upon a thick forest,
> and the wind whirling it about bears it in all directions,
> and thickets fall uprooted when they are attacked by the force of
>   the flames   (11.155).

The simile in book 2 starts with the same formula: 'a destructive fire…' and continues with a similar idea: 'drives/falls on a vast forest'; but here the parallel ends. While the simile from book 11 directly focuses on the wind that whips the fire, the simile in book 2 merely defines the location of the fire, 'on the peaks of a mountain.' Then the notion of distance from danger is reinforced by placing the unnamed observer at a safe distance.

Again a traditional subject, fire, is designed by the poet to express far less than full power. There is an extreme parallel of such diminution of force at *Odyssey* 5.488 where Odysseus, having barely survived the storm at sea, crawls ashore stripped of all but his life. Lying in his nakedness beneath a thorn bush and an olive tree, he is compared to an ember, 'saving a seed of fire'; the fire of the hero is still there though reduced to a mere glow.

2.459

ὥς τ' ὀρνίθων πετεηνῶν ἔθνεα πολλά,
χηνῶν ἢ γεράνων ἢ κύκνων δουλιχοδείρων,
Ἀσίῳ ἐν λειμῶνι, Καϋστρίου ἀμφὶ ῥέεθρα,
ἔνθα καὶ ἔνθα ποτῶνται ἀγαλλόμενα πτερύγεσσι,
κλαγγηδὸν προκαθιζόντων, σμαραγεῖ δέ τε λειμών

as the many families of winged birds,
of geese or cranes or long-necked swans,
fly here and there rejoicing in their wings
on the Asian plain near the streams of the river Kayster
as they move forward with loud cries, and the plain echoes with
    sound

When the actions of warriors are compared to birds, the simile usually focuses on the strength of the attack.[20] Birds of prey attack smaller birds or small animals who are driven in fear before them: a vulture pursues geese, a falcon chases after starlings, an eagle swoops after a hare (17.460, 16.582, *Od.* 24.538, and 17.674). In addition, there are similes where whole groups of attacking warriors are compared to birds of prey; for example, Odysseus and his friends attack the panicked suitors in the final battle at his palace:

οἱ δ' ὥς τ' αἰγυπιοὶ γαμψώνυχες ἀγκυλοχεῖλαι,
ἐξ ὀρέων ἐλθόντες ἐπ' ὀρνίθεσσι θόρωσι·
ταὶ μέν τ' ἐν πεδίῳ νέφεα πτώσσουσαι ἵενται,
οἱ δέ τε τὰς ὀλέκουσιν ἐπάλμενοι, οὐδέ τις ἀλκὴ
γίγνεται οὐδὲ φυγή· χαίρουσι δέ τ' ἀνέρες ἄγρῃ

as vultures with crooked talons and hooked beaks
coming from the mountains rush on small birds
who dart over the plain fleeing away from the clouds,[21]
but the vultures diving down slay them and there is no defense
or flight. And men rejoice in the hunt   (*Od.* 22.302).

The simile at 2.459 is far different. These birds seek no prey; they fly randomly here and there as they delight in the openness of the meadow. In addition, the species cited are traditionally victims. Both Penelope and Telemachus see an eagle attack a single goose or geese, and later the interpretation is immediately offered that Odysseus is the eagle who will overpower and take vengeance on the weaker suitors (*Od.* 15.160–78 and *Od.* 19.536–50); Automedon attacks the Trojans like a vulture in pursuit of geese (17.460). At 3.2 cranes do bear death to Pygmy men, but in this case only the small size of the men allows even these weaker birds to be attackers. Because line 460 is repeated elsewhere in a similar context, it is probable that it is a traditional listing of victims:

ἀλλ᾽ ὥς᾽ τ᾽ ὀρνίθων πετεηνῶν αἰετὸς αἴθων
ἔθνος ἐφορμᾶται ποταμὸν πάρα βοσκομενάων,
χηνῶν ἢ γεράνων ἢ κύκνων δουλιχοδείρων,
ὣς Ἕκτωρ ἴθυσε νεὸς καυνοπρῴροιο

just as a yellow eagle plunges
upon a flock of winged birds who are feeding by the river,
geese or cranes or long-necked swans,
so did Hector rush at the ship   (15.690).

Thus, another dilution in a traditional simile topic by selecting the weaker features of the subject. Once again there is an extreme lowering of heroic potential within this family when Achilles complains of his disadvantaged position in the Greek army: 'as a bird brings food to her unwinged chicks whenever she catches it, but it goes ill for her' (9.323).

2.468 and 469

ὅσσα τε φύλλα καὶ ἄνθεα γίγνεται ὥρῃ.
ἠΰτε μυιάων ἁδινάων ἔθνεα πολλά,
αἵ τε κατὰ σταθμὸν ποιμνήϊον ἠλάσκουσιν
ὥρῃ ἐν εἰαρινῇ, ὅτε τε γλάγος ἄγγεα δεύει

as many as the leaves and flowers in spring.
Just as the many swarms of dense flies
which crowd around the sheep farm
in the springtime when the milk splashes into the pails

Homer juxtaposes these two similes with differing subjects to illustrate the vast number of troops marching against the Trojans. The passage is united internally and externally: it is composed of two juxtaposed spring-time similes and the narrative's need for number is directly expressed both before and after (μυρίοι ὅσσα...τόσσοι, 468 and 472).[22] Both similes join to present an enhanced scene of countryside peace, an effect parallel to the earlier intensifying similes at 2.144 + 147. The short simile of leaves and flowers seems a standard comparison repeated at *Odyssey* 9.51, where the poet describes the numbers of attacking Cicones. Flies also seem a typological subject for this context since there is another simile at 16.641 in which the last line is identical to 2.471 and the rest of the phrasing is similar.

The poet's choice of topics at such a narrative juncture is limited if he wishes to remain within the traditional alternatives. In the places where he uses a simile to illustrate numbers of troops, the tradition – as far as it can be defined – offers only two subjects of consistent usage: insects and leaves.[23] While the subject of leaves is not present often enough in the poems to establish a reliable scaling among its customary elements, the earlier discussion of the insect simile shows that the poet has chosen features which present these insects as an image of nature at peace.[24] Rather than bees or wasps, he uses harmless flies; they flit purposelessly through the farmstead. The rest of the simile diverts attention from them by focusing on the season.

2.474

> ὥς τ' αἰπόλια πλατέ' αἰγῶν αἰπόλοι ἄνδρες
> ῥεῖα διακρίνωσιν, ἐπεί κε νομῷ μιγέωσιν

> as goatherds easily separate the widely roaming flocks
> of goats when they have mingled together in the pasture

This simile describes the leaders among their men, a scene which occurs often in the *Iliad* and *Odyssey*, several times with a simile. In almost every case the tone of the simile reflects the tone of the surrounding narrative. If the men are involved in active fighting, the simile centers on one of the subjects that can be developed into an appropriate parallel for warfare. As the battle-starved Myrmidon commanders arm themselves around Achilles and Patroclus they are compared to wolves:

> οἱ δὲ λύκοι ὥς
> ὠμοφάγοι, τοῖσίν τε περὶ φρεσὶν ἄσπετος ἀλκή,
> οἵ τ' ἔλαφον κεραὸν μέγαν οὔρεσι δηώσαντες
> δάπτουσιν· πᾶσιν δὲ παρήϊον αἵματι φοινόν·
> καί τ' ἀγεληδὸν ἴασιν ἀπὸ κρήνης μελανύδρου
> λάψοντες γλώσσῃσιν ἀραιῇσιν μέλαν ὕδωρ
> ἄκρον, ἐρευγόμενοι φόνον αἵματος· ἐν δέ τε θυμὸς
> στήθεσιν ἄτρομός ἐστι, περιστένεται δέ τε γαστήρ

> flesh-eating wolves,
> in whose hearts is unquenchable fury,
> who having killed a great-horned stag in the mountains
> rip him with their teeth. Their cheeks are red with blood,
> and in a pack they rush to lap water
> from the surface of the dark spring with their slender tongues,
> vomiting up bits of bloody gore. Their spirits
> are unrelenting and their stomachs full   (16.156).

Equally appropriate analogues for a war context are the comparisons of Idomeneus to a boar, of the two Ajaxes to a dark cloud that causes the goatherd to drive his flock to safety, of the men thronging around Diomedes to lions or boars, and the appearance of Hector among his followers as an evil star (4.253, 275; 5.782; and 11.62). In peaceful scenes the tone of the simile usually matches the narrative: Proteus among his seals is likened to a shepherd among his sheep; Nausicaa among her handmaidens is like Artemis sporting in the mountains; and Odysseus' men gather around him like calves around a mother cow (*Od.* 4.413, *Od.* 6.102, and *Od.* 10.410). In the *Iliad* even Odysseus is compared to a ram walking through a flock of white ewes when he is not actually fighting (3.196).

The simile in book 2, however, presents a striking discrepancy between the warrior world of the army and a scene of peaceful nature, a discrepancy paralleled in the aristeia of Idomeneus. Aeneas gathers his comrades to confront Idomeneus and the soldiers follow along:

> ὡς εἴ τε μετὰ κτίλον ἕσπετο μῆλα
> πιόμεν' ἐκ βοτάνης· γάνυται δ' ἄρα τε φρένα ποιμήν·
> ὡς Αἰνείᾳ θυμὸς ἐνὶ στήθεσσι γεγήθει

> as sheep follow after the ram
> going to drink from their feeding place, and the shepherd rejoices
>   in his heart,
> thus did the heart rejoice in the breast of Aeneas   (13.492).

Because this tranquil scene introduces some of the goriest fighting and crudest woundings in the *Iliad*, the role of the simile emerges only from a view of the wider passage. The aristeia of Idomeneus is an episode in the larger battle stretching from the beginning of book 13 to the return of Hector in book 15, a long narrative section directly under the control of Poseidon as he strengthens the Greeks. Throughout this section the two armies are contrasted: the Greeks with the irresistible support of Poseidon vs. the Trojans who have momentarily lost the attention of Zeus. The scene from 424–95 emblematically opposes Idomeneus to Aeneas: the Greek awaits the Trojans like a bristling boar that is eager to defend himself against hunting dogs and men opposed to Aeneas, the leader of the weakened Trojans, who is like a ram among his ewes (13.471 vs. 492).

Likewise in book 2 the mustering of the army for combat would naturally call for a simile appropriate to a warlike context. Instead the poet has developed the simile to stress the non-warlike features of the Greek leaders: the goatherds control the flocks easily, the scene is a pasture, and the flocks have idly mingled together.

2.478 and 480

> μετὰ δὲ κρείων Ἀγαμέμνων,
> ὄμματα καὶ κεφαλὴν ἴκελος Διὶ τερπικεραύνῳ,
> Ἄρεϊ δὲ ζώνην, στέρνον δὲ Ποσειδάωνι.

33

ἠΰτε βοῦς ἀγέληφι μέγ' ἔξοχος ἔπλετο πάντων
ταῦρος· ὁ γάρ τε βόεσσι μεταπρέπει ἀγρομένῃσι

> among them mighty Agamemnon
> like Zeus, who delights in thunder, in his eyes and head,
> Ares in his waist, and Poseidon in his chest.
> Just as a bull is by far preeminent among all in the herd,
> for he stands out among the gathered cattle

Agamemnon is presented as the supreme king of the Greek army with two more juxtaposed similes: in the first the poet chooses to focus on Agememnon's appearance as he prepares for battle; the simile of a god at 7.208 describing Ajax before his single combat with Hector provides a parallel for both context and subject:

σεύατ' ἔπειθ' οἷός τε πελώριος ἔρχεται Ἄρης,
ὅς τ' εἶσιν πόλεμόνδε μετ' ἀνέρας, οὕς τε Κρονίων
θυμοβόρου ἔριδος μένεϊ ξυνέηκε μάχεσθαι.

thus Ajax moved forth like giant Ares,
who goes to battle among men whom the son of Cronos
has sent to fight in the violence of soul-devouring strife.[25]

The simile at 2.478 has several unusual features. First, though there are other similes in which a series of alternatives are offered as comparisons, here Agamemnon is simultaneously likened to three different divinities.[26] Secondly, while heroes are commonly compared to a specific god, never are they said to be like that god in regard to a particular physical feature. With the sole exception of Hector who has the eyes of a Gorgon or of Ares when he is in the act of routing the Greeks (8.349), warriors are not complimented on their eyes, their heads, their waists, or their chests. Usually the comparison is to the action of the god, as in the simile describing Ajax, rather than to his physical appearance. Thus though there are precedents for the simile subject at 2.478, the passage is odd in stressing the surface appearance of the warrior, in identifying him with several gods at once, and in focusing on uncustomary features. Once again choices in the extending elements drain the potential warlike qualities from the simile.

There is even a downscaling of intensity in the choice of the simile form. The simile by its nature is an indirect description. While Homer does not often offer physical descriptions, the strong effect of a direct presentation is evident in the image of Hector as he advances on the Greek ships:

ἀφλοισμὸς δὲ περὶ στόμα γίγνετο, τὼ δέ οἱ ὄσσε
λαμπέσθην βλοσυρῇσιν ὑπ' ὀφρύσιν, ἀμφὶ δὲ πήληξ
σμερδαλέον κροτάφοισι τινάσσετο μαρναμένοιο

foam appeared around his mouth, his eyes
shone from under his ferocious brows, and his helmet
shook fearfully around his temples as he fought
(15.607–10).

Book 2 does not present such a fearful image of Agamemnon.

The second simile centers on a bull, an animal familiar from the simile repertoire. Bulls are usually victims, especially of lions.[27] The simile describing the last moments of Sarpedon is typical:

ἠΰτε ταῦρον ἔπεφνε λέων ἀγέληφι μετελθών,
αἴθωνα μεγάθυμον, ἐν εἰλιπόδεσσι βόεσσι,
ὤλετό τε στενάχων ὑπὸ γαμφηλῇσι λέοντος

as a lion going into a herd destroys a bull –
a tawny, spirited bull among the shambling cattle –
who bellows as he dies in the jaws of the lion
(16.487).

Similes of farm animals usually describe warriors who are helpless or dying (13.571 and 20.403). The simile of the mother cow lowing over her calf that describes Menelaus taking his stand over the body of Patroclus at 17.4 illustrates how effective such a simile can be. Menelaus is always a warrior who causes concern to others when he is exposed to danger. His strength is immediately shown to be sound when he slays Euphorbus – just as a tempest uproots a young olive tree (53), and he is compared to an enraged lion as he terrifies the Trojans cowering around him (61). But then Hector confronts him; he quails and retreats to seek Ajax who returns with him to guard the body of Patroclus. Ajax's action, parallel to the earlier stand of Menelaus, receives a powerful lion simile (133). Thus the simile of the mother cow is the first part of a parallel structure intended to underline the inadequacy of Menelaus as Patroclus' defender.

A related use of a farm animal simile occurs in the passage where Paris returns to battle as a horse racing to the pasture (6.506); when the wounded Hector recovers his strength and reenters battle, he receives the same simile to express his renewed energy, but it is immediately enhanced with a second simile of a lion (15.263 + 271). Though the simile is repeated word for word, the effect is totally different; when the second simile is missing, Paris seems a frivolous creature interested only in warrior-like posturing.

The tone of the bull simile in book 2 can be further contrasted with alternative comparisons at similar junctures. The closest parallel is at 12.41 where Hector urges the Trojans to cross the ditch – another picture of the leader among his men; he is likened to the courageous lion who terrifies the men around him. Also 11.62: Hector stands among the Trojan leaders like an evil star and his armor flashes like the lightning of Zeus (66); elsewhere both subjects stress the impressive appearance of an effective warrior.[28]

From this brief survey it appears that warriors are usually compared to farm animals when the poet presents them as weak, helpless, or pathetic – and there is no warlike word or serious threat added to the image of the kingly bull amid the cattle which describes Agamemnon.

The farm animal simile which is most like that in book 2 occurs when Odysseus returns from Circe's palace to his companions awaiting him on the beach:

ὡς δ᾽ ὅτ᾽ ἂν ἄγραυλοι πόριες περὶ βοῦς ἀγελαίας,
ἐλθούσας ἐς κόπρον, ἐπὴν βοτάνης κορέσωνται,
πᾶσαι ἅμα σκαίρουσιν ἐναντίαι· οὐδ᾽ ἔτι σηκοὶ
ἴσχουσ᾽, ἀλλ᾽ ἀδινὸν μυκώμεναι ἀμφιθέουσι
μητέρας

as when calves on a farm jump around the herd of cows
returning to the farm yard when they are full from grazing –
altogether they frisk around them and the pens no longer hold them,
but lowing endlessly they run around their mothers

(*Od.* 10.410).

This simile suits the infectious joy of men who have been weeping disconsolately on the beach; in addition, the day's activities are done and the returning herd provides an appropriate parallel for the leader who will now neglect the voyage home to settle in with the sorceress. His leadership has ebbed to the point where his men will have to remind him of their goal. A like tone of failed leadership describes the commander Agamemnon as he musters his troops for the catalogue.

If a simile cluster is defined as a grouping of at least three long similes within 30 lines, all of which are focused on a single scene, then there are only three other identifiable simile clusters. In book 11 after Agamemnon departs wounded from the battle (280–3), Hector returns to have the day of glory promised by Zeus. To mark Hector's entrance Homer employs a cluster of four similes:

292: a hunter sets his hounds on a boar or lion
295: Hector is the equal of Ares, the destroyer of men (short)
297: a blustering wind churns the sea
305: two winds clash, raise heavy swells, and the waves scatter spray

Second, in book 15 when the Trojans are on the verge of burning the Greek ships, thus fulfilling the plan of Zeus and putting crucial pressure on Achilles (592 ff.), there is a cluster of six similes, two of which are short comparisons:

592: the Trojans are like flesh-eating lions (short)

605: Hector is like Ares (short) or a destructive fire (extended)

618: the Greeks remain fixed like a cliff which is battered by wind and waves

624: Hector attacks the Greeks like a wave which threatens to sink a ship whose sailors barely escape death

630: Hector attacks like a lion who harasses the inexperienced herdsman[29] and kills a heifer, scattering the herd

The third cluster falls at the end of book 17 describing Menelaus' and Meriones' struggle to remove the body of Patroclus to the Greek camp. In this passage similes respond to the balanced battle between Greeks and Trojans:

725: hounds (Trojans) viciously attack a wounded boar (the two Ajaxes) that scares them away when he turns to fight

737: a fierce fire is driven against a city by the wind and destroys it

742: two mules (Menelaus and Meriones) drag a large beam along a rugged path

747: a ridge (the Ajaxes) holds back several rivers (Trojans) that threaten to burst through

755: a falcon (Aeneas and Hector) attacks smaller birds (Greeks) bringing the threat of death

These four passages in books 2, 11, 15, and 17 show that the simile cluster is a form familiar to the poet. Two rules prevail in such clusters: the tone of all extended similes is subordinated to the direction of the narrative, and each simile acts independently in reinforcing the others in order to underline that direction. Similes in such passages are derived from a variety of subject categories, but there is no need to coordinate the subjects within the cluster so that one will suggest or lead to the next nor is there any necessity for a framing or linking structure created by the same subjects.[30] The grouping of such similes is a clear and economical means of introducing striking poetic background into the narrative. The simile cluster in book 2, the largest and most impressive in the *Iliad* – whether analysed as a series of individual comparisons or as a structured whole – presents a consistent poetic background of the more lyrical and peaceful qualities of nature, even though in this book Homer's goal is to present the army gathering for attack.

The final similes

2.780 and 781

ὡς εἴ τε πυρὶ χθὼν πᾶσα νέμοιτο·

...

Διὶ ὡς τερπικεραύνῳ
χωομένῳ, ὅτε τ' ἀμφὶ Τυφωέϊ γαῖαν ἱμάσσῃ
εἰν Ἀρίμοις, ὅθι φασὶ Τυφωέος ἔμμεναι εὐνάς

as if the whole earth were swept with fire

...

just as when Zeus who delights in thunder
is angry and lashes the land around Typhoeus
among the Arimoi, where they say lies the couch of Typhoeus

While these two similes describing the Greek army on the march are not joined by verbal links as closely as those at 144 + 147 and 468 + 469, they are juxtaposed and their combined effect is greater than either alone. The word 'groan' (στεναχίζω) occurs before and after the second simile – and the repetition gives simile and narrative a common focus. The sound of the fire is not directly reported by 'νέμοιτο', but there is no necessary incompatibility between the idea of a large fire sweeping the earth and a great sound.

Since these two similes immediately follow the Catalogue of the Greek ships, they are parallel to the earlier cluster of seven introductory similes. However they present two separate images – massive fire and earthquake/ thunderstorm – that are radically different from the more restrained, milder pictures throughout the previous lines of book 2.

Fire is a traditional simile subject accompanying the army on the march or in battle.[31] Yet though 2.780 is relatively short, it threatens destruction by stating so openly that all the earth was being consumed by fire; this is no small fire seen at a distance by disinterested observers. This simile does not have to be extended to a great length to emphasize the change in tone both because it is responding to the first simile in the earlier cluster at 455 – the far-removed fire which offered little threat – and because it is imme- diately reinforced by 781.

The image of Zeus lashing the land is insufficiently paralleled in Homeric poetry to construct a pattern of a simile family, but the story is told in Hesiod:

Ζεὺς δ' ἐπεὶ οὖν κόρθυνεν ἑὸν μένος, εἵλετο δ' ὅπλα,
βροντήν τε στεροπήν τε καὶ αἰθαλόεντα κεραυνόν,
πλῆξεν ἀπ' Οὐλύμποιο ἐπάλμενος· ἀμφὶ δὲ πάσας
ἔπρεσε θεσπεσίας κεφαλὰς δεινοῖο πελώρου.

αὐτὰρ ἐπεὶ δή μιν δάμασεν πληγῇσιν ἱμάσσας,
ἤριπε γυιωθείς, στενάχιζε δὲ γαῖα πελώρη.
φλὸξ δὲ κεραυνωθέντος ἀπέσσυτο τοῖο ἄνακτος
οὔρεος ἐν βήσσῃσιν ἀϊδνῆς παιπαλοέσσης,
πληγέντος· πολλὴ δὲ πελώρη καίετο γαῖα
ἀτμῇ θεσπεσίῃ καὶ ἐτήκετο κασσίτερος ὣς

When Zeus gathered his strength and took up his arms,
thunder and lightning, and the smoking thunderbolt,
leaping down from Olympus he struck him (Typhoeus). He burned
all the wondrous heads of the terrible monster.
But when he had overcome him and lashed him with strokes,
he fell lamed and the great earth groaned.
A flame from the king who was struck by the thunderbolt
shot forth in the dark rugged ravines of the mountain.
Much of the huge earth was burned
by the amazing heat and it melted like tin…

(*Theogony* 853–62).

Both the Hesiodic passage and the simile present a scene of massive destruction. Probably the simile refers either to a powerful lightning storm, reminiscent of Zeus' victory over Typhoeus, or an earthquake created by Typhoeus moving under the mountains.[32] In either case the poet has chosen to end the Catalogue with two mutually reinforcing images of nature as overwhelming and awesome in its destructive might.

The role of similes in book 2

For the most part the confused and perplexed reactions of the army to Agamemnon's commands are the physical acts through which the theme of ineffective leadership is presented; but the focus on the army's response to its leader is intensified by similes. Of book 2's twenty similes, fourteen are placed within the first five hundred lines, a rate of one in every thirty-five lines. In addition, since only four of those fourteen are short, similes play an extraordinarily important role in the telling of this tale. It is further significant that the first twelve similes describe the Greek army: its mass, its movements, the noise which it makes, and the gleam from its weapons – all topics for which the tradition offers appropriate subjects that are well designed for a war context. Yet the poet consistently chooses unwarlike features in developing each subject: harmless insects, random winds, wandering flocks of small birds, unthreatening farm animals, leaves, and flowers. The topic of insects traditionally illustrates both the number and ferocity of a group, but both insect similes (87 and 469) stress peaceful, pastoral qualities. In the series of wave similes (144, 209, and 394) the presentation emphasizes both the vastness of the sea and its chaotic

39

qualities; in 144 it is unclear which wind is moving the waves, the East or the South Wind, and this confusion is continued immediately in the simile at 147 where the West Wind blows through the cornfield. At 394 the waves roll 'now here and now there'.[33] Such similes suggest that the Greek army moves in no coordinated manner nor in any one specific direction; thus there is no meaningful threat to humans in either simile or narrative. The fire simile (455) describes a blaze which is seen from afar by men who are unthreatened and the birds at 459 have no goal; they also fly 'here and there'. Not even the locales mentioned in the similes are related to war: the plain with spring flowers, a farm or pastureland; the army musters for the Catalogue 'in the flowering meadow' (467). Two short similes used in speeches to describe the army are highly unwarlike; both Nestor and Odysseus call the warriors children or widow women (289 and 337).[34]

Because the tone of the similes sharply diverges from the war preparations in the narrative, the similes in their consistency strongly support the theme of weakened leadership. From its first scene book 2 is built from intrigue, deceit, and mistaken judgement. The book opens with Zeus instituting the plan that will accomplish his promise to Thetis to weaken the Greeks; he sends a dream to Agamemnon that urges the exact opposite of that promise: arm the Greeks and seize Troy. However, Agamemnon proposes a stratagem to the Greek leaders; he will test the army's mettle by proposing that they abandon the expedition and return home. When the troops seize upon his words and rush to the ships, their actions and thoughts threaten to abort the mission and thus run contrary to the plan of Zeus. The disenabling and weakening of the vast army, which is conveyed through its backward and forward movements, is repeatedly described by similes that make the army seem harmless.

This ironic undercutting reaches its climax in the cluster of seven similes before the Catalogue. Homer introduces this passage with these words:

σὺν τῇ παιφάσσουσα διέσσυτο λαὸν Ἀχαιῶν
ὀτρύνουσ' ἰέναι· ἐν δὲ σθένος ὦρσεν ἑκάστῳ
καρδίῃ ἄλληκτον πολεμίζειν ἠδὲ μάχεσθαι.
τοῖσι δ' ἄφαρ πόλεμος γλυκίων γένετ' ἠὲ νέεσθαι
ἐν νηυσὶ γλαφυρῇσι φίλην ἐς πατρίδα γαῖαν.

(Athena) gleaming rushed through the mass of the Achaeans
urging them to march. In the heart of each man
she roused unshakeable strength for war and fighting.
And war became sweeter to them than returning
to their beloved homes in hollow ships.   (450–4)

But this firm war spirit is immediately sapped by similes – the fire that gleams but does not threaten or destroy, the birds that glory in the freedom of disorganized flight, the leaves and the flowers in springtime, the farmyard flies, and the goats roaming the pastureland.

Once the Catalogue has revealed the actual military might of the Greeks and they begin to move to war, the theme of inadequate leadership ends and the size, talent, and inherent quality of the united mass of the Greek army lends credibility to the terrified Polites/Iris who rouses Hector and his fellow Trojans. The similes closely accompany this change. At 780 and 781 the similes describe massive destruction as Zeus enters the simile world by hurling his thunderbolts at the earth in his wrath, lashing the land. Now there is no mention of springtime nor harmless movements. Here the forces of nature run amok as fire sweeps the land and the earth groans.[35]

The deliberateness with which similes support the narrative of book 2 becomes even more apparent in examining those junctures where the poet chose other means to continue his narrative even though the simile was a traditional option. While it is impossible to know the poet's mind sufficiently to construct a full list of such passages, eight such occasions can be identified in book 2.

1.16ff. and 35f. – the coming and going of the Dream

The tradition suggested four standard means for describing the journey of a divinity: a simple two-line statement (leaving/arriving), the preparation for the trip, the listing of the route, or a simile.[36] For the journeys of the Dream to and from the Trojan camp Homer chose the simplest form of description.[37] Since the theme of the book is the leadership of Agamemnon, the poet introduces the Dream succinctly so that the audience can concentrate on the directions from Zeus to Agamemnon, the key to understanding Agamemnon's 'clever' device in leading – or misleading – his troops.

2.42ff. – Agamemnon enters the action by initiating his plan

There are numerous ways in the Homeric text to bring an important hero into the action including the simple entrance, the statement of the hero's preparation, the ponderings of the hero on possible success or failure, and the simile.[38] In this passage Homer has chosen to describe Agamemnon's appearance as he prepares to go through the camp – his tunic, his cloak, his sandals, his silver-studded sword, and his ancestral scepter – rather than his status, valor, or emotions. At this point an extended simile would offer a parallel scene that would deepen the audience's understanding of the hero.[39] Projections of success or failure would produce a subtler, more sympathetic character, perhaps capable of inner doubt; the Agamemnon of book 2 is misguided and stubborn. Homer chose a description of his entrance which penetrates no deeper than his clothes and equipment in order to direct attention toward the conduct of his office.

3.93 f. – Rumor urges the Greeks

As the Greeks gather to hear the message of Agamemnon, 'Rumor blazed forth in their midst urging them to go to the meeting.' Several divine forces in the Homeric poems are described by similes, such as the river Xanthus (21.12, 237, 257, and 362), the old man of the sea in book 4 of the *Odyssey* (413), or the god Sleep (14.290). Rumor, as the messenger of Zeus, could be emphasized if Homer were stressing the role of the divine plan in the action of this book.[40] But, just as with the Dream, a strong emphasis on divine intervention would destroy the focus on the book's theme. Therefore Rumor enters in a two-line factual report. Such restraint allows Homer to present the eagerness of the army succinctly without diluting the immediately preceding four-line simile describing the human response of the army.

4.100 ff. – the scepter of Agamemnon

This scepter is important in the first two books of the *Iliad*. It is cast to the ground by Achilles in book 1 (234–44), Agamemnon leans upon it as he addresses the Greek army making his misguided proposal to the troops (2.100–8), and Odysseus takes it up when he attempts to stop the chaotic rush to the ships, even beating Thersites into silence with it (2.185–7 and 265–8). An object of such significance is often marked by a simile.[41] In this passage Homer has chosen to detail the genealogy of the scepter, tracing it back through the House of Atreus to the gods Hermes, Zeus, and Hephaestus. By such an extended description Homer presents the divine and ancestral authority associated with the scepter, the very qualities which Agamemnon betrays by his unfortunate plan. By rejecting a simile in this passage, Homer isolates the king and expresses his lack of depth, against the list of previous divine and human authorities.

5.166 ff. – the arrival of Athena

As the Argives rush to their ships (invalidating the plan of Zeus), Hera complains that Troy may go unpunished because of the inept machinations of Agamemnon; Athena descends from Olympus asking Odysseus to urge the Greeks back to the assembly. The alternatives are the same four mentioned in regard to 16 ff. and 35 f. above; here, as there, Homer chooses the simplest of descriptions. Since it has been made clear that Odysseus knows Agamemnon wants the army to advance spiritedly toward Troy, he needs no further motivation from Athena to bring the Greeks back from the ships. Therefore her advice to him cannot be intended to introduce new motivation from another plane; rather the accent provided by the divine message shows that even heaven has been upset by Agamemnon's clumsy scheme. In this case there is not much point in stressing Athena's journey from heaven to earth through a description of elaborate preparation, or by a listing of her route, or by a simile; rather it is more important to demonstrate widespread dismay with Agamemnon's actions.

6.182ff. – the entrance of Odysseus

At this point the narrative spotlight falls directly on Odysseus as he takes the scepter from Agamemnon, rallies the Greeks, squelches all opposition, and finally makes a major speech of encouragement to the whole assembly. Odysseus, more than any other leader, provides new direction to the narrative. Often major figures receive a simile marking their entrance into the narrative,[42] but Odysseus is not parallel to other entrants since he largely seeks to resist a massive movement. Homer describes Odysseus' feelings as he watches the Achaeans stream towards their ships, summarizes his thoughts in Athena's speech, has him take the symbol of authority from Agamemnon, and shows the variety of means which he employs to rally the Greeks. A simile would only call attention to Odysseus, diverting the audience's mind from the complexity of the situation. Odysseus, as rallier of the Greeks, is the contrasting figure who exposes Agamemnon's folly; therefore it is important to focus on the effectiveness of his leadership in order to make him a weighty foil to Agamemnon.

7.212ff. – the entrance of Thersites

Much the same could be said of Thersites in his section of the narrative; he also could receive a simile as he emerges from the background to resist the movement surrounding him. However, since he carries Achilles' criticisms of Agamemnon into this book, it is more important for the poet to emphasize those thoughts over the fact of his resistance. A simile would merely shift attention from the continuing inadequacy of the Greek leader.

8.265ff. – Thersites' tear

When Odysseus strikes Thersites with the scepter, a tear falls from his eye and he sinks to the ground. A simile is often effective in presenting emotions,[43] but in this passage Homer does not call attention to Thersites' emotions. The narrative requires that the audience focus on the actions of Odysseus which will reinvigorate the Greeks' spirit. In addition, by enhancing the sorrow of Thersites through a simile, Homer would build sympathy for a character whose subjugation is cheered by the other Greeks.[44] The continuing focus on the contrast between Agamemnon and Odysseus as leaders directly furthers the theme of the book (2.270–7).

The poet and his audience

In general, individual phrases derived from the traditional diction, while seemingly indispensable to the poet, are not a satisfactory guide to the poet's thought processes. Homer has themes, conceptions, and imaginative images that must be expressed within the language that he inherited from the tradition, a language which is largely designed to describe concrete objects and physical actions; in designing the comparisons the materials which he uses are the repeated elements which appear in each simile family – even though the same element is not necessarily expressed in identical language. In some similes the poet can include simultaneously a series of suggestive parallels ranging from the literal to the metaphoric; as a result each simile reveals a mind striving to communicate particularized complex images, more or less parallel to the surrounding narrative, through the generic verbal building blocks offered by the tradition.[45] After choosing the shape and content which will enhance the narrative, he puts the abstractly planned simile into words by creating a vivid picture that includes only compatible objects and suppresses alternatives which he felt were inappropriate.[46] It is the role of the audience to appreciate the individual simile as the mental product of deleted alternatives – and then to embed the decoded comparison into the developing larger narrative.[47]

How should one describe this mental construct carried by the poet and his audience as part of their inheritance from the tradition although probably impossible to express fully in any single example? In analyzing Homeric composition Nagler has suggested a generative process dependent on Gestalt psychology.[48] But a Gestalt (= 'mental template') is based on a wide variety of human experiences and perceptions while the Homeric construct is mostly verbal, is drawn from a fairly limited variety of scenes, and has been developed almost solely to suit narrative needs.[49] An alternate concept has been the semantic frame which is defined as a 'system of categories structured in accordance with some motivating context';[50] but such contexts are often based on perceptions of finely-detailed scenes or images. In similes, however, the physical scenes seem mostly derived from literary typologies.[51] Both these theories empower an observer to extend and expand the basic form in new and more original ways; but the traditional form underlying the simile encourages the production of highly limited scenes which often comprise repeated motifs in formulaic language. Thus although there are features of simile composition which are made understandable by parallels to both Gestalt structures and frame semantics, neither is a precise guide, fully adequate to define the Homeric simile as the individual poet's creation formed from traditional diction, customary placement, and repeated topics. In addition, in spite of Homer's creative instincts there is a much more mechanical quality that is fundamental to each simile since it is necessary that the basic elements of the family have been created and shaped to parallel recurring actions in early Greek narrative. Just as Homeric Greek is an artificial language developed to sing effectively the old stories of Greece, so also the customary simile families are limited to subjects and forms that will provide easy comparison to the common scenes in such stories. The application of Gestalt psychology or frame semantics opens the individual simile to wide areas of interpretation, but it is truer to Homeric phrasing and audience psychology to base the decoding of traditional language on a finite set of repeated literary phrases. For these reasons I find that the theory of scripts, developed by Schank and Abelson, offers a more precise parallel to the reception and interpretation of similes.

Through decades of use the simile families remained constantly developing entities through their continual redeployment in familiar contexts. The most important feature of each family is its flexibility; there is no impediment to the poet creating a wide variety of individual similes by a process of recombination, deletion, or addition. Nagler has well described the special quality of Homeric expression: 'All is traditional on the generative level, all original on the level of performance.'[52] In drawing on the knowledge of simile families shared by poet and audience, the poet is exercising his artistic choice within the traditional devices and language of early Greek narrative in order to tell his own story.[53]

An awareness of the customary elements shared by poet and audience places several problems regarding Homeric similes into a new perspective:

1. The delineation of the families' components permits a clearer understanding of the process of poetic composition both in regard to the similes and to the larger narrative. Because of a combination of features inherent in their form the similes provide a concentrated and circumscribed body of evidence within the Homeric epics: their relative shortness and separateness, their clear demarcation as discrete poetic units, their close references to a parallel scene, and their flexibility. In forming the individual simile the poet makes many artistic choices that are like those he makes in composing other, less defined and neatly framed elements of his larger epic. The joining of two scenes drawn from radically different areas expands a critic's ability to see the poet's artistic processes with a clarity available at few other places in the poems: first the poet is describing the same moment twice

in different words and from different perspectives; second it is possible to compare parallel narrative passages where the poet employs a different subject or even chooses not to use a simile.

2. There is reality to the classifications of simile families that various critics have developed. However, if critics are to deal with Homer's creative processes, they must avoid statements which are based solely on the phrasing and language of the individual similes, thus classifying similes only by the the the first animal mentioned or the one who is the active subject. To analyse an individual simile properly a critic must compare the maximum number of similes composed of parallel elements in order to identify the family. While there is no law against continually subdividing the individual simile into increasingly discrete units, the establishment of elements repeated through a series of similes is a test which has a chance of bringing critics close to dealing with the categories in which Homer himself thought.

3. Scholars have long felt that there was more being expressed through certain similes than the simple surface meaning of the words. The awareness that the simile families are the shared property of poet and audience allows more open discussion of this silent language of powerful communication; it also permits a measure of control over impressionistic responses to those similes which have been appreciated as though they were free-standing small lyrics with high emotional charge. In spite of the limitations of the inherited traditional diction, which tends to tie the simile to the narrative through one and only one contact, it becomes mandatory for a critic to press for a broader interpretation which acknowledges that the components of the family as a whole were present to both poet and audience whenever its subject was introduced.[54]

4. The difference between long and short similes is not as important as some have thought. The choice is largely aesthetic; a short simile can add a degree of emphasis to the narrative without injecting the full weight of an expanded simile into a passage.

The creative processes that produced the final formation of each simile can never be adequately defined; thus it is easy for critics to speak in ways which diminish them. The talent, poetic brilliance, and remarkable abilities of later poets should not be denied to Homer as though he were mindlessly dependent on modes of expression which were prevalent in his own time. To the extent that his verse-making is viewed as a mechanical process, the fault is ours for underestimating his creations on the basis of criteria developed from the study of later poetry. The derivation of traditional modes of expression and categories of thought from the *Iliad* and the *Odyssey* themselves comes as close as possible to establishing the phrasing,

46

the typological categories, and the customary associations which were present in the mind of Homer as he composed his two epics.[55]

Notes

[1] The following publications have been of special importance in preparing this discussion: Edwards 1991, Jachmann 1958, Kirk 1985, Minchin 1992 and 2001, Nagler 1967 and 1974 , Schank and Abelson 1977, Schank 1999, Scott 1974, and Taplin 1990.

[2] Throughout this discussion I will refer to similes only by the opening line number. I will prefix *Od.* to all references to the *Odyssey*; otherwise references are to the *Iliad*.

[3] For a detailed discussion of traditional simile families and their customary placement see Coffey 1955 and 1957, Lee 1964, and Scott 1974.

[4] Applicable research into the use of memory in narrative communication appears in Schank and Abelson 1977 and Schank 1999. These studies of mental preconditioning from previous performances focus on scripts; see Shank and Abelson 1977, p. 41: 'a script is a structure that describes appropriate sequences of events in a particular context. They are not subject to much change, nor do they provide the apparatus for handling a totally novel situation' and p. 55: 'A script is a generalization. It is a structure with an implicit, built-in assumption, namely that because something has happened many times in a similar way, one should expect that thing to happen in the same way next time.' See also Minchin 2001, esp. 32–72.

[5] There are a series of parallels between books 1 and 2 which suggest that Homer intended these two books to be a continuous characterization of Agamemnon, just as books 23 and 24 provide a continuous presentation of Achilles (Scott 1997):

Book 1	Book 2
8–52: Agamemnon proposes to do the reverse of a priest's wishes.	1–75: Agamemnon proposes to do the reverse of Zeus' instructions.
53–307: a meeting in which Nestor supports Agamemnon.	76–85: a meeting in which Nestor supports Agamemnon.
308–57: Agamemnon asserts his will over Achilles.	86–154: Agamemnon asserts his will over the army.
	155–210: Odysseus and Athena restore order
357–427: Achilles complains to Thetis about Agamemnon's arrogance.	211–42: Thersites complains to the army about Agamemnon's arrogance.
427–56: Odysseus restores order by returning Chryseis.	243–77: Odysseus restores order.
	278–393: Odysseus and Nestor encourage men to a continued war effort.
457–75: Sacrifice to Apollo.	393–432: Sacrifice to Zeus.

[*1.458–69 = 2.421–32 (except 425–6)*]

493–530: Thetis and Zeus = unity	486–760: Catalogue of Greek ships = unity

[6] Even Agamemnon talks about the army in terms of numbers at 2.123–30.

[7] Bluntly stated in line 2.38–40. For a recent discussion of the status and performance of Agamemnon see Taplin 1990 with its bibliography.

[8] All translations are my own and are designed to reflect the phrasing in Greek as closely as possible.

[9] The simile at 12.167 places wasps and bees within the same family by offering them as alternatives.

[10] See Scott 1974, 58–68 and 76–7.

[11] This sense of the simile is confirmed in the description of the meeting place as confused (95) and filled with noise (96).

[12] Leaf (on 1.146) entertained the possibility that one of these two similes (probably 144–6) would have to be rejected. However, the juxtaposition of such different subjects within a tight narrative frame demonstrates the ability of each simile family to be adjusted in order to emphasize the varied tonal qualities of specific narrative situations; see Edwards 1991, 40.

[13] Probably this structure is related to those similes which offer alternative topics, such as: 'Not so great is the might of a leopard or of a lion or of a wild boar…' (17.20–1); see Edwards 1991, 37. Each of these alternatives has appeared alone, but the series of nouns suggests that the poet is striving to emphasize the narrative direction by repeating elements of like tone.

[14] Nimis 1987, 50–5 finds a different potential in the similes at 11.548 and 558 which describe the same subject (Ajax) in close proximity: 'A simile is generated to handle the development (548–55), but the lion simile gets the appetite seme wrong…Homer…leaves it and takes another shot, this time focusing on the woodman simile more sharply and adjusting the transformation of the appetite seme in the lion simile (558–63)' (p. 55). This seems his general approach to double similes (p. 111): 'Homer's similes are often attempts to exercise control over the course of the narrative; for this reason, they are at one level symptomatic of a certain *lack of mastery*. In fact, a dense accumulation of similes in Homer often signifies textual complexities.' I can find no good parallels to this type of juxtaposition; most joined similes reinforce the surrounding passage.

[15] The best examples are those already discussed, but add 9.4, 11.297, and 11.305.

[16] The similarities of items in 2.209 and 13.795 show that they both arise from the same model; the items added to 13.795 are: the thunder of Zeus (source), the scale of the wind which is not only at the beach but blows over the plain (location), the mixing of wind and water (alternatives within the simile family), the succession of waves (repetition), and the addition of adjectives (ἀργαλέων, θεσπεσίῳ, πολλά…παφλάζοντα). Through these choices the simile at 13.795 illustrates the controlling force of Zeus and the appropriately enhanced scope of the action.

[17] 15.618 is, in fact, a double simile opening with 'they held fixed like a wall' (πυργηδόν), thus focusing on the army's resistance. See comment by Janko 1992 on 618–36 for the structure of the larger passage.

[18] ἠλίβατος is a word that also suggests great size and strength: e.g. the massiveness of the rock with which Polyphemus seals his cave, and the size of the cliffs which protect a harbor (*Od.* 9.243, *Od.* 10.88, and *Od.* 13.196).

[19] This is a suggestively complex simile allowing the audience to structure a unified

48

'plot' from the juxtaposed elements: the sailors have put to sea and are being driven further away from the shore by a storm; they can only see the distant fire in the hills marking their friends' farm. The sentimental tone in the unwilling journey away from friends has roots in the surrounding narrative: 365–7 ('into his heart entered unendurable grief'), 387–91 = 16.140–4, and 407–17 (all reminders of Achilles' role in Patroclus' death). See de Jong 1985, 276 (revealing the desires of the Greeks around Achilles) and Edwards 1991 on 372–80 ('the longing with which the defeated Greeks…are looking towards this sign of safety').

[20] Scott 1974, 77–9. 2.459–63 seems to stress both the size of the Greek army and the noise of its advance; see Kirk 1985 on 465–6.

[21] 304 is difficult to understand; see Fernández-Galiano 1992 on *Od.* 22.204–6 for alternate interpretations.

[22] Leaves within similes have other connotations, but in 2.468, 2.800, and *Od.* 9.51 they are marked in the passage as referring to numbers. Both 6.146–7 and 21.464 are likewise marked within their passages as referring to natural qualities of the leaves; *Od.* 7.106 is ambiguous.

[23] See Scott 1974, 74–5 and 81.

[24] See discussion above about 2.87. Kirk 1985 on 473 notes that Homer returns to the narrative with a sentence which ends with διαρραῖσαι μεμαῶτες, 'a deliberately harsh formula in contrast with the pastoral scene.'

[25] Also 13.298 (although the extension of this simile adds Phobos as a mark of warrior spirit) and *Od.* 6.102.

[26] There is one other triple comparison at 14.394–9.

[27] In addition to the similes here cited see 5.161, 12.293, and 17.542. However similes of farm animals are not used with consistency in the Homeric poems; see Scott 1974, 79–80. In 21.237 and *Od.* 21.48 the bull is not a victim but is used to describe sound, and in the later example the bull is grazing peacefully in the meadow.

[28] See 13.242 and 22.26.

[29] 'The lack of a qualified herdsman' may be a motif in book 15 representing the Greek army without Achilles; see 15.325. Achilles' absence is emphasized at 59–65 and 395–404.

[30] Moulton 1977, 27–33 provides an extended discussion of the signs of internal organization in the full series of seven similes in book 2: 'The entire movement…clearly exhibits a contraction of the frame, until the audience is finally brought to concentrate on the supreme leader of the expedition' (33). He bases this conclusion on a series of words which seem repeated from earlier similes. On the verbal level it is highly likely that such repetitions may take place. But the choice of topics and the development of those topics seem less ordered and are more likely the results of the poet seeking a common effect through a series of different simile families, all of which can be organized into a unity under the general concept: 'images of peace undercutting the army's potential in war.' Moulton insists that the series develops until 'Agamemnon is at last singled out in glory'; although he further states: 'whatever equivocal impressions we may have of him after his foolish conduct earlier in this book seem to give way to the description of his powerful external image' (33). I would argue that the sequence shows no such development when each simile is considered against the audience's familiarity with the more customary directions in which each simile family has been developed elsewhere in support of battle scenes; I have the same problem with his

discussion of the repeated simile subjects from 87–394 on pp. 38–42.

For a more reasonable discussion of the repetition of words and phrases within the simile cluster see Kirk 1985 on 2.467–8.

[31] Scott 1974, 66–8.

[32] Van der Valk 1964, v. II, 475–7 interprets this simile as an element in a strategy to show Homer's judgment against the Trojans, who are thus the parallels to Typhoeus defeated by Zeus. Such a reading does not sit well with the role of Zeus at the end of the *Iliad* where he considers saving Hector, presses Achilles to return the body, and sends Iris to urge Priam to go to Achilles' tent (22.168–76; 24.104–19 and 144–58). It seems to me that the evidence of judgment against the Trojans is not developed consistently enough to define it as a pervasive theme in the poem.

[33] In book 2 the phrase 'here and/or there' seems a sign of weak leadership: see 90, 397, 462, and 476 (all in similes). In confirmation see 778–9 where the Myrmidons are singled out as roaming 'here and there yearning for their leader'. 812 uses the phrase in a different sense.

[34] For the consistent attitude toward children in simile and narrative see Ingalls 1998.

[35] There are only short similes in the rest of the book. 764 and 800 recall topics from earlier in the book, birds, leaves, and sand. When Iris describes the Greek army, she says that they are as numerous as leaves and sand, borrowing a simile from the first part of the book which talks of leaves, flowers, and springtime (800 vs. 468). Because most subjects after the Catalogue echo similes earlier in the book, the audience that has heard the description of flowers, leaves, and birds earlier can realize how terse and direct the simple unmodified description is. 754 and 872 are inside catalogues – thus providing too little content or context to contribute meaningfully to the book's ongoing theme.

[36] See Scott 1974, 15–20.

[37] As contrasts there are scenes where the passing from one area to another is a sufficiently important event in the narrative to receive an extended simile, e.g. *Od.* 5.51 or 5.864.

[38] See Scott 1974, 38–41.

[39] As examples, see 11.548 and 558 (Ajax) and 17.4 (Menelaus).

[40] As examples see 8.18–27 (the Golden Chain speech to emphasize the power of Zeus) or the first three similes in book 15 at ll. 80, 170, and 237 (reinstatement of Zeus' plan).

[41] See 8.555, 22.317, and *Od.* 21.406 + 411.

[42] Scott 1974, 38–41.

[43] Scott 1974, 28–31. For a discussion of Homer's use of similes to explore facets of human psychology, see James V. Morrison's chapter in this volume.

[44] The potential complexities which could be opened by enhancing the scene with Thersites are discussed by Thalmann 1988.

[45] Yet these building blocks because of their variety of previous associations have their own kind of complexity; see Schank 1999, 12: 'In script-based memory what we know in a given situation comes from what we have experienced in more or less identical situations; using more general structures allows us to make use of information originally garnered from one situation to help us in a quite different situation.'

[46] See Schank and Abelson 1977, 55: 'Every act in the restaurant script is potentially

subject to obstacles and errors, each of which suggests its own appropriate prescriptions or loops; a few of these will occur with sufficient frequency that a person repeatedly exposed to the script situation will learn them along with the rest of the script.'

[47] J.A. Notopoulos, 'Parataxis in Homer: a new approach to Homeric literary criticism', *TAPhA* 80 (1949) 1–23: 'neither the poet nor his audience can divert their attention for any period of time to the whole; they cannot pause to analyse, compare and relate parts to the whole; the whole only exists as an arrière pensée which both the poet and his audience share as a context for the immediate tectonic plasticity of the episode' (15) and 'The poet selects his material and the unity of the larger whole may be in the minds of the audience... The oral recitation thus becomes a selection of parts whose whole is the inexpressed context of the traditional material' (21).

[48] Nagler 1974.

[49] Nagler 1967, 281: 'The Gestalt itself...would seem to exist on a preverbal level of the poet's mind, since we have found it impossible to define other than as a comprehensive list of all the allomorphs which happen to exist in the recorded corpus. But to approach accuracy this would have to be made an infinitely open-ended list, leaving room for all the allomorphs that escaped recording (the vast majority!) and even all possible allomorphs; it would not really be a definition at all.' See the criticism by Nimis 1987, 1–22: 'Interpretive strategies based on such a notion of language focus on finding meaning "in" the text or "under" the text, and generally end up minimizing the historical determinants of the process of meaning production and conferring some more abstract and ahistorical significance on works of "literature"'. (6).

[50] Fillmore 1982, 119.

[51] Of course, there must be an original imaging which is reflected in Homer's similes, yet they are the result of a long tradition of development and arise from pressure to use repeated language. I feel that the pictorial source argued by Minchin 2001 as the major basis for the similes must be augmented by the descriptions that Homer derived from the existing preverbal and verbal simile subjects offered to him by the literary tradition; see the review by Rabel. This is clearest in the case of the repeated similes; see Scott 1974, 127–40. Given the formulaic nature of the language in the similes, I find the simile closer to a type scene, thus far more a literary construct than a visual experience to both poet and audience. See also the discussion of artifacts as models for similes by Damon 1961.

[52] Nagler 1967, 291.

[53] The theory of scripts opens the possibility for such restructuring by revealing the variety of categories in which elements can be stored; see Schank 1999, 119: 'most episodes are broken apart in terms of the structures employed in understanding them (during processing), stored in terms of those same structures in memory, and are reconstructable by various search techniques.' For special reference to Homer see Minchin 1992.

[54] Such recall of elements is common in remembering previous performances: 'for stories to be told without a great deal of effort, they must be stored away in a fashion that enables us to access them as a unit. If this were not the case, stories would have to be reconstructed each time they were told, a process that would become more and more difficult with time as a particular event faded from memory' (Schank 1999, 105).

[55] I am grateful for the criticism so generously offered in preparing this study by John Foley, Carolyn Higbie, and Lindsay Whaley.

51

Bibliography
Coffey, M.
1955   'The similes of the *Odyssey*', *BICS* 2, 27.
1957   'The function of the Homeric simile', *AJP* 78, 113–132.
Damon, P.
1961   'Modes of analogy in ancient and medieval verse', in *University of California Publications in Classical Philology* 15.6, 261–71, Berkeley and Los Angeles.
de Jong, I.J.F.
1985   'Fokalization und die homerischen Gleichnisse', *Mnemosyne* 38, 257–80.
Edwards, M.W.
1991   *The* Iliad: *A commentary*, vol. V: Books 17–20, Cambridge.
Fernández-Galliano, M., Russo J. and Heubeck, A. (eds.)
1992   *A Commentary on Homer's* Odyssey, vol. III, Books XVII–XXIV, Oxford.
Fillmore, C.J.
1982   'Frame semantics', in The Linguistic Society of Korea (ed.) *Linguistics in the Morning Calm*, Seoul, Hanshin Publishing Co.
Fränkel, H.
1921   *Die homerischen Gleichnisse*, Göttingen.
Ingalls, W.B.
1998   'Attitudes towards children in the *Iliad*', *Echos du monde classique* 17, 13–34.
Jachmann, G.
1958   *Der homerische Schiffskatalog und die* Ilias, Köln and Opladen, 218–34.
Janko, R.
1992   *The* Iliad: *A commentary*, vol. IV: Books 13–16, Cambridge.
Kirk, G.S.
1985   *The* Iliad: *A commentary*, vol. I: Books 1–4, Cambridge.
Leaf, W.
1900   *The* Iliad, London.
Lee, D.J.N.
1964   *The Similes of the* Iliad *and the* Odyssey *Compared*, Melbourne.
Minchin, E.
1992   'Scripts and themes: cognitive research and the Homeric epic', *CA* 11, 229–41.
2001   *Homer and the Resources of Memory: Some applications of cognitive theory to the* Iliad *and the* Odyssey, Oxford. (Reviewed by R.J. Rabel 2001, *BMCR* 12.09.)
Moulton, C.
1977   *Similes in the Homeric Poems*, Göttingen.
Nagler, M.N.
1967   'Towards a generative view of the oral formula', *TAPA* 98, 269–311.
1974   *Spontaneity and tradition: A study in the oral art of Homer*, Berkeley, Los Angeles, London.
Nimis, S.A.
1987   *Narrative Semiotics in the Epic Tradition: The simile*, Bloomington and Indianapolis.

Notopoulos, J.A.
  1949   'Parataxis in Homer: a new approach to Homeric literary criticism', *TAPA* 80, 1–23.
Schank, R.C.
  1999   *Dynamic Memory Revisited*, Cambridge.
Schank, R.C. and Abelson, R.P.
  1977   *Scripts, Plans, Goals, and Understanding: An inquiry into human knowledge structures*, Hillsdale, N.J.
Scott, W.C.
  1974   *The Oral Nature of the Homeric Simile*, Leiden.
  1997   'The etiquette of games in *Iliad* 23', *GRBS* 38, 213–27.

Taplin, O.
  1990   'Agamemnon's role in the *Iliad*', in C. Pelling (ed.) *Characterization and Individuality in Greek Literature*, Oxford, 60–82.
Thalmann, W.G.
  1988   'Thersites: comedy, scapegoats, and heroic ideology in the *Iliad*', *TAPA* 118, 1–28.
Van der Valk, M.
  1963–4   *Researches on the Text and Scholia of the* Iliad, Leiden.

3

HOMER ON AUTOBIOGRAPHICAL MEMORY: THE CASE OF NESTOR

Elizabeth Minchin

To what extent was an oral poet like Homer aware of the reliance he placed on memory, as he performed stories from his traditional repertoire? What was the extent of his understanding of the workings of memory? We might conclude that he attributed some of his talent for storytelling to the Muse of epic song, to whom he appealed for inspiration at the outset of each epic and, in the *Iliad* at least, at frequent points in its course.[1] But it is highly likely that he and no doubt other singers before him had thought a great deal about the workings of memory and were well aware that, Muse or no Muse, their own memories could either serve them well or let them down badly.

We have abundant evidence for these singers' preoccupation with memory. In a number of ways and at a number of levels in his songs Homer acknowledges its nature, its power – and its value. We see this concern on the very surface of the poems. We observe, for example, that the heroes of the *Iliad*, most notably Hektor, are anxious for the future. They are anxious that their names should live on; and that their deeds and triumphs be remembered by generations to come.[2] In the course of the *Odyssey*, on the other hand, Homer's characters, in particular Odysseus and Penelope, look back in time; they dwell on the pain so often associated with memories of things past.[3] But, as Odysseus and Penelope learn, it can ultimately be a source of pleasure to turn one's mind back to one's troubles – once they are over.[4] Furthermore, we observe that in Homer's world, just as in ours, people employed – or perhaps we might say they institutionalized – a range of stratagems designed to prompt memory, in order to reduce the burden placed on it and to increase its effectiveness. Think of the burial mounds of heroes to which Homer on occasion refers, or of the gifts which they exchange with so much ceremony.[5] The role of these grave markers or these gifts is clearly, as Ruth Scodel has argued, to *cue* memories, whether of individuals or of significant moments from times past.[6]

Homer, therefore, as a representative of this particular oral tradition, often remarks on or alludes to the activities of reminding, remembering, forgetting, and its opposite, the inability to forget. This present study is a first attempt at assessing the poet's understanding of the workings of memory and to compare it with our own. I shall concentrate in this first instance on autobiographical memory. It is an aspect of memory which appears to be one of the poet's (and, perhaps, the tradition's) special interests, since at a number of points in the epics his characters engage in personal reminiscence and find a certain satisfaction in doing so. The principal focus of the discussion will be Nestor, the old warrior who, in his appearances in both the *Iliad* and the *Odyssey*, is characterized by his readiness to share lengthy and detailed reminiscences of his earlier years. The frequency, the length, and the content of these reminiscences, as we shall see, shape the way we perceive him. In order to compare the understanding of poets in this oral tradition with our own, I have turned to a number of recent studies of memory and its functions in everyday activities, including the work of Daniel Schacter, who draws together, very usefully, wide-ranging research into the practical aspects of memory.[7]

Homer tells us (*Il.*1.250–2) that Nestor is remarkably old: all his age peers have died, as have some of their sons;[8] but Nestor is still alive and full of energy, as we observe at each of his appearances in the narrative. There is something very appealing about this portrait of someone who is in fact too old for the rough and tumble of battle but who simply cannot retire; he is still eager to participate in whatever way he can – and he does so by contributing accumulated knowledge based on years of experience. On a number of critical occasions in the *Iliad*-story, Nestor comes forward to advise his companions. And he backs up his advice, as older people are wont to do, with a story from his early days. Let us look at four such instances.

At the beginning of the *Iliad* Achilleus and Agamemnon are quarrelling bitterly, Nestor intervenes; he tells them to give up their anger and put an end to their disagreement; and he reminds them that in days past, as a much younger man, he gave advice to people far more distinguished than they could ever be – and these people at that time heeded his advice:[9]

ἀλλὰ πίθεσθ'· ἄμφω δὲ νεωτέρω ἐστὸν ἐμεῖο·
ἤδη γάρ ποτ' ἐγὼ καὶ ἀρείοσιν ἠέ περ ὑμῖν
ἀνδράσιν ὡμίλησα, καὶ οὔ ποτέ μ' οἵ γ' ἀθέριζον.
οὐ γάρ πω τοίους ἴδον ἀνέρας οὐδὲ ἴδωμαι,
οἷον Πειρίθοόν τε Δρύαντά τε, ποιμένα λαῶν,
Καινέα τ' Ἐξάδιόν τε καὶ ἀντίθεον Πολύφημον,
Θησέα τ' Αἰγεΐδην, ἐπιείκελον ἀθανάτοισι·

56

...

καὶ μὲν τοῖσιν ἐγὼ μεθομίλεον ἐκ Πύλου ἐλθών,
τηλόθεν ἐξ ἀπίης γαίης· καλέσαντο γὰρ αὐτοί·
καὶ μαχόμην κατ᾽ ἔμ᾽ αὐτὸν ἐγώ· κείνοισι δ᾽ἂν οὔ τις
τῶν οἳ νῦν βροτοί εἰσιν ἐπιχθόνιοι μαχέοιτο·
καὶ μέν μευ βουλέων ξύνιεν πείθοντό τε μύθῳ·
ἀλλὰ πίθεσθε καὶ ὕμμες, ἐπεὶ πείθεσθαι ἄμεινον·

Yet be persuaded. Both of you are younger than I am.
Yes, and in my time I have dealt with better men than
you are, and never once did they disregard me. Never
yet have I seen nor shall see again such men as these were,
men like Peirithoös, and Dryas, shepherd of the people,
Kaineus and Exadios, godlike Polyphemos,
or Theseus, Aigeus' son, in the likeness of the immortals.

...

I was of the company of these men, coming from Pylos,
a long way from a distant land, since they had summoned me.
And I fought single-handed, yet against such men no one
of the mortals now alive upon earth could do battle. And also
these listened to the counsels I gave and heeded my bidding.
Do you also obey, since to be persuaded is better.

Il. 1.259–65, 269–74[10]

The contrasts that Nestor himself perceives, not only between the excellent qualities of the men of past times (κάρτιστοι[266]...κάρτιστοι [267]...) and the lesser men of the present, but also between his former self and his own present state, colour his tale.[11] It is a theme which runs through almost all of Nestor's reminiscences in the *Iliad*, as we shall observe below. The point which is crucial to his tale is that he gave advice to the Lapiths, who – even they – heeded his counsel (273). This narrative is a lengthy and emphatic preface to the advice he is about to give Achilleus and Agamemnon:[12] to resolve their differences for the sake of a successful outcome of the war (274–84). Unfortunately, Nestor's advice on this occasion was not taken. The quarrel between the two men escalated and Achilleus decided to withdraw from the fighting.

Battle was resumed. Hektor, leader of the Trojans, then threw down a challenge to the Achaians, to single combat. There was much hesitation on the Achaian side; no one was prepared to stand against him. Nestor was dismayed; he reproved his fellow warriors, reminding them that years before, despite his youth, he alone had had the courage to take the field against the Arkadian Ereuthalion – and in doing so he had felled a mighty warrior (*Il.* 7.132–57). He was the youngest of the Pylian heroes (153) and yet it was he who responded to Ereuthalion's challenge to fight (150–3).[13]

He begins and ends his story of that encounter with what will become familiar themes:

αἲ γάρ, Ζεῦ τε πάτερ καὶ Ἀθηναίη καὶ Ἄπολλον,
ἡβῷμ᾽ ὡς ὅτ᾽ ἐτ᾽ ὠκυρόῳ Κελάδοντι μάχοντο
ἀγρόμενοι Πύλιοί τε καὶ Ἀρκάδες ἐγχεσίμωροι,
Φειᾶς πὰρ τείχεσσιν, Ἰαρδάνου ἀμφὶ ῥέεθρα.
...
εἴθ ὣς ἡβώοιμι, βίη δέ μοι ἔμπεδος εἴη·
τῷ κε τάχ᾽ ἀντήσειε μάχης κορυθαίολος Ἕκτωρ.

If only, O father Zeus, Athene, Apollo,
I were in my youth as when the Pylians assembled
and the spear-fighting Arkadians battled by swirling Keladon,
by the streams of Iardanos and before the ramparts of Pheia.
. . .
If only I were as young now, as then, and the strength still steady
  within me;
Hektor of the glancing helm would soon find his battle.

Il. 7.132–5, 157–8

In subsequent fighting the Trojans temporarily gained the upper hand, the losses on the Greek side were heavy, and there was anxiety in the Greek camp. At this point Achilleus sends Patroklos to talk to Nestor to get some news about the Achaians' position (*Il.* 11.611–15). Nestor, who has just now been brought off the field, is having a recuperative drink and a comfortable chat with Machaon (618–43). But when Patroklos arrives unexpectedly (644) he springs into action. He uses this encounter with the young man to try to persuade him, at least, to return to the fighting. As he speaks to Patroklos he attempts to impress on him the satisfaction one feels in doing a good day's work on the battlefield, the justifiable pride one can take in one's achievements, and the sense of responsibility one must feel to one's companions who are fighting for the same cause. This he does by telling a long story (670–762) about his own brilliant achievements in the distant days of his youth, when he had first engaged in battle as a young hero, and triumphed, even though his father had decreed that he was too young to go off to fight. Here is its beginning:

εἴθ᾽ ὣς ἡβώοιμι βίη δέ μοι ἔμπεδος εἴη,
ὡς ὁπότ᾽ Ἠλείοισι καὶ ἡμῖν νεῖκος ἐτύχθη
ἀμφὶ βοηλασίη, ὅτ᾽ ἐγὼ κτάνον Ἰτυμονῆα,
ἐσθλὸν Ὑπειροχίδην, ὃς ἐν Ἤλιδι ναιετάασκε,
ῥύσι᾽ ἐλαυνόμενος· ὁ δ᾽ ἀμύνων ᾗσι βόεσσιν
ἔβλητ᾽ ἐν πρώτοισιν ἐμῆς ἀπὸ χειρὸς ἄκοντι,
κὰδ δ᾽ ἔπεσεν, λαοὶ δὲ περίτρεσαν ἀγροιῶται.

ληΐδα δ' ἐκ πεδίου συνελάσσαμεν ἤλιθα πολλήν,
πεντήκοντα βοῶν ἀγέλας, τόσα πώεα οἰῶν,
τόσσα συῶν συβόσια, τόσ' αἰπόλια πλατέ' αἰγῶν,
ἵππους δὲ ξανθὰς ἑκατὸν καὶ πεντήκοντα,
πάσας θηλείας, πολλῇσι δὲ πῶλοι ὑπῆσαν.
καὶ τὰ μὲν ἠλασάμεσθα Πύλον Νηλήϊον εἴσω
ἐννύχιοι προτὶ ἄστυ·

If only I were young now, and the strength still steady within me,
as that time when a quarrel was made between us and the Eleians
over a driving of cattle, when I myself killed Itymoneus,
the brave son of Hypeirochos who made his home in Elis.
I was driving cattle in reprisal, and he, as he was defending
his oxen, was struck among the foremost by a spear thrown from my
    hand
and fell, and his people who live in the wild fled in terror about him.
And we got and drove off together much spoil from this pastureland:
fifty herds of oxen, as many sheepflocks, as many
droves of pigs, and again as many wide-ranging goatflocks,
and a hundred and fifty brown horses, mares all of them
and many with foals following underneath. And all there
we drove inside the keep of Neleian Pylos, making
our way nightwise to the town.   *Il.* 11.670–83

At the end of his long tale the old man perceives that Patroklos is swayed, at least a little, by his indirect appeal, so he moves in with a more direct argument. He again consults his memory and selects a narrative from a more recent time. This is a memory which Nestor and Patroklos have in common: he reminds him of the occasion when Nestor had gone to Phthia to invite Achilleus and Patroklos to join the forces which would sail to Troy. Nestor then had watched and listened as first Achilleus' father, Peleus, and then Patroklos' father, Menoitios, made their farewells. As they parted Menoitios advised his son that because he was the elder of the two warriors, it was his responsibility to speak 'solid words to Achilleus, and give him good counsel and to point his way' (788–9). This recollection is an inspired choice. It wins the day. Through this shared reminiscence Nestor persuades Patroklos (804–5) to return to the fighting, in Achilleus' place, with, as we know, disastrous results.

We see Nestor in the *Iliad* for the last time during the funeral games which Achilles holds in memory of Patroklos. The first event of the games is a chariot race in which one of the participants is Nestor's son, Antilochos. As the participants step forward to compete, Nestor comes over to Antilochos. He himself will not be competing, but, as on other occasions, he wishes to participate in the only way he can. Now he gives detailed instructions to his son on how to handle the horses to tactical advantage.

The race is run. Antilochos – eventually – takes out second prize. After the final distribution of all prizes for this competition, there is one prize left over. In a spontaneous gesture Achilles takes up this prize, a two-handled jar, and presents it to the old man:

τῆ νῦν, καὶ σοὶ τοῦτο, γέρον, κειμήλιον ἔστω,
Πατρόκλοιο τάφου μνῆμ’ ἔμμεναι· οὐ γὰρ ἔτ’ αὐτὸν
ὄψῃ ἐν Ἀργείοισι· δίδωμι δέ τοι τόδ’ ἄεθλον
αὔτως· οὐ γὰρ πύξ γε μαχήσεαι, οὐδὲ παλαίσεις,
οὐδ’ ἔτ’ ἀκοντιστὺν ἐσδύσεαι, οὐδὲ πόδεσσι
θεύσεαι· ἤδη γὰρ χαλεπὸν κατὰ γῆρας ἐπείγει.

This, aged sir, is yours to lay away as a treasure
in memory of the burial of Patroklos; since never
again will you see him among the Argives. I give you this prize
for the giving; since never again will you fight with your fists nor wrestle
nor enter again the field for the spear-throwing, nor race
on your feet; since now the hardship of old age is upon you.

Il. 23.618–23

Nestor is clearly gratified by Achilles’ recognition of his contributions over the years; and in this moment of joy he remembers his past triumphs in events just like this, at other funeral games. He thinks back to the games for Amaryngkeus, when he won all the events except the chariot race. And, as before, he prefaces his description of this event with familiar words:

ναὶ δὴ ταῦτά γε πάντα, τέκος, κατὰ μοῖραν ἔειπες·
οὐ γὰρ ἔτ’ ἔμπεδα γυῖα, φίλος, πόδες, οὐδέ τι χεῖρες
ὤμων ἀμφοτέρωθεν ἐπαΐσσονται ἐλαφραί.
εἴθ’ ὡς ἡβώοιμι βίη τέ μοι ἔμπεδος εἴη
ὡς ὁπότε κρείοντ’ Ἀμαρυγκέα θάπτον Ἐπειοὶ
Βουπρασίῳ, παῖδες δὲ θέσαν βασιλῆος ἄεθλα.
...
ὣς ποτ’ ἔον· νῦν αὖτε νεώτεροι ἀντιοώντων
ἔργων τοιούτων· ἐμὲ δὲ χρὴ γήραϊ λυγρῷ
πείθεσθαι, τότε δ’ αὖτε μετέπρεπον ἡρώεσσιν.

Yes, child: all this you said to me was true as you said it.
My limbs are no longer steady, dear friend; nor my feet, neither
do my arms, as once they did, swing light from my shoulders.
I wish I were young again and the strength still unshaken within me
as once, when great Amaryngkeus was buried by the Epeians
at Bouprasion, and his sons gave games for a king’s funeral.
...
This was I, once. Now it is for the young men to encounter
in such actions, and for me to give way to the persuasion
of gloomy old age. But once I shone among the young heroes.

Il. 23.626–31, 643–5

So this is Nestor: eager, irrepressible even, although now physically not the man he once was; he is a man with a store of treasured memories which he delights in sharing, with very little provocation. How does this portrait compare with what psychology tells us about old age, memory, and reminiscence?

One of the important functions of memory is that it underpins for each of us our sense of self.[14] Every one of us holds in memory a sequence of stories about himself or herself and the things he or she has done.[15] These stories, taken together, amount to an informal life-history. We can update this autobiography or revise it at any point during our lifetime.[16] We have sole editorial control. The stories we include in our personal history are likely to be the stories that exemplify the characteristics that we want to attribute to ourselves; they construct the identity which we prefer.[17] It is clear that there may be inconsistencies amongst the perceptions which we entertain about ourselves; it is also clear that when we revise our self-concept we may be obliged to revise, reconfigure, or reconstruct substantial holdings in our memory store.[18]

The functions of autobiographical memory are not only of this intrapersonal kind, which relates to self-definition. We also draw on our personal reminiscences in talk as a way of maintaining and extending our relationships with others.[19] The sharing of autobiographical stories, for the most part, establishes goodwill in others. Such stories can be used as strategic moves in an exercise in persuasion or counselling: they may, for example, take the form of self-disclosure, when we relate personal experiences and invite our listeners' sympathy; or they may be stories about events in which our listeners were also participants. By evoking a shared past we aim to increase their receptivity to our proposals.[20]

So how much do people remember of their lives? We don't remember every detail, but we do remember a great deal. And, of course, the older we are the more memories we have. Until recently it had been assumed that elderly people retained clearer memories of remote events than of recent events. But the reality is a little more complicated than this. If we consider the way in which memories are distributed across a person's lifespan we see, first of all, evidence of childhood amnesia. That is, we have very few memories from the period before age 3 (the pre-school years) and few memories for the years before age 7. Second, there is a peak of memories for a period that runs between the decades that cover adolescence and early adulthood, approximately age 11 to age 30. Third, we must take into account a simple retention component for the most recent 20 years of our lives. That is, we have a relatively large number of memories from most recent decades. Fourth, studies show that in subjects in the age-range 35–50 a process called life review begins – that is, people begin to reminisce.[21]

A study of reminiscence, that is, of spontaneous memory in older people, has revealed a surprising lack of memories for the age range 30–40 and a return to memories from earlier decades.[22] The apparent freshness of memories from the earlier period, ages 11–30, may be attributed to several factors. This is the period in which so many of the conventional landmarks in life occur: in our own times education; first job; the formation of long-term friendships; falling in and out of love; relationships; possibly marriage; the birth of children. Many of these events are marked by strong emotional responses, which ensure that associated memories are securely encoded.[23] All these memories therefore take a central place in a person's life-history. We should bear in mind also that events in which we played an active role, such as the landmark events which I identified a moment ago, being more vivid are likely to be more enduring.[24] The vividness of memories, however, does not remain constant. Vividness decreases as the age of the memory increases, for about 20–30 years. After this interval there is little change.[25]

So how is it that people in their 70s and 80s have such clear memories of their youth? As we grow older we establish and preserve a repertoire of favourite memories which stem from that period of landmark events. It is the process itself, of accessing memory, of reliving in our mind's eye this or that event, of establishing its relevance to the current situation, and talking about it, which counteracts a decline in vividness.[26] Hence the apparent freshness of memories from youth and early adulthood in the elderly.

To return now to Nestor – an old man whose vast experience of life has equipped him with a host of memories. When any crisis arises in the Greek camp, his memory is, naturally, prompted: he has seen it all before. A parallel circumstance from his earlier years comes readily to mind and Nestor is able to remember precisely how he handled it. We should note that most, but not all, of Nestor's memories are of himself as the actor; it was he who nearly always played the leading role in his tales. These autobiographical stories depict him as a man of action, a man of energy and talent, who earned the respect of the great men of his time. Events from his life-history, as he tells them, illustrate salient traits in his self-image – and validate it.[27] These recollections give him an identity which is a source of pride. We note also that on all but one of the occasions I described earlier Nestor returns in memory to that period which we would describe as the prime of life, late teens to early adulthood. From the readiness with which the old man launches into these tales we have the sense that in his later years he has more than once shared these particular memories of the past with his family, his friends, and his comrades; and that he has found much pleasure in doing so.[28] And so these memories from long ago, through their salience (as memories marking significant points in his career) and through his active preservation of them (as favourites in his repertoire),[29] retain a freshness and a vividness which engage us all as we hear them, even if they do not always succeed as tools of persuasion within the story itself.[30]

It is interesting to observe that whenever Nestor returns in memory to that distant time, he announces it. Every time that Nestor reminisces about events in his youth, he introduces his tale with the lament of old age – a 'nostalgic wish', as de Jong describes it: 'I wish I were as young and as strong as I was when…'; or 'never again will I see men of the calibre of…'[31] By contrast, on those few occasions when his memory takes him back to his later years, to a time closer to the present (that is, the years of the Trojan War), he does not. When, for example, the old man recollects the advice that Menoitios gave to Patroklos when he and Odysseus had visited Phthia (*Il.* 11.764–88), he does not present his narrative as a memory from long ago, from his vigorous youth. This is a memory which dates to the gathering of the forces before the assault on Troy, just ten years before; and it is a 'bystander memory' – a second person story, in which Nestor reminds Patroklos of what was said to him by his father.[32] What is significant is that this story is not framed by feelings of regret such as those which have prefaced the stories which I have examined above. In this respect the Patroklos-story resembles Nestor's reminiscences as presented in the *Odyssey*. These reminiscences also relate to his later years – they are his recollections of the Trojan War and its immediate aftermath (that is, events of the previous two decades) – and are never introduced by those nostalgic phrases that we hear in other contexts.[33] Nestor's lament for times past, therefore, is not simply a routine speech habit. It is used only as appropriate.

As for instances in which other heroes use such a 'nostalgic wish', I note that Phoinix inverts the idea in the same kind of context when he is trying to persuade Achilleus not to return to Phthia but to return to the fighting (he would not be willing to be left behind, not even if the god were to make him 'a young man blossoming' [νέον ἡβώοντα, *Il.* 9.446]). Phoinix prefaces his appeal to Achilleus to give up his anger – this is to be followed in turn by the paradeigmatic story of Meleagros – with a long account of his youthful adventures, when he all but killed his father Amyntor, who had dishonoured his mother, and had escaped the protective custody of his kinsmen and cousins. Phoinix is using personal reminiscence in the same way as Nestor had used it: to win a sympathetic hearing, and, in this case, to strengthen his case by drawing on the bond between himself and Peleus in the first instance and himself and Achilleus in the second. But he avoids actively wishing for those days, because they were not always happy. Before he tells the tale of Meleagros, however, he prefaces it too with a nostalgic lament for a time when heroes acted appropriately (524–8, and especially at 526). Laertes expresses the same idea in the same kind of context, when he speaks with his son at the end of the *Odyssey*:

αἲ γάρ, Ζεῦ τε πάτερ καὶ Ἀθηναίη καὶ Ἄπολλον,
οἷος Νήρικον εἷλον, ἐϋκτίμενον πτολίεθρον,
ἀκτὴν ἠπείροιο, Κεφαλλήνεσσιν ἀνάσσων,
τοῖος ἐών τοι χθιζὸς ἐν ἡμετέροισι δόμοισι,
τεύχε' ἔχων ὤμοισιν, ἐφεστάμεναι καὶ ἀμύνειν
ἄνδρας μνηστῆρας· τῷ κε σφέων γούνατ' ἔλυσα
πολλῶν ἐν μεγάροισι, σὺ δὲ φρένας ἔνδον ἐγήθεις.

O father Zeus, Athene and Apollo, if only
as I was when, lord of the Kephallenians, I took
Nerikos, the strong-founded citadel on the mainland
cape; if only I could have been such yesterday in the palace,
with armour upon my shoulders, to stand beside you and fight off
the suitors' attack; so I would have unstrung the knees of many
there in the hall, and your heart within you would have been gladdened.

Od. 24.376–82

And there is a light-hearted example, to prove the point. When Odysseus himself, in his disguise as a beggar weathered by time and circumstance, is about to 'reminisce' about an exploit in his fictitious youthful past to Eumaios, he frames his tale with just this nostalgic wish. He has set his false tale in a more remote world of times past, and implies that these events happened in his (invented) youth. The tale is persuasive: the disguised Odysseus' references to his active youth (engaged in the siege at Troy, at the side of Odysseus) appeal to Eumaios, because the behaviour described is true of his master – Odysseus:

εἴθ' ὣς ἡβώοιμι βίη τέ μοι ἔμπεδος εἴη,
ὡς ὅθ' ὑπὸ Τροίην λόχον ἤγομεν ἀρτύναντες.
ἡγείσθην δ' Ὀδυσεύς τε καὶ Ἀτρεΐδης Μενέλαος,
τοῖσι δ' ἅμα τρίτος ἄρχον ἐγών· αὐτοὶ γὰρ ἄνωγον.
...
ὣς νῦν ἡβώοιμι βίη τέ μοι ἔμπεδος εἴη·
δοίη κέν τις χλαῖναν ἐνὶ σταθμοῖσι συφορβῶν,
ἀμφότερον, φιλότητι καὶ αἰδοῖ φωτὸς ἑῆος·
νῦν δέ μ' ἀτιμάζουσι κακὰ χροῒ εἵματ' ἔχοντα.

I wish I were as young again and the strength still steady within me,
as when, under Troy, we formed an ambush detail and led it.
The leaders were Odysseus and Atreus's son, Menelaos,
and I made a third leader with them, since they themselves asked me.
...

> I wish I were young like that and the strength still steady within me.
> Some one of the swineherds in this house would give me a mantle,
> both for love and out of respect for a strong warrior.
> Now they slight me because I wear vile clothing upon me.
>
> *Od.* 14.468–71, 503–6

Each man returns in memory to a time of youth and vigour and action – to the highlights of his life. My point here is that the poet is consistent, in psychological terms, in drawing a distinction between memories of self-defining landmark events, when his characters are in their youth and life is full of promise, and of events which have happened subsequently.

Does Nestor live in the past? This is an accusation frequently levelled against the elderly today. In Nestor's case, the answer is 'not at all'. Neither do most of the elderly in our own world.[34] We must acknowledge that as a person ages the more memories he or she has stored. Thus it is more likely that *any* event in the present will cue a memory from the past. An accumulation of memories is an inevitable consequence of age and it goes some way towards explaining the habit of reminiscence that we see in the elderly. This factor, naturally, plays its part in Nestor's habit of reminiscence. But Nestor, for all that, lives very much in the present: all the stories he tells have present application.[35] Of course, he tells each one in part for the pleasure of reminiscence but he tells it also to influence the decisions of his comrades. It is his goal, in his later years, to make his mark by guiding the decisions of the Achaian leaders at the present time and for the future.

Homer's Nestor, as we have seen, is a persuasive figure. The fact that for the most part his reminiscences are of events from early adulthood is, as we observe from psychological studies, true of life. And the fact that his memories of these events which took place so long ago are clear and vivid – and that they bear the marks of rehearsal and repetition – is also authentic. We recognize the old man's habit of drawing on his reminiscences for interpersonal functions – in the *Iliad*-story, to exhort and persuade; and we recognize his management of them for intrapersonal functions – to exemplify the characteristics that he wishes to attribute to himself. At *Il.* 11.669–761 he portrays himself as the most distinguished fighter on the battlefield, despite his youth and inexperience. At *Il.* 7.132–156 he presents us with the image of a very young man who did not flinch from battle with a warrior who inspired terror in the hearts of all others. At *Il.* 1.260–73 he remembers himself as a young man who is prepared to take on the most difficult challenges on the battlefield and whose advice, despite his youth, was heeded by the great warriors of the day. Nestor, according to Nestor, is a man of rare energy and talent. He is a man of action, a great warrior in single combat and in sustained fighting, who is also respected for his counsel.[36] All his memories, in sum, illustrate salient traits in Nestor's self-image, as he has fashioned it. They give him authority, through his immediate experiential link with traditions of the past;[37] and they give him his identity. As he shares his memories with his comrades, through the agency of the poet, these reminiscences contribute to the sum of his character in their eyes – and in our eyes as well. But we, the audience, may sense that Homer's Nestor has taken advantage of his editorial control over his 'actual' life-history in order to adjust, refashion, or reorientate the focus of his experiences for present purposes.[38] The fact that his triumphs on the battlefield are far more substantial and far more glorious than those of any Achaian at Troy leads us to suspect a degree of 'epic inflation'.[39] Nevertheless, Homer's depiction of the readiness of an old man to refer to memory and to try to turn his recollections to advantage (with both himself and others in mind) is an observant and affectionate portrait of one of society's elders, drawn, I suggest, from life.[40]

There is, however, one possibly *inauthentic* element in the portrayal of Nestor. I refer here to the fluency of his speech. This is uncharacteristic of the elderly today, who tend to suffer temporary failures (such as forgetting everyday terms). The poet, however, is quite emphatic that Nestor is a good speaker (he is ἡδυεπής [*Il.* 1.248]; a λιγὺς ἀγορητής [*Il.* 2.246; 4.293; 19.82; *Od.* 20.274]). Old age, he asserts, has not affected Nestor's capacity for fluent speech.[41]

In the light of the unrelenting demands of composition in performance, we might have expected Homer's characterizations to be crudely stereotypical. There is, on the contrary, a remarkably rich vein of psychological insight in the poet's recreation of everyday behaviour patterns in his principal actors. Certainly, Homer knew a great deal about the processes of memory (drawing on popular wisdom, on the tradition in which he worked, on his experience as a singer, and on his own observation of life). It was perhaps only natural that he, who enjoyed so constructive a relationship with memory in his professional life, should have been attentive also to the ways in which both he and people around him worked with memory on an everyday basis, in its practical applications. It is to our delight that he found ways of recreating these behaviours in his songs.

Acknowledgements

I thank colleagues attending the conference of the Australian Society for Classical Studies (Sydney, February 2003) and that of CAMWS (Lexington, April 2003) for their comments and suggestions regarding this paper. I also thank Bob Rabel for his invitation to CAMWS and the University of Kentucky at Lexington for hosting my visit.

Notes

[1] For these invocations see *Il.* 1.1–7; 2.484–7, 761–2; 11.218–20; 14.508–10; 16.112–13; and *Od.* 1.1–10. For discussions of Homer and his relationship with his Muse, see Murray 1981; Finkelberg 1998; Minchin 2001, 161–4.

[2] See, for example, *Il.* 7.87–91; 22.301–5; and see also Helen's – negative – words at *Il.* 6.354–8.

[3] On Odysseus's sorrows, see *Od.* 8.83–95, 521–34; 9.12–15; on Penelope's, see *Od.* 19.204–9, 249–60.

[4] See especially 15.390–401 (the words of Eumaios to his master); 23.300–9 (the narrator's commentary).

[5] On burial mounds, see, for example, *Il.* 7.87–91. On gifts, see, for example, *Od.* 15.125–9.

[6] See Scodel 2002; and see also Tatum 2003.

[7] See Schacter 2001. And see also, for example, Cohen 1989; Gruneberg, Morris, and Sykes 1988; Gruneberg and Morris 1992.

[8] For comment on Nestor's possible age, see Kirk 1985, 79. Here Kirk appears to endorse the comment of the scholiast bT, who argues that since his father has perished, as have his brothers, Nestor is ruling over a third generation of men. Assuming thirty years as the span of a generation, Nestor must be at least seventy years of age. On Nestor's uniqueness in the *Iliad* in terms of both longevity and the command of persuasive speech, see Dickson 1995, 10–13. For further discussion on this latter point, see below.

[9] On Nestor as a representative of a remote past unfamiliar to his fellow-warriors, see Dickson 1995, 65, 71–2; Kullmann 2001, 394–5.

[10] Translations are from Lattimore 1951 and 1965.

[11] For comment on some of the rhetorical features of the tale, see Kirk 1985, 80–1; Kirk's observation of the purposefulness of Nestor's exemplum (80) perhaps indicates that the old man has told this story before. Taplin (1992, 90), however, is critical of Nestor's portrayal. He points out that although Nestor is eloquent he fails to persuade Agamemnon and Achilles; and he cites another instance of Nestor's failure, at *Il.* 2.336–68. For a well-argued and sympathetic appraisal of Nestor's abilities in counsel, see Schofield 1986, 22–30. I believe, with Schofield, that this particular exemplum was quite appropriate. No one – not even Nestor – would have predicted that such an extremity of passion would have been aroused in Achilleus and Agamemnon.

[12] For comment on the origins of the tale, see Willcock 1976, 10, who believes that this tale has been invented by our poet for the purpose of the present speech. This does not affect my argument. Nestor presents this as a tale from his past. He judges it to be consistent with his character and therefore plausible.

[13] We might have heard this tale earlier, at *Il.* 4.319. Instead, Nestor alluded to it there without giving a fuller account. Note that the old man has framed even this earlier story fragment with what will become a familiar theme (see 4.318 and 321) whenever he turns to memories from his early years. Note also Willcock's comments (1976, 77–8): he believes that this story, like others, is an ad hoc invention of the poet to suit the circumstances. See also Willcock 1964, 146. And see above.

[14] Robinson 1992, 243; and see also his comment (at 246), that past, present, and future are integrated in a personal history which is unique to each one of us.

[15] These stories may be true and accurate autobiographical memories; but it is more likely that they will undergo gradual changes each time those memories are revisited, without the subject being aware of the changes. Provided that the tale is consistent with his self-image, the subject will be satisfied with its accuracy: cf. Nestor's tales to the Achaians at *Il.* 1.259–74 and 7.132–58, above, which may – or may not – be absolutely accurate. On this see Miller 1994, 175; Hagberg 1995, 61–2.

[16] Robinson 1992, 244.

[17] Robinson 1992, 243; and see also Bruner 1994, 46–7 and 53.

[18] Robinson 1992, 243. And see also Neisser 1994, 2–9; and Ross and Buehler 1994.

[19] Robinson 1992, 241; see further Neisser 1988, 555.

[20] Homer's Nestor is particularly resourceful in his use of personal reminiscence, as a preliminary to advice or a tool of persuasion. Robinson 1992, 242, notes also that autobiographical memory may contribute to our ability to interpret the behaviour of those around us. That is, our own self-awareness may assist us in coming to terms with the inner life of others.

[21] The distribution can be characterized 'by a combination of a simple retention component for the most recent 20–30 years of a subject's life; a childhood amnesia component for the earliest years; and, if and only if the subject is older than about 35, a reminiscence component for the subject's youth': see Rubin, Wetzler, and Nebes 1986, 212–13 (on reminiscence) and 220. See also Cohen 1989, 131–4 (on childhood amnesia); Cohen and Faulkner 1988, 277; and Robinson 1992, 225–6.

[22] See Rubin, Wetzler, and Nebes 1986, 212–13.

[23] See Cohen and Faulkner 1988, 280. On the relationship between emotion and memory, see Schacter 2001, 163–5.

[24] See Cohen and Faulkner 1988, 280. In this study subjects were asked to describe and date their most vivid memories. Cohen and Faulkner note that 75% of memories elicited were classified as 'actor memories', by contrast with 25% 'bystander memories'.

[25] See Cohen and Faulkner 1988, 281–2.

[26] See Cohen and Faulkner 1988, 282; and see Rabbitt and Winthorpe 1988, 306–7, who note (at 307) that 'subjective vividness of memories is directly determined by the recency and frequency of their rehearsal.'

[27] For a discussion of the ways in which we interpret events about which we reminisce, see Kovach 1995. Kovach uses the Autobiographical Memory Coding Tool (AMCT) to conceptualize autobiographical reminiscences as either positive or negative memories, which she codes using the terms 'validating' or 'lamenting'. Nestor's reminiscences are on the whole extremely positive – their primary force is a validating one; but they are often framed by a negative comparison (in which the hero laments that in the past he was physically more able than he is in the present). On this moment of nostalgia and its points of occurrence, see also below. For reminiscences that may be coded as laments pure and simple, see, for example, Helen's words at *Il.* 6.344–53, 24.762–6. Such laments are commonly characterized by the wish that things had been different.

[28] It is the vividness of his memory which leads the old man to recount his exploits in all their detail: hence their length. Hainsworth 1993, 295, comments on Nestor's 'logorrhea' and declares it to be a symptom of senility (cf. also Mugler 1980, 429–33;

Dickson 1995, esp. 15–16). This may be so, if Nestor were so deficient in self-awareness that delight in sharing his memories of the past were to override his caution about holding the conversational floor for an inappropriate length of time. But it is also the case that younger men's respect for their elders (in the Homeric world and still, I like to think, in the Western world) urges them to be patient and to listen politely while their seniors speak. Patroklos, for example, listens to Nestor's lengthy monologue (*Il.* 11.670–803) without any conspicuous restlessness, even though he is anxious to report back to Achilleus. Achilleus, too, will listen to the old man's story at *Il.* 23.626–50 with good grace. Indeed, Nestor does not ramble; he always speaks to the point: see Finlay 1979, 267–73; Minchin 1991. Homer, I suggest, does not make a facile identification of loquacity and old age. Even if he sees loquacity as a fault, it is not exclusively connected with senility. It seems to me that the character who truly suffers from 'logorrhea' is the Menelaos of the *Odyssey*. As he is clearly much younger than Nestor or Phoinix, we cannot attribute his post-Trojan war wordiness to old age. Of course, the young men who visit him, Telemachos and Pisistratos, treat Menelaos with great respect (thereby encouraging his reminiscences); but even so his response to Telemachos' question regarding his father (*Od.* 4.316–31) is delivered in a most circuitous fashion (333–586, with relevant information only at 551–60). Finally, to return to Nestor: it is true that Telemachos famously avoids a second visit to Pylos (*Od.* 15.193–214), but we must remember that he is not at this point acting entirely of his own volition; he is acting in obedience to Athene, who has prompted him to return home as quickly as possible (15.10–19).

[29] As I have noted above, Homer shows us that Nestor, like all elderly people, can tell the same story twice: when he is speaking with Agamemnon (4.318–21) and when he speaks to the assembled Achaian leaders (7.132–58). Memories of his victory over Ereuthalion have been triggered on both occasions.

[31] Nestor's plea to Agamemnon and Achilleus in *Il.* 1, as we have noted, falls on deaf ears.

[31] On the term 'nostalgic wish', see de Jong 2001, 32. On the evaluative force of such laments within reminiscence, see also above.

[32] We do not normally tell another person about his or her life, since we assume that s/he is in a better position than we are to know what s/he has experienced. But there are occasions when such stories are appropriate: when the hearer could not remember, or know of, an event which concerned him; when s/he has forgotten an incident from the past; or when he does remember but fails to see the relevance of the event, or his interpretation of what happened differs from that of the speaker. An example of the first instance is Phoinix's story to Achilleus in which he details his care for him as a small child, 9.485–95; an example of the second (or, possibly, the third) is Nestor's story to Patroklos discussed here. For brief discussion, see Linde 1981, 98–9.

[33] For Nestor's reminiscences in the *Odyssey*, see *Od.* 3.103–98, 254–312. We should note, however, that these memories have been requested specifically by Telemachos (92–101); they are not memories arising spontaneously.

[34] See on this, for example, Conway 1990, 151–7.

[35] This is consistent with research into memory. As Rabbitt and Winthorpe 1988, 306, observe: 'we do not passively rehearse our memories, but rather use them to try to understand and control our lives.'

[36] His reminiscence at *Il.* 23.629–43 confirms his all-round skills as a man of action. This is a story told for no other purpose than to rejoice in – to validate – his life and his triumphs.

[37] See Dickson 1995, 71, 90, 108.

[38] Cf. Dickson 1995, 214: 'Nestor is engaged in the essentially autobiographical act of composing and recomposing his own history out of the tales he tells others'.

[39] For the term, see Dickson 1995, 172 and 179 (and n. 36).

[40] See Burke 1988, 127, who notes that the elderly are more inclined than are younger people to forget the names of items in daily use, or people's names; hence their more frequent use of pronouns instead of nouns (and noun substitutes, such as 'whatsit' and 'thing') in order to cope with this temporary failure. For discussion of Homer's representation of Nestor's speech, see Dickson 1995, 25–38.

[41] For comment on Nestor's rhetorical prowess, see above.

Bibliography

Bruner, J.
    1994   'The "remembered" self', in U. Neisser and R. Fivush (eds.) *The Remembering Self: Construction and accuracy in the self-narrative*, Cambridge.

Burke, D.
    1992   'Memory and aging', in Gruneberg and Morris (eds.) *Practical Aspects of Memory*.

Cohen, G.
    1989   *Memory in the Real World*, Hove and London.

Cohen, G., and Faulkner, D.
    1988   'Life span changes in autobiographical memory', in Gruneberg, Morris and Sykes (eds.) *Practical Aspects of Memory*.

Conway, M.
    1990   *Autobiographical Memory: An introduction*, Milton Keynes and Philadelphia.

de Jong, I.J.F.
    2001   *A Narratological Commentary on the* Odyssey, Cambridge.

Dickson, K.
    1995   *Nestor: Poetic memory in Greek epic*, New York and London.

Finkelberg, M.
    1998   *The Birth of Literary Fiction in Ancient Greece*, Oxford.

Finlay, R.
    1979   'Patroklos, Achilleus, and Peleus: fathers and sons in the *Iliad*', *Classical World* 73, 267–73.

Gruneberg, M. and Morris P. (eds.)
    1992   *Aspects of Memory*, 2nd edn, vol. 1: *The practical aspects*, London and NewYork.

Gruneberg, M., Morris, P. and Sykes, R. (eds.)
    1988   *Practical Aspects of Memory: Current research and issues,* vol. 1: *Memory in everyday life*, Chichester and New York.

Hagberg, B.
    1995   'The individual's life history as a formative experience to aging', in

B. Haight, and J. Webster (eds.) *The Art and Science of Reminiscing: Theory, research, methods, and applications*, Washington D.C.

Hainsworth, B.
1985   *The* Iliad: *A commentary*, vol. 3, Cambridge.

Kirk, G.
1985   *The* Iliad: *A commentary*, vol. 1, Cambridge.

Kovach, C.
1995   'A qualitative look at reminiscing: using the autobiographical memory coding tool', in B. Haight and J. Webster (eds.) *The Art and Science of Reminiscing: Theory, research, methods, and applications*, Washington D.C.

Kullmann, W.
2001   'Past and Future in the *Iliad*', tr. L. Holford-Strevens, in D. Cairns (ed.) *Oxford Readings in Homer*'s Iliad, Oxford.

Lattimore, R.
1951   *The* Iliad *of Homer*, Chicago.
1965   *The* Odyssey *of Homer*, New York.

Linde, C.
1981   'The organization of discourse', in T. Shopen and J. Williams (eds.) *Style and Variables in English*, Cambridge, Mass.

Miller, P.
1994   'Narrative practices: their role in socialization and self-construction', in U. Neisser and R. Fivush (eds.) *The Remembering Self: Construction and accuracy in the self-narrative*, Cambridge.

Minchin, E.
1991   'Speaker and listener, text and context: some notes on the encounter of Nestor and Patroklos in *Iliad* 11', *Classical World* 84, 273–85.

2001   *Homer and the Resources of Memory: Some applications of cognitive theory to the* Iliad *and the* Odyssey, Oxford.

forthcoming   'Can one ever forget? Homer on the persistence of painful memories', *Scholia* 15.

Mugler, C.
1980   'La loquacité sénile chez Homère', Centre des recherches comparatives sur les langues de la Méditerranée ancienne: *Documents* 6, 428–38.

Murray, P.
1981   'Poetic inspiration in early Greece', *Journal of Hellenic Studies* 101, 87–100.

Neisser, U.
1988   'Time present and time past', in Gruneberg, Morris and Sykes (eds.) *Practical Aspects of Memory*.
1994   'Self-narratives: true and false', in U. Neisser and R. Fivush (eds.) *The Remembering Self: Construction and accuracy in the self-narrative*, Cambridge.

Rabbitt, P., and Winthorpe, C.
1988   'What do old people remember?', in Gruneberg, Morris and Sykes (eds.) *Practical Aspects of Memory*.

Robinson, J.
  1992   'Autobiographical memory', in Gruneberg and Morris (eds.) *Aspects of Memory*.
Ross, M., and Buehler, R.
  1994   'Creative remembering', in U. Neisser and R. Fivush (eds.) *The Remembering Self: Construction and accuracy in the self-narrative*, Cambridge.
Rubin, D., Wetzler, S. and Nebes, R.
  1986   'Autobiographical memory across the life span', in D. Rubin (ed.) *Autobiographical Memory*, New York.
Schacter, D.
  2001   *The Seven Sins of Memory: How the mind forgets and remembers*, Boston and New York.
Schofield, M.
  1986   'Euboulia in the *Iliad*', *Classical Quarterly* 36, 6–31.
Scodel, R.
  2002   'Homeric signs and flashbulb memory', in I. Worthington and J. Miles Foley (eds.) *Epea and Grammata: Oral and written communication in Ancient Greece*, Leiden.
Taplin, O.
  1992   *Homeric Soundings: The shaping of the* Iliad, Oxford.
Tatum, J.
  2003   *The Mourner's Song: War and remembrance from the* Iliad *to Vietnam*, Chicago and London.
Willcock, M.
  1964   'Mythological Paradeigma in the *Iliad*', *Classical Quarterly* 14, 141–54.
  1976   *A Companion to the* Iliad, Chicago and London.

4

SIMILES FOR ODYSSEUS AND PENELOPE: MORTALITY, DIVINITY, IDENTITY

James V. Morrison

This paper will examine comparisons applied to Odysseus and Penelope in Books 19–23 of the *Odyssey*. My initial interest concerns whether similes describe physical appearances or inner psychological states. After this survey, I would like to relate Homer's use of similes to the Odyssean themes of mortality, divinity, and identity. While Odysseus is often described as godlike, it is possible to see certain similes as a corrective to this view of heroes. Several key similes emphasize Odysseus' and Penelope's humanity rather than their heroism or near-divinity. Or, to put it another way, these similes show that an essential part of Odysseus' heroism is his humanity.[1]

A second function of similes is to offer insight regarding Penelope, 'the most enigmatic of Odyssean characters.'[2] Homer's audience is privy to the plot of Odysseus and Telemachus against the suitors; but for an inordinately long time we do not learn definitively what Penelope is thinking or planning. The similes, however, allow us – even without knowing what Penelope is thinking – to know what she is feeling.

Similes: inner and outer

Let us look first at the four comparisons describing Penelope in Bk. 19. The poet says that she looked like a goddess, Artemis or Aphrodite.

> ἡ δ' ἴεν ἐκ θαλάμοιο περίφρων Πηνελόπεια,
> Ἀρτέμιδι ἰκέλη ἠὲ χρυσέῃ Ἀφροδίτῃ.

> And wise Penelope came from her bedchamber
> like Artemis or golden Aphrodite.
> (19.53–4 = 17.36–7)

This first simile concerns physical appearance – what we might call the *outer* Penelope, that is, how she appears to others.[3]

Then Odysseus compares Penelope's fame to that of a prosperous and just king.

ἦ γάρ σευ κλέος οὐρανὸν εὐρὺν ἱκάνει,
ὥς τέ τευ ἢ βασιλῆος ἀμύμονος, ὅς τε θεουδὴς
ἀνδράσιν ἐν πολλοῖσι καὶ ἰφθίμοισιν ἀνάσσων
εὐδικίας ἀνέχῃσι, φέρῃσι δὲ γαῖα μέλαινα
πυροὺς καὶ κριθάς, βρίθῃσι δὲ δένδρεα καρπῷ,
τίκτῃ δ' ἔμπεδα μῆλα, θάλασσα δὲ παρέχῃ ἰχθῦς
ἐξ εὐηγεσίης, ἀρετῶσι δὲ λαοὶ ὑπ' αὐτοῦ.

For your fame reaches broad heaven,
like that of a blameless king, who godlike
rules among many strong men and
upholds just decisions: and the black earth brings forth
wheat and barley, the trees are heavy with fruit,
the flocks dependably bear young, and the sea provides fish
– all from good government, and the people flourish under him.

(19.108–14)

This second comparison concerns Penelope's reputation.[4]

When Odysseus in disguise describes his meeting with Penelope's husband, Penelope's weeping is compared to snow melting on a mountain and swollen rivers.

τῆς δ' ἄρ' ἀκουούσης ῥέε δάκρυα, τήκετο δὲ χρώς·
ὡς δὲ χιὼν κατατήκετ' ἐν ἀκροπόλοισιν ὄρεσσιν,
ἥν τ' Εὖρος κατέτηξεν, ἐπὴν Ζέφυρος καταχεύῃ·
τηκομένης δ' ἄρα τῆς ποταμοὶ πλήθουσι ῥέοντες·
ὡς τῆς τήκετο καλὰ παρήϊα δάκρυ χεούσης,
κλαιούσης ἑὸν ἄνδρα παρήμενον.

She listened, and tears poured down soaking her cheeks.
As snow melts on lofty mountains,
which the east wind melts after the west wind pours it down.
As it melted, the swollen rivers flow on.
Just so did she shed tears flooding her beautiful cheeks,
weeping for her husband sitting beside her.

(19.204–9)

In this passage, we find an outer manifestation – Penelope's tears – of her inner suffering as she remembers her husband.[5]

Finally, Penelope herself introduces the comparison of Pandareus' daughter in an attempt to describe her own feelings. During the day, Penelope says she 'mourns and wails as she goes about her tasks,' but at night she lies in bed, sleepless and tormented by worry (19.513–17). Penelope then compares herself to Pandareus' daughter, Philomela, who is changed into a nightingale after recklessly killing her own son. This bird sings a beautiful song at the start of spring, yet it is a song of sorrow for her lost child.

ὡς δ' ὅτε Πανδαρέου κούρη, χλωρηῒς ἀηδών,
καλὸν ἀείδησιν ἔαρος νέον ἱσταμένοιο,
δενδρέων ἐν πετάλοισι καθεζομένη πυκινοῖσιν,
ἥ τε θαμὰ τρωπῶσα χέει πολυηχέα φωνήν,
παῖδ' ὀλοφυρομένη Ἴτυλον φίλον, ὅν ποτε χαλκῷ
κτεῖνε δι' ἀφραδίας, κοῦρον Ζήθοιο ἄνακτος,
ὥς καὶ ἐμοὶ δίχα θυμὸς ὀρώρεται ἔνθα καὶ ἔνθα,
ἠὲ μένω παρὰ παιδὶ καὶ ἔμπεδα πάντα φυλάσσω,
κτῆσιν ἐμήν, δμῶάς τε καὶ ὑψερεφὲς μέγα δῶμα,
εὐνήν τ' αἰδομένη πόσιος δήμοιό τε φῆμιν,
ἦ ἤδη ἅμ' ἕπωμαι Ἀχαιῶν ὅς τις ἄριστος
μνᾶται ἐνὶ μεγάροισι, πορὼν ἀπερείσια ἕδνα,
παῖς δ' ἐμὸς ᾖος ἔην ἔτι νήπιος ἠδὲ χαλίφρων,
γήμασθ' οὔ μ' εἴα πόσιος κατὰ δῶμα λιποῦσαν.

As when Pandareus' daughter, the greenwood nightingale,
sings beautifully at the start of spring,
sitting in the trees on thick leaves,
and it pours forth much-echoing song with frequent variety
lamenting her own son Itylus, whom she had killed
with bronze in her recklessness, the son of lord Zethus,
so for me my spirit hurdles in division here and there,
whether I should remain beside my son and keep all secure,
my property – both servants and the great high-roofed house –
honoring the bed of my husband and reputation of the people,
or should I follow one of the Achaeans, the best
who woos me in the house, bringing a vast dowry,
for my son, while he was young and foolish,
did not allow me to marry and leave my husband's house.

(19.518–31)

Regarding the points of comparison between this simile and Penelope's description of her own indecision, commentators have pointed to the nightingale's continuous song of lament matching Penelope's grief, all in the context of facing a dilemma: should she stay and protect her home and reputation, or marry one of the suitors?[6]

Within these 500 lines, we observe, first, that these comparisons describe various aspects of Penelope: her appearance, her fame, and her emotions. In fact, this series begins with her physical appearance (she looked like a goddess), moves on to what others say about her (her fame), then turns to a physical manifestation of her trauma (weeping), and ends with Penelope's own description of her inner emotional turmoil.

Second, when we say that some similes 'describe' Penelope's inner feelings, this is rather loose. Strictly speaking, Homer uses the third simile that describes snow melting on a mountain and swollen rivers to focus our attention on Penelope's tears. Her weeping – expanded by the simile – suggests her feelings. But only the outer manifestation – tears – is described; then the simile amplifies, explores, and intensifies what has been presented in the main narrative.[7]

We now examine four similes applied to Odysseus in Books 19–22. When Penelope weeps, Odysseus pities her but his eyes remain like horn or iron.

> αὐτὰρ Ὀδυσσεὺς
> θυμῷ μὲν γοόωσαν ἑὴν ἐλέαιρε γυναῖκα,
> ὀφθαλμοὶ δ' ὡς εἰ κέρα ἕστασαν ἠὲ σίδηρος
> ἀτρέμας ἐν βλεφάροισι· δόλῳ δ' ὅ γε δάκρυα κεῦθεν.

> And Odysseus
> pitied his wife as she lamented in her spirit,
> but his eyes stood like horn or iron –
> steady between his eyelids. And he hid his tears by stealth.
> (19.209–12)

Odysseus' pity is explicitly stated, but this inner emotion is not openly revealed. Unlike Penelope, he hides his tears. This simile in fact does not *elaborate* on Odysseus' feelings – named explicitly by the poet – but on his self-restraint, how he checks those powerful feelings.[8]

At the start of Book 20 as female servants go off to sleep with the suitors, Odysseus' heart is said to bark.

> κραδίη δέ οἱ ἔνδον ὑλάκτει.
> ὡς δὲ κύων ἀμαλῇσι περὶ σκυλάκεσσι βεβῶσα
> ἄνδρ' ἀγνοιήσασ' ὑλάει μέμονέν τε μάχεσθαι,
> ὣς ῥα τοῦ ἔνδον ὑλάκτει ἀγαιομένου κακὰ ἔργα.

> And his heart within barks,
> as a dog, protecting her young pups
> and failing to recognize a man, barks and stays to fight,
> so within Odysseus, his heart barks angrily at their evil deeds.
> (20.13–16)

Here two poetic devices portray Odysseus' psychological state: first a metaphor (the 'barking' heart), then a simile triggered by that metaphor (the mother dog protecting her pups against a stranger).[9]

Odysseus' tossing in bed is then likened to the flipping of food over an open fire.

> ἀτὰρ αὐτὸς ἑλίσσετο ἔνθα καὶ ἔνθα.
> ὡς δ' ὅτε γαστέρ' ἀνὴρ πολέος πυρὸς αἰθομένοιο,
> ἐμπλείην κνίσης τε καὶ αἵματος, ἔνθα καὶ ἔνθα
> αἰόλλῃ, μάλα δ' ὦκα λιλαίεται ὀπτηθῆναι,

ὡς ἄρ' ὅ γ' ἔνθα καὶ ἔνθα ἑλίσσετο, μερμηρίζων
ὅππως δὴ μνηστῆρσιν ἀναιδέσι χεῖρας ἐφήσει
μοῦνος ἐὼν πολέσι.

> But he rolled to and fro.
> As when over a large blazing fire a man
> quickly turns a pudding full of fat and blood
> to and fro, desiring to roast it very quickly;
> so Odysseus rolled to and fro considering
> how he would lay his hands upon the shameless suitors –
> one man alone against many.   (20.24–30)

Here the outer action (Odysseus tossing in bed) serves as a guide to Odysseus' emotional distress (to which we might compare Penelope's tears as the outer manifestation, the guide to her inner feelings). Russo comments that the sequence of metaphor, simile, second simile, and divine intervention (20.10–35) 'achieve[s] an unusually strong intensification of the description of the hero's inner turmoil.'[10]

In Book 22 after the suitors are slaughtered and Eurycleia returns, Odysseus is compared to a lion with blood on its face and chest.[11]

εὗρεν ἔπειτ' Ὀδυσῆα μετὰ κταμένοισι νέκυσσιν,
αἵματι καὶ λύθρῳ πεπαλαγμένον ὥστε λέοντα,
ὅς ῥά τε βεβρωκὼς βοὸς ἔρχεται ἀγραύλοιο·
πᾶν δ' ἄρα οἱ στῆθός τε παρήϊά τ' ἀμφοτέρωθεν
αἱματόεντα πέλει, δεινὸς δ' εἰς ὦπα ἰδέσθαι·
ὡς Ὀδυσεὺς πεπάλακτο πόδας καὶ χεῖρας ὕπερθεν.

> She then found Odysseus among the slain corpses,
> splattered with blood and filth like a lion
> who comes after devouring a field ox:
> all its chest and cheeks on both sides
> are bloody, and its face is terrifying to look upon;
> so was Odysseus splattered on his feet and hands above.
>   (22.401–6)

The comparisons of Odysseus demonstrate his ability to hide his inner emotion; they also indicate his outrage and frustration – first the inner feeling (his barking heart); then the outer action (tossing and turning in bed) which reveals his internal emotional upset – and finally comment upon his appearance with the image of a triumphal and bloody lion.[12]

In Book 23 Telemachus and Odysseus attempt to understand Penelope. When Penelope sits silently facing Odysseus, Telemachus says to his mother:

σοὶ δ' αἰεὶ κραδίη στερεωτέρη ἐστὶ λίθοιο.

> Your heart is always harder than stone.
>
> (23.103)

After bathing and putting on fresh clothes, Odysseus also describes Penelope's heart:

> ἢ γὰρ τῇ γε σιδήρεον ἐν φρεσὶ ἦτορ.
>
> For indeed, the heart in your breast is iron.
>
> (23.172; cf. 23.72)

Both of these passages indicate the frustration son and husband feel at Penelope's self-restraint.

Regarding Odysseus, when he bathes and puts on clean clothes, Athena adds beauty to his appearance, making him look like a god.

> αὐτὰρ κὰκ κεφαλῆς κάλλος πολὺ χεῦεν Ἀθήνη
> μείζονά τ' εἰσιδέειν καὶ πάσσονα· κὰδ δὲ κάρητος
> οὔλας ἧκε κόμας, ὑακινθίνῳ ἄνθει ὁμοίας.
> ὡς δ' ὅτε τις χρυσὸν περιχεύεται ἀργύρῳ ἀνὴρ
> ἴδρις, ὅν Ἥφαιστος δέδαεν καὶ Παλλὰς Ἀθήνη
> τέχνην παντοίην, χαρίεντα δὲ ἔργα τελείει·
> ὣς μὲν τῷ περίχευε χάριν κεφαλῇ τε καὶ ὤμοις.
> ἐκ δ' ἀσαμίνθου βῆ δέμας ἀθανάτοισιν ὁμοῖος.
>
> But Athena poured much beauty down onto his head,
> so that he looked taller and broader. And he let loose his thick hair
> from his head, like a hyacinth blossom.
> Just as when a skilled man pours gold around silver,
> a man whom Hephaestus and Pallas Athena has taught
> complete mastery, and he finishes charming objects.
> So then did she pour charm upon his head and shoulders,
> and he stepped out of the bath like an immortal in body.
>
> (23.156–63 ~ 6.229–37)[13]

Clearly this simile concerns Odysseus' outward appearance: physically he looked like a god.

What happens next captures everyone's attention. Until now, comparisons have ranged widely over the realms of the divine, the animal world, and the inanimate realm of nature, but rarely are Odysseus or Penelope compared to human beings in these five Books.[14] Yet after Penelope is convinced that Odysseus sits before her, home after twenty years away, Homer introduces a simile that emphasizes the humanity of these two.

> κλαῖε δ' ἔχων ἄλοχον θυμαρέα, κεδνὰ ἰδυῖαν.
> ὡς δ' ὅτ' ἂν ἀσπάσιος γῆ νηχομένοισι φανήῃ,
> ὧν τε Ποσειδάων εὐεργέα νῆ' ἐνὶ πόντῳ
> ῥαίσῃ, ἐπειγομένην ἀνέμῳ καὶ κύματι πηγῷ·

παῦροι δ᾽ ἐξέφυγον πολιῆς ἁλὸς ἤπειρόνδε
νηχόμενοι, πολλὴ δὲ περὶ χροῒ τέτροφεν ἅλμη,
ἀσπάσιοι δ᾽ ἐπέβαν γαίης, κακότητα φυγόντες·
ὣς ἄρα τῇ ἀσπαστὸς ἔην πόσις εἰσοροώσῃ,
δειρῆς δ᾽ οὔ πω πάμπαν ἀφίετο πήχεε λευκώ.

He wept, holding his like-minded, careful-thinking wife.
As when land joyfully appears to swimmers
whose well-built ship, driven by wind and heavy waves,
Poseidon shatters on the sea.
Only a few escape the gray sea, swimming
toward land. Much brine is caked on their skin,
and joyfully they step onto land, fleeing hardship.
So then did her husband joyfully appear to her looking at him,
nor did she ever let go of his neck with her white arms.

(23.232–41)

Here the simile describes inner emotion; for once it is not trauma, but joy. This simile comes close to recapitulating Odysseus' adventures: a shipwreck sent by Poseidon, swimming for his life, sea-salt clogging his pores, finally emerging gratefully onto dry land. Yet when Homer begins the simile, it is not clear whether Odysseus or Penelope is the subject of the comparison–they are simply left in an embrace. Only as the simile concludes do we realize that it is *Penelope* who looks at her husband with the same joy that a shipwrecked survivor feels upon reaching shore. This is a *reversal simile*, which de Jong analyses:

> a character is cast in a role which is the reverse of his true status (parent becomes child, man becomes woman, victor becomes victim), and/or which recalls another character in the story.[15]

The point is that Penelope has undergone adventures and endured suffering equal to that of her husband. She, too, is like a shipwrecked survivor – she, too, has suffered in her soul and now feels joy just as Odysseus did when he emerged from the sea.

Mortality: suffering and death
Our analysis remains in Book 23 but moves from similes to the theme of suffering and mortality that immediately follows Penelope's recognition of Odysseus. Once reunited, Odysseus and Penelope confront the life awaiting them. Odysseus tells Penelope that his sufferings are not over: he must journey further, ultimately planting an oar and establishing an inland site of worship for Poseidon. He emphasizes the challenges and toil:

ὦ γύναι, οὐ γάρ πω πάντων ἐπὶ πείρατ᾽ ἀέθλων

79

ἤλθομεν, ἀλλ' ἔτ' ὄπισθεν ἀμέτρητος πόνος ἔσται,
πολλὸς καὶ χαλεπός, τὸν ἐμὲ χρὴ πάντα τελέσσαι.

Oh wife, we have not yet come to the end of our challenges,
for still there is immeasurable toil to come hereafter,
great and grievous. And I must complete it all.

(23.248–50)

In addition to further suffering – which he hyperbolically describes as 'immeasurable' (ἀμέτρητος) – amazingly one of the first things Odysseus says to his wife after she recognizes him concerns his own death.

θάνατος δέ μοι ἐξ ἁλὸς αὐτῷ
ἀβληχρὸς μάλα τοῖος ἐλεύσεται, ὅς κέ με πέφνῃ
γήρας ὕπο λιπαρῷ ἀρημένον· ἀμφὶ δὲ λαοὶ
ὄλβιοι ἔσσονται· τὰ δέ μοι φάτο πάντα τελεῖσθαι.

Death will come to me away from the sea,
a gentle death, which will take me
in rich old age. Around me, our people
will be blessed. All this [Teiresias] told me would take place.

(23.281–4; cf. 11.134–7)

The mortality of Odysseus is again emphasized when he mentions to Penelope Calypso's offer of immortality: she promised to make Odysseus a god (ἀθάνατος), yet he refused (23.333–6).[16]

A great deal of characterization in the *Odyssey* is built upon 'characterization-by-comparison': Menelaus, Agamemnon, Achilles, and Odysseus' crew are foils to Odysseus; Penelope is contrasted explicitly and implicitly with Nausicaa, Circe, Calypso, Clytemnestra, and Helen.[17] Regarding the theme of mortality, there is an implicit contrast early in the epic, suggested in the juxtaposition of Books 4 and 5. In Sparta, Helen's drug does not permit suffering, not even if a relative dies (4.220–6). On top of this, Proteus promises that Menelaus and Helen will not die, but rather will go to the Elysian field (4.561–9). At the beginning of the next book, in our first encounter with Odysseus, he is at his lowest point, yet he explicitly rejects Calypso's offer of immortality (5.203–24). Menelaus and Helen are exceptional: though mortal in some sense, they escape the usual lot of humanity which includes pain and death. Odysseus by contrast is offered such an escape, but he embraces his mortality, choosing to see his wife once more. When reunited with Penelope in Book 23, Odysseus defines himself not only as husband, but also as a man who suffers and inevitably will die.

Divinity, humanity, identity

Let us return to the dichotomy of inner and outer similes. I would now like to link Homer's use of similes and the themes of suffering and mortality to a question raised in the opening lines of the epic: Who is this man, unnamed for the first 20 lines? At pivotal moments in the epic, various characters proclaim Odysseus' divinity. To her companions, Nausicaa describes Odysseus as a god (6.243); Alcinous speculates that Odysseus may be immortal (7.199–203); when Odysseus appears to Telemachus, his son's first reaction is that he must be a god (16.183); and even Penelope, when she learns of the battle with the suitors, is convinced only a god could achieve such a victory (23.63; cf. 22.413). But time and again when the divinity of Odysseus is asserted, he emphatically rejects it. To Alcinous, he enumerates his sufferings with a great emphasis on the hunger of his shameless stomach (7.208–21).[18] In Book 16, Odysseus tells Telemachus:

> οὔ τίς τοι θεός εἰμι· τί μ' ἀθανάτοισιν ἐΐσκεις;
> ἀλλὰ πατὴρ τεός εἰμι, τοῦ εἵνεκα σὺ στεναχίζων
> πάσχεις ἄλγεα πολλά, βίας ὑποδέγμενος ἀνδρῶν.

> I am not a god, I tell you. Why do you liken me to the immortals?
> No, I am your father, for whom you have groaned and
> suffered much from submitting to the violence of men.

> (16.187–9)

Throughout the epic, the poet explores the tension between appearance and reality. In terms of physical appearance, Odysseus is described as 'godlike' both in the narrative and by several characters, but these descriptions concern how Odysseus looks. At times, Odysseus may appear to be a god – but that is on the outside (often Athene looks like a mortal). Similes, strategically placed, serve to reveal the inner feelings, the pain – and the humanity – of Odysseus. A similar point could be made about Penelope. Homer contrasts inner and outer perspectives by setting how she appears ('godlike', like Artemis or Aphrodite) against what she is feeling.[19]

The first word of the epic is 'man' (ἄνδρα – 1.1) and the immediately succeeding lines describe this man's travels, suffering, and struggles. Odysseus is a human being, not a god. Homer employs similes for a variety of purposes, but at climactic moments similes – emphasizing Odysseus' and Penelope's humanity, mortality, and suffering – correct the concept of 'godlike Odysseus' and 'godlike Penelope.'[20]

Conclusion

I close with one final instance in which the idea of Odysseus as a god is juxtaposed with his 'inner' experience. In Book 8, just before Odysseus reveals himself to the Phaeacians, Demodocus sings about the sack of Troy.

In this song by the court singer, Odysseus is described as being like a god, in particular Ares, the war god.[21]

αὐτὰρ Ὀδυσσῆα προτὶ δώματα Δηιφόβοιο
βήμεναι, ἠΰτ' Ἄρηα, σὺν ἀντιθέῳ Μενελάῳ.

But Odysseus came to the house of Deiphobus,
like Ares, with godlike Menelaus.   (8.517–18)

Yet here, too, Homer uses a simile to overrule Demodocus' glorification. While hearing this song, Odysseus breaks down in tears and Homer introduces a remarkable simile to describe Odysseus' state of mind. Odysseus weeps like a woman trying to embrace her husband, who has been mortally wounded defending his homeland.

αὐτὰρ Ὀδυσσεὺς
τήκετο, δάκρυ δ' ἔδευεν ὑπὸ βλεφάροισι παρειάς.
ὡς δὲ γυνὴ κλαίῃσι φίλον πόσιν ἀμφιπεσοῦσα,
ὅς τε ἑῆς πρόσθεν πόλιος λαῶν τε πέσῃσιν,
ἄστεϊ καὶ τεκέεσσιν ἀμύνων νηλεὲς ἦμαρ·
ἡ μὲν τὸν θνήσκοντα καὶ ἀσπαίροντα ἰδοῦσα
ἀμφ' αὐτῷ χυμένη λίγα κωκύει· οἱ δέ τ' ὄπισθε
κόπτοντες δούρεσσι μετάφρενον ἠδὲ καὶ ὤμους
εἴρερον εἰσανάγουσι, πόνον τ' ἐχέμεν καὶ ὀϊζύν·
τῆς δ' ἐλεεινοτάτῳ ἄχεϊ φθινύθουσι παρειαί·
ὣς Ὀδυσεὺς ἐλεεινὸν ὑπ' ὀφρύσι δάκρυον εἶβεν.

And Odysseus
melted, and tears from his eyes wet his cheeks.
As a woman falls upon and weeps for her husband
who has fallen before his city and people,
warding off the pitiless day from city and children;
seeing her husband dying and gasping for breath,
she clings to him and shrilly cries out. But those behind her
beat her with spear-butts in her back and shoulders,
and drag her off to slavery to have toil and misery.
Her cheeks are wasted with the most pitiful pain;
so Odysseus wept pitiful tears from his eyes.   (8.522–31)

The explicit point of comparison is that Odysseus weeps like a woman in a defeated city. On the face of it – and in common with other reversal similes – Odysseus is nothing like the person to whom he is being compared, save that they both weep. Odysseus, a man, is compared to a woman. Odysseus was on the winning side at Troy, yet this woman has seen her city sacked and her husband dying, and is being led off to slavery. Homer does not explicitly say that this is how Odysseus felt, but that is the effect of the simile. The implication is that, although Odysseus is a man and a victor and she is a woman from a conquered city, at this moment Odysseus is going through the pain and suffering she experiences.[22]

The singer Demodocus has been seen as a stand-in for Homer himself.[23] Yet I wonder whether in this instance Demodocus might instead be considered Homer's rival. Demodocus says that Odysseus was like the god Ares (8.518), yet Homer's simile revealing his inner feelings demonstrates that Odysseus is anything but godlike. Just as many figures in the *Odyssey* mistake Odysseus for a god, so in a sense does Demodocus.[24] By means of this simile – outside Demodocus' tale of Troy, but linked to it by unmistakable echoes – Homer reveals the inner pain and trauma Odysseus suffers as he relives the war, correcting Demodocus' inaccurate description of 'godlike' Odysseus.[25]

In some ways, Homer's presentations of Odysseus and Penelope are quite different. We know of Odysseus' plans and deliberations. Athena's plan is introduced at 13.375–428 when it is revealed to Odysseus; then it is passed on to Telemachus, Eurycleia, Eumaeus, and Philoetius. Naturally it comes as a surprise to the suitors, but not to Homer's audience. Penelope, on the other hand, remains a puzzle – there is much we do not know about her. Homer's ambiguous presentation has led readers to insist that she knows Odysseus has returned (in Book 19, say) or at least that she subconsciously realizes this.[26] I would make the following distinction. We do not know what Penelope is thinking, what she knows, what she is planning, or what her true motivation is, say, for getting gifts from the suitors or setting up the bow contest – only that 'she wished for something else' (18.283).[27] Yet Homer does make clear what she is *feeling*: her emotions, her pain, her desperation. The effect of Homer's similes is to take us within the heart, if not the mind, of Penelope.

It is easy to be impressed by the variety and invention of similes used by Homer to describe Odysseus and Penelope. The contention of this paper is that while Homer reveals character in a variety of ways, inner psychological states may be subtly revealed by means of similes. Of course we can only speculate concerning the extent to which Homer may be criticizing other singers' treatments of heroes as godlike. Yet the poet has placed a few similes – describing inner psychological states – in such a way as to reorient our consideration of Odysseus and Penelope. These similes are a means for the poet to resist what may well have been a common portrayal of heroes in previous poems and in those by Homer's contemporaries. As in the songs of Demodocus, heroes may have been distant, impressive, and 'godlike' – both in traditional diction and in terms of heroes' superhuman abilities. Homer's exploration of human psychology, revealed most brilliantly by similes, demonstrates the human side of Odysseus and Penelope.[28]

Notes

[1] For the use of similes in the *Iliad* to reveal the psychological state of the army, see Scott's paper in this volume.

[2] de Jong 2001, 36, who remarks 'her inner thoughts…remain a secret.'

[3] de Jong (2001, 411) comments: 'The double comparison might suggest her ambiguous status during Odysseus' absence: she wants to be chaste (Artemis), but is desired by the Suitors (Aphrodite).'

[4] Moulton (1975, 131–2) argues that the simile of the good king ruling a prosperous people foreshadows Odysseus' homecoming (cf. 2.230–4 ~ 5.8–12; cf. 4.687–93). Note that the king in the simile is 'godlike' (*theoudēs* – 19.109), discussed below.

[5] Russo et al. (1992, 87) notes that the verb τήκω contains both the meaning of melting and overflowing: 'overflowing is the surface phenomenon; melting is what happens internally…as melting snow produces a liquid overflow, so the dissolving of her energies spent in the repression of emotion produces an overflow of feeling whose *concrete manifestation is tears* [my italics].' Cf. de Jong 2001, 471. For the connection between outer description and inner feeling in this passage, see Riezler 1936, 254–5.

[6] Stanford (1964–5 I, 336–7) remarks that 'in these constant changes of direction in the bird's song lies part of the similarity with the condition of Penelope, whose mind is constantly distracted and changed by the thronging anxieties and worries that beset her. Besides this, the nightingale and Penelope have a similar share of sorrow.' See also Russo et al. (1992, 100) on 'the frequency and intensity of lamentation;' cf. de Jong (2001, 479) and Coffey (1957, 130–1). Interestingly, Anhalt (2001–2) finds the comparison 'particularly inappropriate' (149), almost a 'counter-paradigm' (153): 'Procne's story appears to be the antithesis of her own. Procne kills her son; Penelope has, thus far, preserved hers. Procne takes revenge on her husband; Penelope has remained faithful to hers. Procne weaves in order to deceive; Penelope has unraveled her weaving in order to deceive' (156). And yet Anhalt allows that the 'simile provides a clue, then, to Penelope's state of mind during her interview' with Odysseus (156) and concludes that 'the nightingale's grief at murdering her own son parallels Penelope's grief at confronting simultaneously two terrible alternatives, either of which entails self-inflicted pain' (157). Moulton (1975, 118 n. 8) feels that the later description of Procne at 20.66–82 (a somewhat different story apparently) 'functions as mythical paradigm, rather than as a simile.'

[7] Scott (1974, 31) distinguishes four methods for revealing human feelings or emotions: the poet 'could state the emotion directly; he could modify the individual theme with a simile; he could describe the character's physical movements; or he could have the character tell his own emotions.' In this instance, no emotion is mentioned for Penelope – we must deduce the inner feeling from her weeping.

[8] Russo et al. (1992, 88) finds this to be 'a paradigmatic example of the power of self-control… Homer uses horn and iron to represent the hardness of the hero's will, just as in the simile of the melting snow (204–8) the physical world was used to represent, through externalization, the inner, psychic reality that is normally not accessible to observation.' Cf. Rutherford 1986, 158.

[9] Stanford (1964–5, II 341) says that the barking metaphor 'emphasize[s] the terrific strain placed on Odysseus' self-control by the sight of his disloyal and shameless

servants tripping gaily off to meet his deadliest enemies.' On Odysseus' barking heart and dogs in the *Odyssey*, see Rose (1979). de Jong (1994, 34) makes an obvious point: 'barking inwardly is almost a paradox, since barking normally involves quite a bit of noise.' This makes the image all the more arresting.

[10] Russo et al. 1992, 108; he later comments on 'the poet's wish to explicate or illustrate a striking detail in his description of Odysseus' emotional turmoil' (110). de Jong (2001, 485) remarks upon 'the sustained insight into our hero's mind.'

[11] On Eurycleia's focalization of Odysseus as bloody lion, see de Jong (2001, 541).

[12] I have passed over the singer simile, Penelope's dream of the eagle and twenty geese, and her 'paradigm' of Procne (21.406–10, 19.535–69, 20.66–80).

[13] See Scott (1974, 131) on the purpose of deliberately repeating this simile; cf. Moulton 1975, 139 n. 10 and 152–3.

[14] Comparisons to other people include those of the good king and the singer (19.108–14, 21.406–10).

[15] de Jong 2001, 144, which continues: 'Telemachus compared to a traveler = Odysseus, Penelope compared to a king = Odysseus, Penelope compared to ship-wrecked sailors = Odysseus.' Moulton (1975, 129) remarks that 'it is Penelope who is explicitly equated with the shipwrecked swimmers who struggle to land.' Podlecki (1971, 90) says: 'It is as if Penelope had been the victim of long wandering and shipwreck, as if she had been physically present with Odysseus in his travels as she surely was in spirit.' Foley (1988, 98–9) remarks: 'Penelope takes on the mature Odysseus' experiences as her own…the reverse simile and the dream express more precisely the ambiguity of Penelope's position and her inner life.' Moulton (1975, 134) comments on placement of reversal similes: 'Through association, or allusion, some of his major images may simultaneously evoke response to two or more levels of the poem's meaning. It is noteworthy that he reserves these images for particularly climactic moments: Odysseus' sight of Scheria in 5, the point just preceding his self-revelation to the Phaeacians in 8, his reunion with Telemachus, his first speech to Penelope in the Homilia, and his revelation to his wife in 23. In each passage, through surprising reversals in the similes' details, the poet directs some portion of our attention to another facet, or plot strand, of the epic.'

[16] In distinguishing between god and mortal, Odysseus also says that 'no living mortal'(οὔ…τις ζωὸς βροτός) could move their bed from its spot (23.187–9), while Penelope comments that 'no other mortal' (οὐ βροτὸς ἄλλος) had seen their bed (23.225–6).

[17] See, e.g., Taplin 1988.

[18] See de Jong 2001, 182 on the 'accursed belly' motif, that not only anticipates Odysseus' 'masquerade as a beggar in the second half of the *Odyssey*, but it also characterizes him as a man who has acquired a broader view of the world than the heroic one of the heroes in the *Iliad*…by the time he returns to Ithaca, Odysseus has become painfully familiar with the phenomenon of hunger.' Later she comments on how Odysseus refers to himself: 'self-identification of Odysseus [is expressed] in terms of much suffering and return home in the twentieth year' (396 – cf. 16.205–6, 19.483–4, 21.207–8, 23.101–2 = 23.169–70).

[19] And when Penelope is indirectly described as godlike (*theoudes*) in Odysseus' simile of the good king (19.109), like Odysseus, Penelope also rejects such an idea by

emphasizing her suffering (19.124–36).

[20] Homer may also be 'correcting' the undoubtedly inherited formulae. de Jong (2001, 278) observes that Penelope is the only female referred to as 'godlike' (ἀντιθέην – by Teiresias at 1.117 and by Athena at 13.378). And a majority of the traditional formulae referring to Odysseus label him 'godlike' (θεῖος) or 'divine' (δῖος). I am particularly interested in the expression 'much suffering godlike Odysseus' (πολύτλας δῖος Ὀδυσσεύς), used 37 times in the epic; cf. Austin 1975, 26. Is it possible to see Homer exploring this almost paradoxical combination? Might we see *dios* as describing the outer, 'godlike' Odysseus and the *polutlas* as the inner man who suffers yet endures that suffering? Are these the two sides of Odysseus, both of which Homer wishes to explore? Scott's paper in this volume attempts to distinguish traditional uses of similes from Homer's innovations, though this is not my intention here. On other functions of similes, see, e.g., Magrath 1982, 206 on the progression of lion simile 'from anticipation to climax.'

[21] See Moulton 1975, 121 n.14 and Coffey 1957, 128–9. For similes comparing heroes to gods, see Fränkel 1921, 96–7.

[22] This is another reversal simile, as in Book 23. Stanford (1964–5, 1. 345) surmises that 'Here Odysseus presumably weeps for his lost comrades and for the sad sequels to the victory.' Rohdich (1987, 48) connects Odysseus' weeping at Demodocus' song to Penelope's reaction to Phemius' tale in Book 1. Macleod (1982, 4–5) remarks that it is 'as if her [the captive woman's] suffering has through the poet's art become his [Odysseus'] own.' Foley (1988, 100) comments upon 'how close Odysseus has come in his travels...to the complete loss of normal social and emotional function which is the due of women enslaved in war.' Rutherford (1986, 155) agrees: 'It needs the eloquence and the compassion of a Homeric poet to open the springs of pity in Odysseus and to make him see that the victory he won all those years ago has become a matter for history and poetry; that the profits which he gained have slipped through his fingers; and above all that his own sufferings and his own separation from wife, child and home are not *more* important than the sufferings of the Trojans, but mirror-images of them (as is brought out by the marital theme in the simile).' On Odysseus' own recognition that 'nothing is more frail than man' (18.130–2), see Rutherford (1986, 156); cf. Moulton (1975, 131–2).

[23] Segal 1992, 6.

[24] In fact, in his request to the singer, Odysseus asks to hear of 'godlike Odysseus' (δῖος Ὀδυσσεύς – 8.494), so maybe Demodocus is just giving him what he asked for; see Rohdich (1987, 50). Wyatt (1989, 243) believes that Demodocus' third song is 'in Homer's words, not in those of Demodocus himself.' I am not persuaded that this distinction holds. Rutherford (1986, 155) makes a different discrimination: 'Here we see Homer contrasting different ideas of what poetry does and what it is for. What Odysseus expects is, in effect, a panegyric of his own strategic and military successes. There seems no reason to doubt that in the aristocratic society of early Greece and Ionia, such poems would be common, as in many other oral traditions, and familiar to Homer (cf. Hes. *Th.* 80–93). But what Odysseus actually gets is something deeper and more characteristically Homeric: not a partisan version, but one that sees both sides, Trojan and Greek.' I would differ in emphasizing that what *we* get – outside Demodocus' tale – is 'something deeper and more characteristically Homeric,' though Odysseus may also share in this empathy. On possible antagonism of a good-natured

sort between Odysseus and Demodocus, see Harrison (1971) and Wyatt (1989, 247–8). Rabel (2002, esp. 79 and 85) argues that Homer's (and Odysseus') songs are superior to those of Demodocus and Phemius, both of whom are interrupted by their audiences.

[25] Nagy (1979, 222) thinks that 'the simile re-enacts one of the scenes implicit in Demodocus' narrative.' Cf. Segal 1992, 9–10. Rohdich (1987, 52) sees Odysseus as 'disenchanted from the intoxication of traditional heroic.' Segal (1992, 10) agrees that 'there is little in the heroic code that would encourage Odysseus to identify with his conquered enemy, especially one of the opposite sex.'

[26] For bibliography on divergent interpretations of what Penelope knows, see de Jong (2001, 460 nn. 2 and 3). The interpretation that she is ignorant of Odysseus' return is supported by her hopes and fears, especially her wish to die (18.201–5, 20.61–82). Amory (1966, 113) observes that 'the poet cannot pause for a detailed explanation of Penelope's state of mind and reasons for deciding to set the contest now.' On a modern analogy for Penelope's conflict, see Morrison (2003, 145–6).

[27] Emlyn-Jones (1984, 11) supports Hölscher's interpretation that νόος δὲ οἱ ἄλλα μενοίνα (18.283) means 'she wants something else passionately, namely the return of her husband.' For a full discussion on 'unspoken thoughts', see de Jong 1994.

[28] Certainly, Odysseus is like a god in other ways – in terms of his disguise and his penchant for testing others – yet this contrasts with his intermittent lack of detachment and his anger. Concerning Penelope's order to move their bed outside, Rutherford (1986, 160) comments on Odysseus' 'moment of angry passion, of uncontrolled emotion. As commentators have pointed out, a god could have known the truth, but no mortal in the Homeric poems can trick or deceive a god; and the automatic, unthinking surge of anger at the thought of *his* bed, his wonderful creation, being violated, is wholly human. As often in Homer, the emotions of human relationships are more intense and more precious than those shared between god and man.' On Odysseus' reunion with his father, Rutherford also remarks: 'the analogy between god and man also highlights the contrasts... Here again, as in those scenes and when he heard the song of Demodocus, others' grief and pain bring home his own emotion, his own *humanity*, more acutely. Since he lacks the detachment of a god, Odysseus' own distress (318–9) answers that of Laertes (as we have seen, the hero's moments of open, unsuppressed emotion form a significant sequence in the poem)' (162).

Bibliography

Amory, A.
   1966   'The reunion of Odysseus and Penelope', in C.H. Taylor, Jr. (ed.) *Essays on the* Odyssey. *Selected modern criticism*, Bloomington, 100–36.

Anhalt, E.K.
   2001–2   'A matter of perspective: Penelope and the nightingale in *Odyssey* 19.512–54', *CJ* 97, 145–59.

Austin, N.
   1975   *Archery at the Dark of the Moon*, Berkeley.

Coffey, M.
   1957   'The Homeric simile', *AJP* 78, 116–32.

de Jong, I.J.F.
  1994   'Between word and deed: hidden thoughts in the *Odyssey*', in I.J.F. de Jong
          and J.P. Sullivan (eds.) *Modern Critical Theory and Classical Literature*,
          Leiden, 27–50.
  2001   *A Narratological Commentary on the* Odyssey, Cambridge.
Emlyn-Jones, C.
  1984   'The reunion of Penelope and Odysseus', *G&R* 31, 1–18.
Foley, H.P.
  1988   ' "Reverse similes" and sex roles in the *Odyssey*', in H. Bloom (ed.) *Homer's*
          The Odyssey, New York, 87–101 = *Arethusa* 11 (1978) 7–26.
Fränkel, H.
  1921   *Die homerischen Gleichnisse*, Göttingen.
Harrison, E.L.
  1971   'Odysseus and Demodocus: Homer, *Odyssey* θ 492 f.', *Hermes* 99, 378–9.
Lloyd, M.
  1987   'Homer on poetry: two passages in the *Odyssey*', *Eranos* 85, 85–90.
Macleod, C.W.
  1982   *Homer. Iliad, Book XXIV*, Cambridge.
Magrath, W.T.
  1982   'Progression of the lion simile in the *Odyssey*', *CJ* 77, 205–12.
Morrison, J.V.
  2003   *A Companion to Homer's* Odyssey, Westport, Connecticut.
Moulton, C.
  1975   *Similes in the Homeric Poems*, Göttingen.
Podlecki, A.J.
  1971   'Some Odyssean similes', *G&R* 18, 81–90.
Rabel, R.J.
  2002   'Interruption in the *Odyssey*', *Colby Quarterly* 38, 77–93.
Riezler, K.
  1936   'Das homerische Gleichnis und der Anfang der Philosophie', *Die Antike*
          12, 253–71.
Rohdich, H.
  1987   'Ein Gleichnis der *Odyssee*', *A&A* 33, 45–52.
Rose, G.P.
  1979   'Odysseus' barking heart', *TAPA* 109, 215–30.
Russo, J.
  1968   'Homer against his tradition', *Arion* 7, 275–95.
Russo, J., Fernandez-Galiano, M. and Heubeck, A.
  1992   *A Commentary on Homer's* Odyssey, vol. III, Oxford.
Rutherford, R.B.
  1986   'The philosophy of the *Odyssey*', *JHS* 106, 145–62.
Scott, W.C.
  1974   *The Oral Nature of the Homeric Simile*, Leiden.
Segal, C.
  1992   'Bard and audience in Homer', in R. Lamberton and J.J. Keaney (eds.)
          Homer's Ancient Readers. The hermeneutics of Greek epic's earliest exegetes,
          Princeton, 3–29.

Stanford, W.B.
   1964–5   *The* Odyssey *of Homer*, 2 vols., 2nd edn, London and New York.
Taplin, O.
   1988   'Reading differences: the *Odyssey* and juxtaposition', *Ramus* 17, 1–31.
Wyatt, W.F. Jr.
   1989   'The intermezzo in *Odyssey* 11 and the poets Homer and Odysseus', *SMEA*
        27, 235–53.

5

TELEMAKHOS' ONE SNEEZE
AND PENELOPE'S TWO LAUGHS
(*ODYSSEY* 17. 541–50, 18.158–68)

Donald Lateiner

This paper concerns irresistible urges, not the sexual or food-related ones, but two types of involuntary spasms: the sneeze and the laugh at something not in any way funny. Reflex behaviors in Homer could include the tired yawn, the anxious blink, the digestive fart, hiccoughs, and the barely controllable belch that arises from rapid or excessive consumption of food (cf. the *Homeric Hymn to Hermes* 294–7). The fastidious Homer, however, unlike the transgressive comic Aristophanes, excludes most of these symptomatic expressions and excretions. He allows the questionable joy of eructation only to sub-human Polyphemos (9.373–4).

Whether or not 'anatomy is destiny', I claim that apparent human 'accidents' are prophetic, signs of divine participation. Specifically, this *Odyssey* both explicitly recognizes kledonomancy,[1] casually uttered words with unintended power, and also utilizes *palmike*, divination from involuntary movements. *Palmike* was the subject of more than one lost treatise, the most famous written by the Stoic Poseidonios.

The cornered mother Penelope explicitly interprets Telemakhos' unique, inexplicable, and alarmingly loud sneeze as a sign confirming her wish for Odysseus' return and the suitors' death. One can explain in two ways her laugh here and her second 'queer' laugh (appearing only 228 verses later). Either they are psychologically apt responses in two moments that allow her fantasies of an improved situation, an approach that suits our rational, post-Freudian inclinations. Or, the laughs are themselves involuntary signs of divine perturbation in the human realm, an interpretation supported by the puzzling descriptor *akhreion*, 'pointless,' that is, I think, 'humanly unmotivated in the circumstances.'

1. A fortunate sneeze

Those who have entertained one hundred and eight rowdy 'guests'[2] for weeks on end, or even for one evening, sympathize with hostess Penelope's frenzied fury.

> [They party, eat and drink the gleaming wine]
> indecently. Most of our stores are consumed, for there is no man around
> Such as Odysseus was, to ward off harm from the household. (17.537–8)

> μαψιδίως· τὰ δὲ πολλὰ κατάνεται· οὐ γὰρ ἔπ' ἀνήρ,
> οἷος Ὀδυσσεὺς ἔσκεν, ἀρὴν ἀπὸ οἴκου ἀμῦναι.

In desperation at the suitors' carouse, in a cross between a wish, a possibility, and a prayer (as the optatives make clear), the trapped widow/wife speaks her desire to Eumaios, trusty swineherd (17.539–40, Lattimore's transl.; cf. Telemakhos at 1.115–17):

> If Odysseus could come back to his fatherland,
> soon, with his son he could punish [pay back] the violence of these people.

> εἰ δ' Ὀδυσεὺς ἔλθοι καὶ ἵκοιτ' ἐς πατρίδα γαῖαν,
> αἶψά κε σὺν ᾧ παιδὶ βίας ἀποτείσεται ἀνδρῶν.

Then an odd, indeed Homerically *hapax*, event occurs. At this moment, Telemakhos somewhere nearby (but not in the conversation) sneezes Homeric epic's only sneeze.[3] It is a big, thunderous, violent[4] sneeze:

> ὣς φάτο, Τηλέμαχος δὲ μέγ' ἔπταρεν, ἀμφὶ δὲ δῶμα
> σμερδαλέον κονάβησε· γέλασσε δὲ Πηνελόπεια...

Penelope, like her marital antithesis Helen, is no slouch at divinatory interpretation. She uncharacteristically laughs at the outburst. Her quick perception proclaims a meaning for the seemingly unconnected sneeze, that is an 'involuntary spasm resulting from irritation of the nasal mucosa' (*American Heritage Dictionary* [1979 edn] s.v.). Her cheerful reading echoes her son's first recorded thought or day dream, the punishment of the suitors (1.113–17). Just what punishment might Penelope have in mind? She finds the theological significance and explains it to Eumaios (17.545–7):

> Do you not see how my son *sneezed in confirmation* of everything I said?
> May it mean that death, accomplished in full, befall the suitors
> each and all, not one avoiding death and destruction.

> οὐχ ὁράᾳς, ὅ μοι υἱὸς ἐπέπταρε πᾶσιν ἔπεσσι;
> τῷ κε καὶ οὐκ ἀτελὴς θάνατος μνηστῆρσι γένοιτο
> πᾶσι μάλ' οὐδέ κέ τις θάνατον καὶ κῆρας ἀλύξει.

'The origin of the importance attached to sneezing...is primarily due to [its] arbitrary nature.' The normal body, in the confident words of positivist science and A.S. Pease, is 'the slave and instrument of its owner's will and intention,' but here it behaves independently or serves as a human instrument of the gods, as sacrificial animals and their informative liver organs do. The body obeys predictable biological clocks – necessities of breathing, eating, sleeping, aging, death and so forth – but the involuntary accident, an arbitrary interruption of the foreordained pattern, such as sneezing, proves that things can be different, hope is reasonable, divinity can splotch or swerve the immutable design.[5] Kledonomancy depends on meaningful accidental speech, spontaneous words, but *palmike manteia* describes involuntary emotional expressions and twitches, as of the eyebrow, the nose, and ringing in the ears.[6] It is a 'cledonisme sans parole' (Bouché-Leclercq 1879, 1.159). The Sneeze-God Hermes warrants both types of divine interference. A.S. Pease, the scholar of the sneeze, and the magisterial annotator of Cicero's *De Divinatione*, observed elsewhere (1911, 437–8): 'That the deity which communicated its future designs to mortals through so great a variety of mediums…should have spoken in this particular form also need occasion us little surprise…'. All body openings have a peculiar importance because spirits might exit or enter through them. The Greeks usually considered the enigmatic sneeze a good omen, although it required a prophylactic responsive salute from Greeks and Romans (Apul. *Metam.* 9.25). Sternutatory spasms also have the capacity to ratify the truth of any preceding utterance, to identify another person's words as ominous.[7]

The nasal eructation's ominous nature is noted in many cultures (Russo 1992 ad loc.). Utterances whose significance is not fully understood by the emitter but grasped or posited by an interlocutor, observer, and/or by the external audience, are called, if identified at all, *kledones*. Another related term, less often employed and less specific in denotation, is *pheme* (κληδών, φήμη: 18.117, 20.120, [4.317= 'news']; 20.100, 105; 2.35). The process of identifying such omens is a form of domestic and therefore non-professional divination.

Penelope immediately identifies the significance of her son's[8] sneeze. No other woman in early Greek literature, so far as I can determine, grabs and identifies a spasmodic omen, a non-verbal *kledon*.[9] The act corroborates her wish and predicts its fulfillment – the two functions of kledonic omens (cf. Xen. *Anab.* 3.2.8–9). She laughs,[10] asserting to Eumaios that Telemakhos has just *'sneezed for* everything I have spoken' (17.542: ὅ μοι υἱὸς ἐπέπταρε[11] πᾶσι ἔπεσσι). Penelope is not a light-hearted, or light-headed, or optimistic woman. This smile or laugh is her first in the *Odyssey*, and perhaps her first in twenty years.[12] Her recurrent tears,[13] of course, manifest non-verbally her loyalty to Odysseus and her love of Telemakhos. In her claustrophobic situation, neither virtue can achieve its desired effects. Why is this sad woman suddenly laughing?

Penelope's two laughs are necessarily highly marked – given her typed role, indeed a folktale motif, of the grieving widow under serious pressure while vainly awaiting the long-gone, homecoming husband. She is not a happy hospitality provider.[14] The first laugh, after Telemakhos' unique, big sneeze, then marks a significant change of heart and expectation: realization of divine support and, consequently, a new and stiffened resolve to manage the plot. The omen of the sneeze, following Penelope's statement of Odysseus' potential to set the house aright, confirms godly approval. The omen's recipient, then, in the words of Professor Bruce Heiden (*per litt.*), must 'make a wish' – so that the divinity will know how to assist the human in need. Penelope's aggressive interpretation of her son's sneeze is a more active response than scholars have remarked. Indeed, they understate when they do not decry her role in the recuperation of Odysseus' authority.

Her subsequent laughing smile signifies her growing confidence in several members of the Laërtid family – an increase in confidence that they too share. Odysseus has already revealed himself to his son. His rapid advance as beggar into the house and *megaron*, into *the* center of power, presages the family's re-integration. The stranger's oddly familiar appearance, voice, and presence itself soon encourage the war-widow. Her next irregular, and rather masculine move, is to order Eumaios to summon the mysterious stranger to the hearth, to an unaccompanied fireside chat (544). Clearer evidence yet, however, is her explicit interpretation of the *palmic* 'accident'.

A skeptical age regards such noted coincidences of the present type as 'wishful thinking' before the outcome, or 'the victor's chosen explanation' afterwards. Studying the appendix of sneezes below, nevertheless, one observes that the extensively attested ancient belief in predictive *kledonic* and *palmic* omens rewards active participation in ominous events, not merely passive recognition after the fact. A participant's recognizing that a seemingly chance occurrence provides a window on the future seems to *help bring about that result*. The phrase δέχομαι τὸν οἰωνόν, 'I accept the [kledonic] omen', a parallel example from later historiography, welcomes and participates in shaping the future. Herodotos, Dionysios of Halikarnassos, and Plutarch, among others, report such incidents.[15] The instantly sequential, if seemingly disconnected, unintentional event, a corroborating unexpected *palmic* event or a *kledon, and* someone's prompt discernment of its ominous quality, encourage confidence in its interpretation as an omen. The quick acknowledgment of an omen turns an ambiguous event into one of the desired meaning (Pease [1911] 441, citing Plin. *HN* 28.16).[16] The god responds to the expressed human 'need'.

When Telemakhos sneezes, involuntarily, of course, and without a knowing or intended connection to his mother's outburst, weepy Penelope laughs first and reads the sneeze as ominous. Soon after, her second and last laugh should somehow be related to the first (18.163; cf. Levine [1983] 172; [1987] 26; see part II). Before that connection becomes clear, early in *Odyssey* 18 the vagrant and modest beggar Aithon/Odysseus flattens the impudently possessive and arrogant house-beggar Iros, a pre-echo of the suitors. After this parody of heroic combat, and as a reward for his knockout victory, he receives a multi-faceted (and specified) *kledon*/omen from the suitors. They state a hope (unintentionally cursing themselves) that he will obtain whatever he most wants from Zeus. Further, they say that the other, worsted beggar, Iros, will be hauled away to the evil ogre King Echetos who [like Hades] preys on *all* men (18.112–17; cf. 21.308–9). Since they too are men, the thought seems poorly conceived.

Odysseus rejoices in this *kledon* for his deepest wish, vouched for explicitly to be such a meaningful utterance by the narrator: Ὥς ἄρ' ἔφαν, χαῖρεν δὲ κλεηδόνι δῖος Ὀδυσσεύς.

Penelope, after Athene's impulse, soon laughs again – allegedly 'uselessly' – for the plan of exhibiting herself flirtatiously and uncharacteristically to the hateful suitors.[17] As so often, the goddess Athene seconds pre-existing and already percolating human plans and intentions. 'Double determination' (Dodds 1951, 14) itself usually signals a merely apparent lack of 'logical', humanly psychological, explanation. Penelope now plans, in fact, in an active Odyssean manner, to deceive the suitors about her sexual availability, her nubility, in order to excite them and to extract gifts from the *faux* husbands-to-be (18.158–68) – another sign of her increasing confidence. Her second laugh also characterizes her more recently acquired, optimistic emotional condition.

Thus, behold the sneeze sequence. Penelope wishes for the suitors' destruction, and Telemakhos sneezes corroboratively (out of a nearly clear blue sky, cf. 20.98–105). Then, Penelope laughs appreciatively and divines palmically, and she simultaneously, and for reasons obscure to some critics, decides to have Eumaios summon the mysterious beggar to her presence alone (τὸν ξεῖνον ἐναντίον κάλεσσον). The sequence shows the divine affirmation of a human wish by means of the active, perhaps supernaturally tweaked, human identification of the divine omen.[18] Penelope wants the suitors exterminated – and she promotes that result in several ways; one might call it theological *jiu-jitsu*. This quick-witted sneeze divination 'on the fly' is one, the superficially flirty but false encouragement of the suitors' marriage hopes is the second, the bow-contest planned for – and against – them is a third. Less obviously, Penelope's insistence on allowing the beggar's participation at some level in that decisive form of athletic and agonistic divination is an important fourth (21.336–42).[19] His 'turn,' as Eurymakhos recognizes (21.321–6), would shame them by equating them to lower-status wooers (χείρονες). She employs and enjoys here a moral and legal authority that was long ago delegated to her by Odysseus (18.259–70). She has carved out some real power and autonomy for herself, *faute de* husband (Felson-Rubin 1994, 155 n. 29). She insults the suitors by moving the beggar into play.

The laugh is Penelope's nonverbal sign of a new phase in her emerging assertiveness to shape her final 'plot', or *dolos*. Inviting the beggar to chat with the 'queen' in her women's quarters is a verbal sign. The death wish for the suitors, not first enunciated here (cf. 4.681–95, 17.499, 19.569), has been ratified by the still-maturing scion of the house, the now-bearded (18.176) beneficiary of her wish and Odysseus' estate. She truly makes the most of his sneeze. All three chief members of the house of Odysseus receive divine signs and wonders (15.531–4, 17.155–9, 18.112–17, 20.102–21, 13.392–6, 16.170–1, 20.47–51) that portend the coming victory.

Every muscle of the antique body was capable of spasmodic signals (Bouché-Leclercq 1879, 1.165; texts collected at 160 n.). As epilepsy, the so-called 'sacred disease,' proved divine influence on human comportment, so any involuntary impulse or spasm, however brief and widely shared, invited interpretation. Consequently, the ancients erected their 'fragile scaffold of explanation' for the sneeze (see Aristotle, *Problems* and other texts collected in the appendix; cf. Bouché-Leclercq 1879, 1.163). But the interest in this branch of physiological psychology, a reflex that is neither entirely of the autonomic system nor entirely of the somatic system, is – nothing to sneeze at (an English idiom first attested in 1806, *Oxford English Dictionary*).

2. A 'useless' laugh?

'Strong-handed' (five times) Penelope's second, later ἀχρεῖον laugh (18.153), often translated as an 'idle' or 'useless' laugh, has attracted more attention than Telemakhos' puzzling sneeze.[20] The polysemic but very rare[21] adverb ἀχρεῖον invites clarification. Translators and readers have suggested the following English translations: 'cunning', 'gleeful', 'inappropriate', 'unnecessary', 'strange', 'idle', 'insidious', 'uncharacteristic', 'uncomfortable', 'forced', 'embarrassed', etc. She laughs when describing to her maid Eurynome her odd, unexpected urge, her arguably immodest plan for sexual deception and profitable depredation of the suitors (166: κέρδιον). She will display herself, adorned as if for (re-)marriage, and flirt with the heretofore – and still – loathed suitors (165: ἀπεχθομένοισί περ ἔμπης).

Subsequent bourgeois generations with their different manners, table and otherwise, read this second and last recorded laugh as a sign of her discomfort with her (and Athene's, 158) seemingly disloyal flirtation project. One should view this cautious 'think around' or *periphron* (159) coquetry as an additional nonverbal indicator (another 'palmic' spasm) of her changed heroic strategy. The elusive adjective *akhreion* may be focalized correctly as servant Eurynome's ignorant judgment, or as Penelope's confused one, but more likely it provides the narrator's own rare but not unprecedented editorial comment. *Akhreion* perhaps suggests that this chuckle is not characteristic of her usual, purely human and rational, means for dealing with threats to herself, her house, her husband, and her son. An unexpected inspiration, comparable to her son's earlier unexpected nasal expectoration, leads to a parallel, unreadable response from her (ἐγέλασσεν). Under pressure from within and without (suitors, son, reports about Odysseus' whereabouts, but here, especially, Athene), Penelope responds to an external, and/or sudden internal, impulse. The activity of Athene,[22] the 'illogical' laugh, and the behavior out of character determine and characterize the Homeric heroic synergy of goddess and human. Penelope moves – as already Odysseus has by his pugilism – from disadvantaged, trapped victim to a wily, trapping victimizer.

Penelope manipulates the social space of the household. Thus, her proxemic strategy takes her from her self-chosen periphery to social dead center in the *megaron* – just like the now homecome, non-person Odysseus. She will solicit, extract, or even extort, gifts from the suitors – whatever her intention (18.283 – this is Odysseus' educated homophrosynic guess). She thus manipulates, by her beauty and self-advertisement, the *hedna* or bride-gift system. Here the underdog female finds an advantage available from her assets in the fixed and loaded rules of a patriarchal society. Athene (or prescient Penelope) wants the wife to look even better, to be more valued (τιμήεσσα μᾶλλον), in the eyes of her husband and her son (18.160–2). Odysseus, better than Homer's censorious critics, appreciates her feminine (or homophrenetic) wiles. Her teasing deceit and her beauty enhanced by Athene (18.190–7) recall both Hera's seductive *apate* of Zeus himself in *Iliad* 14 and Odysseus' two-step seduction of Nausikaa the ballplayer (6.90–246).[23] The guest-friend is mightily pleased with the house mistress's bride-commerce success (18.282: γήθησεν).

97

Penelope, before and after conversing with the disguised guest, *acts* as if she believes her guest's prophetic claims about Odysseus' proximity, while suddenly[24] and repeatedly denying them in her words any credence. Thus, she decides, in the beggar's presence, after some comic dream-(mis-)interpretation, to hold the bride-contest by stringing the bow and shooting for herself as prize. Since the interlocutor certainly does know Odysseus' precise whereabouts, the privileged vagrant warmly encourages her to put her body on the line and hold the courtship (con-)test (19.584). *Cunning Odysseus* alleges to her that *Cunning Odysseus* will arrive before the bow is strung (19.582–7). The coincidence of the narrator and the speaker using the same epithet (πολύμητις) of the present absence is striking and unusual. The foretold event has already come true! The homecomer has come home.

Smiling is a visible sign of heroic confidence (4.609, 16.476, 23.111). Odysseus' inwardly laughing heart and his sole, unseen sardonic smile also make this clear.[25] Laughter conveys self-assurance, or over-assurance, to others. Alternatively, laughter, like Penelope's supposed vanity, is a woman's cover-up, a veil for Penelope's deadly intentions. These two Penelopean laughs signal to internal audiences, and to external ones like us, that the duplicitous house of Odysseus now has the confidence and sufficient person-power to help itself. The three unintended spasms further signify – insofar as they are incomprehensibly motivated at the time – that the gods are also ready for resolution. Detective Penelope has begun to see the light at the end of the long tunnel (at 17.452). Her focal interrogations, her hilarious discussion of a self-decrypted dream,[26] her bizarrely self-arranged bride-contest, and finally her oblique reference to moving the immovable bed expose the limits of the cunning but not equally clever homecoming-husband. Her last laugh has a sharp point. She is truly περίφρων, 'thinking around' her husband.

Conclusion

Divination in the Odyssey, the book that Anne Amory Parry (1963, 130 n. 1) intended to produce but unfortunately never wrote, drenches the fifth tetrad (Books 17–20, 21 also). Omens pullulate through different channels: most unnatural are the prodigies (such as eerie radiance: 19.39–40, or clear sky thunder: 20.100–4). Other examples include portents, augury, both waking visions and dreams, mysterious epiphanies (22.205–10), hopes and prayers that become prophecies (e.g. 21.402–3), perverted toasts (18.112–22), and the contest itself. Further manifestations include wishes that repeatedly rebound on their authors – the suitors – and many other words that when spoken teem with kledonic, i.e. unintended, significance for the privileged internal audience of omen-seeking (e.g. 17.541–6, 20.97–102) Laërtids and for external ears, Homer's omen-attuned listeners.

This paper has demonstrated three points:

1. Greek divination actively seeks omens, natural and 'accidental,' as Odysseus explicitly requests (20.97–102: *pheme* and *teras*) and Penelope implicitly hopes for.

2. The veriest muscular twitch as well as verbal slip can provide such an unintentionally portentous omen.

3. Finally, the mental acuity to recognize arbitrary events such as sneezing and laughing as omens validates and activates them, and thus creates an ominous power in, and for, the cryptanalyst, here Penelope.

Often the speech or act that literary critics term 'ironic' is in fact 'palmic' or 'kledonic,' prophetic, a self-fulfilling prophecy. So, Telemakhos' most timely sneeze (and Penelope's seemingly untimely laughs) helps bring about the afflicted parties' desired outcome – poetic justice, bloody revenge, and the reinstallation of Laërtid primacy on Ithaka.

APPENDIX[27]

Other ancient sneezes for ptarmoscopes to consider

Greek: πταρμοί

Hom. Hymn to Hermes 294–8: Hermes reacts to Apollo's rough handling.

Herodotos 6.107.3: Hippias happened to sneeze and cough.

Aristoph.

  Birds 720: a word-omen (*pheme*) is a 'bird' [omen].

  Kn. 639: sausage-seller hears a wide-assed pathic fart on right; pun on ἐπέπταρε/ἐπέπαρδε.

  Lysist. 389–97: ill omened Adonis was cried out during assembly vote for Sicilian expedition.

Thuc. 2.49.3: a symptom of plague.

Xen. *Anab.* 3.2.8–9: a soldier sneezes at Xenophon's phrase πολλαὶ ἡμῖν καὶ καλαὶ ἐλπίδες εἰσὶ σωτηρίας. Xenophon interprets the spasm as confirmation of Zeus Soter's deliverance of his expedition.

Hippocr. *Prog.* 14 (= 1.103 Kuhn): sneezing beneficial in many illnesses.

Plato *Symposion* 185, 189a: sneezing as a cure of hiccoughs, a sign of recovery.

Aristotle *Hist. Anim.* 1.11.7–10 (492b8): human sneezes are regarded as ominous.

[Aristotle] *Problemata* 33.7–11 (962b19): humans sneeze more than other animals; sneezes deemed important when projects begun, etc.

Philokhoros (*FGrHist* 328 F 192): Demeter credited with discovery of significance of sneezes and other *kledones.*

Philemon F 100 (Kock): a character is unusually skeptical of the significance of sneezing.

Theokr. 7.96 with scholia (Halliday 1913, 176): Erotes' sneeze for Simikhidas.

Theokr. 18.16: sneezes portend happiness for marrying lovers.

Athenaios *Deipnos.* 2.66c: sneezes are deemed sacred (*hierous*).

Plut. *Them.* 13, from Phainias of Eresos, the Peripatetic biographer (?): a sneeze on the right before the battle of Salamis forces Themistokles to acquiesce in human sacrifices.

Plut. *Genio Socr.* 11 (581a–b): a sneeze or similar *kledon* is trivial but somehow a *daimon.*

Polyain. 3.10.2: Timotheus turns an ambiguous omen into a positive one for his sailors off Kerkyra; cf. Frontinus *infra.*

Anth. Pal. 11.268: the proper response to sneeze: Ζεῦ σῶσον.

Anth. Pal. 6.333: a lamp 'sneezes' thrice; lover Antigone comes to visit? If so, lamp is mantic.

Latin: sternumenta

Cic. *De Div.* 2.84: scorns a preposterous concept, but *sternumenta erunt observanda* (*cf.* Pease 1920–3 ad loc., 487–8).

Catull. 45.8–9, 17–18: favorable Love omen [orientation relative to speaker is of questionable relevance, thus probably humorous; cf. Gratwick 1992].

Prop. 2.3.24: *Amor* sneezes shrilly at beloved's birth ['shrilly' may translate the unexpected adverb used of Telamakhos' sneeze: σμερδαλέον].

Ovid *Heroid.* 18.151–2: a lamp sneezes [sputters] for Hero's love of Leander.

Frontinus *Strat.* 1.12.11: Timotheus at Corcyra in 373 BCE: discounted his ship-pilot's alarm at a sneeze.

Petron. *Sat.* 98.4: Giton under the bed sneezes thrice.

Plin. *HN* 2.24: sneezes and stumbles are small but ominous events.
HN 7.42: a sneeze after copulation causes abortion.
HN 28.23, 26: advises an apotropaic *Gesundheit* for a sneezer with sneezer's name.

Apul. *Metam.* 9.25: Sulfur makes the young adulterer sneeze repeatedly; fuller cries out the apotropaic phrase [*salve!*] for his wife.

Biblical and Patristic

2 Kings 4:35: a dead child awakes and sneezes seven times.

Augustine *De Doctr. Chr.* 2.20: return to bed if you sneeze while donning shoes.

Notes

[1] The word, when meaning 'unconscious, verbal presage,' occurs only at 18.117 and 20.120 (the mill woman's prayer/curse), where the text most clearly describes and warrants it as a divine message (and one equated to φήμη, 100, 105; cf. 2.35. In the elderly mill-grinder's case, Odysseus requests such a sign, and gladly receives it, but she is unaware of that aspect of the 'unnatural' transaction.

[2] Let us note *their* servants too, *Od.* 16.247–53.

[3] The *Homeric Hymn to Hermes* 294–8 juxtaposes the baby's mysterious burp/fart as an omen with an equally ominous sneeze: is this double palmic determination? Podlecki (1967, 17) mentions the *Odyssey's* sneeze as an unexpected occurrence that one could interpret as divine.

[4] The adverb may be mock-heroic, as Leaf suggested but Stanford contested (see both, in their commentaries, ad loc.). The adverb, 'dauntingly', 'violently', 'piercingly', usually modifies paralinguistic, non-verbal human war cries or shouts of supernatural or monstrous beings: Odysseus, 24.537 (cf. Eurymakhos, 22.81), Hephaistos, 8.305, Kyklops Polyphemos when poked in the eye, 9.395, but also Odysseus' groaning crew, 10.399. The adjective can refer to disconcerting sights such as Skylla's head, 12.91.

[5] The discerning reader may discover the assistance here of Bruce Heiden in my paper.

[6] Posidonios wrote a *Palmikon* (Suda, s.v. *oionistiken*), as did the Ptolemaic diviner Melampous.

[7] Some Greeks thought that the sneeze revealed temporary demonic residence (Plut. *Gen. Socr.* 11; Orig. *Con. Cels.* 4.94; Pease 1911, 429–43 with ethnographic parallels; Lawson [1910] 329–30). See also Dodds 1951, 13, 24 n. 87: trivial departures from normal behavior. Sonin 1999 examines Aristophanes' spasms in Pl. *Symp.*

[8] We say in English that 'out of the mouths of babes' comes unexpected truth. Plut. *Is. et Osir.* 14 (356e) notes the power of children's words as omens. The very old Aegyptios' words are interpreted as ominous of success by the young Telemakhos (*Od.* 2.32).

[9] Helen is adept at recognizing resemblances and at augury (4.141–4, 247–50; 15.171–81). Telemakhos ratifies the last example.

[10] *Meid-* words (e.g. 23.111; 20.302 – very quiet) are more clearly marked as soundless facial expressions than *gel-* words that often indicate voiced amusement: Odysseus 9.413 (in his heart); Telemakhos 21.105; Penelope 18.163, 17.542 [our passage]; Suitors: 18.40, 100, 111, 320, 350; 20.346–7 [prodigy!], 358, 374, 390; 21.376; 2.301. Others: gods in one cluster: 8.307, 326, 343, [344: Poseidon does *not* laugh at Ares' predicament]; 14.465 [wine produces singing, laughing, dancing, and loose words]; the maids 20.8.

[11] Both the words for 'sneeze' and for 'sneeze in behalf of' are *hapax* in Homer.

[12] One folklore student at Ohio Wesleyan in 1999, Brenda Williamson, suggested this point in a brief but minor paper on Penelope's recognitions entitled 'Penelope, Private Eye.' Levine (1982/3, 97) points out that the suitors always laugh

and never smile, while the family of Odysseus enjoys affectionate and superior smiles. Penelope's laugh verb is the emphatic *gelasse* both times.

[13] e.g., see 1.363, 4.703–5, 16.450, 17.31–40, 19.251, 603; 21.56–7.

[14] Twelve of the twenty-two occurrences of the *gel-* stem appear in *Odyssey* 18–20, but most of these refer to the concentrated merry-making of the befuddled suitors.

[15] Lateiner 2005 discusses how the Greeks portray welcome kledonic omens in historiography.

[16] See Halliday (1913, 47–51); Riess in PWK *RE*, s.v. omen; LSJ⁹ s.v. *kledon*, *symbolon* iii.2; Parker in *OCD*³, s.v. divination, Greek; cf. Lateiner 2005. One might appropriate for oneself another's omen. Nestor calls for Zeus to send a reassuring thunderbolt (*Il.* 15.377); but the *Trojans* gain confidence from this portent. Bouché-Leclercq (1879) claims that Homer has rejected omens, but his citation, 12.25, must be a misprint.

[17] We bypass the long-standing analytic-unitarian controversy about her several motives for this appearance. Without arguing through the matter here, I believe that she wants to observe for herself the well-referenced, recent arrival. Further, she already suspects (and is encouraged so to do: 17.539–40) that he may be the husband that Telemakhos, Theoklymenos, and the stranger himself (*via* Eumaios) report as alive and now near (17.141–3, 18.155–9, 17.525–7).

[18] At *Od.* 17.595–601, Eumaios expresses a wish for Zeus to destroy the suitors and Telemakhos helpfully asserts 'So it shall be, Pops' (ἔσσεται οὕτως, ἄττα). Since Eumaios may still be ignorant that Odysseus has returned (the usual view), Telemakhos may be practicing his own kledonomancy, theological *jiu-jitsu*.

[19] The *agon* reveals the divine will and divine favor, as surely as a lottery does. Odysseus is victor in the beggars' slugfest contest, the Penelopean recollection of Odysseus' appearance test (19.215), the bow-stringing contest, the ax-shooting contest, and the megaron mêlée battle. He loses only the last contest, of wits, with Penelope, by insisting that he is the person that he had so long pretended not to be, and by being properly surprised and outwitted about his allegedly portable bed.

[20] 18.163; Hölscher 1939; Büchner 1940; Levine 1983; Clay 1984; Russo 1992 ad loc.; de Jong 2001, 445, inter alios.

[21] The adverb appears elsewhere in Homer only for Thersites' helplessness, *Il.* 2.269. Cf. Levine 1983: 'confident'; Clay 1984: 'uncharacteristic'; and R. van Bennekom, *LfgrE* 'not necessary', followed by Russo 1992. These views ignore or play down the divine impulse that I argue for (cf. Hölscher 1939, 62). Amory (1963, 131 n.6) thinks the laugh marks Penelope's intuition that Odysseus is now back.

[22] The formulaic verse, τῆι δ' ἄρ' ἐπὶ φρέσι θῆκε θεὰ γλαυκῶπις Ἀθήνη, is rarer than one might imagine. The only exact repetition comes at 21.1, the vital 'inspiration' for the bow contest, and the closest similar formula appears at 5.427, where Athene saves Odysseus from the Skherian rocks by a sudden, radically different plan.

[23] Note that here too Athene manages the stage movements (6.112–14) and alters the seductive one's appearance for the better (6.229–37) – taller, 'thicker', and more graceful (not 'whiter', a gender discriminator).

[24] Before the news of the stranger's strange arrival, Penelope persistently expected her husband's return. She eagerly questioned every visitor to the island (14.122–30). At this inopportune instant, the idea has become stale and silly. How odd!

[25] 9.414, 20.302; Lateiner 1995; cf. Kalypso's and Athene's superiority: 5.180,

13.287; Levine 1984.

[26] Harsh (1950) explains (persuasively to me, although to few others) many of the cryptic and encrypted elements of the disguised stranger's conversation with Penelope – supposedly beyond hope. Winkler (1990) improves on elements of Harsh's pre-feminist case. Both John Vlahos (unpubl.) and I discuss in other papers the related, long-debated but misconstrued issue of Odysseus' recognition(s). We both argue for Penelope being conscious of the stranger's identity from Book 17. Pratt (1994) and Rozokoki (2001) with bibliography recently discussed the important topic of Penelope's dreams (4.795–841, 20.87–90, 19.535–53).

[27] Pease (1911) and Halliday (1913) have already collected many of these examples.

Bibliography

Amory, A.
  1963   'The reunion of Odysseus and Penelope', in C. Taylor (ed.) *Essays on the*
          Odyssey, Bloomington, 100–21, 130–6.
Bouché-Leclercq, A.
  1879   *Histoire de la divination dans l'antiquité*, Paris, I.161–5, with refs.
Büchner, W.
  1940   'Die Penelopeszenen in der Odyssee', *Hermes* 75, 129–67.
Clay, J.S.
  1984   'Homeric ἄχρειον', *AJP* 105, 73–6.
de Jong, I.J.F.
  2001   *A Narratological Commentary on the* Odyssey, Cambridge.
Dodds, E.R.
  1951   *The Greeks and the Irrational*, Berkeley and Los Angeles.
Felson-Rubin, N.
  1994   *Regarding Penelope. From character to poetics*, Princeton.
Gratwick, A.S.
  1992.   'Those sneezes: Catullus 45, 8–9, 17–18', *CPh* 87, 234–40.
Halliday, W.R.
  1913   *Greek Divination*, London, 174–5 (repr. Chicago).
Harsh, Ph.W.
  1950   'Penelope and Odysseus in *Odyssey* xix', *AJP* 71, 1–21.
Hölscher, U.
  1939   *Untersuchungen zur Form der Odyssee*, Leipzig.
Lateiner, D.
  1995   *Sardonic Smile*, Ann Arbor.
  2005   'Signifying names and other ominous accidental utterances in classical
          historiography', *GRBS* 45, 35–57.
Lawson, J.
  1910   *Modern Greek Folklore and Ancient Greek Religion*, Cambridge.
Levine, D.
  1982/3 'Homeric laughter and the unsmiling suitors', *CJ* 78, 97–104.
  1983   'Penelope's laugh: *Od.* 18.163', *AJP* 104, 172–8.
  1984   'Odysseus' smiles: *Od.* 20.301, 22.371, 23.111', *TAPA* 114, 1–9.

1987   '*Flens matrona et meretrices gaudentes*: Penelope and her maids', *CW* 81, 23–7.

Pease, A.S.

1911   'The omen of sneezing', *CP* 6, 429–43.

1920–3   *Ciceronis De Divinatione*, Urbana. With folkloric bibliography.

Podlecki, A.J.

1967   'Omens in the *Odyssey*', *G&R* 14, 12–23.

Pratt, L.

1994   '*Od.* 19.535–50: On the interpretation of dreams and signs in Homer', *CPh* 89.2, 147–52.

Rozokoki, A.

2001   'Penelope's dream in Book xix of the Odyssey', *CQ* 51.1, 1–6.

Russo, J. et al.

1992   *A Commentary on the* Odyssey, vol. 3, Oxford, esp. p. 44.

Sonin, J.

1999   *The Verbalisation of Non-Verbal Communication in Classical Greek Texts*, diss. Cambridge, esp. 166–76.

Vlahos, J.B.

unpublished   'Homer's *Odyssey*, The case for early recognition'.

Winkler, J.

1990   'Penelope's cunning and Homer's', in *The Constraints of Desire*, New York, 129–61.

OLD MEN AND CHIRPING CICADAS
IN THE *TEICHOSKOPIA*

Hanna M. Roisman

For the most part, the focus of the ample commentary on the *teichoskopia* in lines 161–244 of Book 3 of the *Iliad* has been on what Kirk terms its anachronism.[1] The 'viewing from the wall' takes place in the tenth year of the siege, yet Priam is depicted asking Helen who Agamemnon, Odysseus, and Aias are. Realistically, he should have been able to identify them, especially since his observation that Agamemnon is handsome (3.169) and, even more, his rather detailed description of Odysseus – as short and broad-shouldered, with his battle gear on the ground as he ranges through the ranks (3.194–6) – make it clear that he has no visual problem.[2]

The anomaly has led scholars to regard the episode as a relic from another epic that told of the first years of the war, and was transposed to its present place in the version that has come down to us.[3] Kirk claims it would have been easy enough to redraw the scene to remove Priam's ignorance, but that this wasn't done because the anomaly, which stands out strikingly in the written version, could be overlooked or tolerated in the oral version, so there was no need to correct it.[4]

Although such historical speculation has engaged many scholars, it remains inconclusive. One may also wonder how apt it is here, and whether the seeming anomaly cannot be better accounted for within the text itself. Tsagarakis, for one, has argued that Priam's questions stem not from ignorance but from kindness and politeness: he wanted to set Helen at ease when she appeared at the Scaean Gates.[5] I share Tsagarakis' view that Priam's questions do not stem from ignorance. In this paper, I would like to suggest another interpretation of Priam's questions and of the scene as a whole.

This is a scene mainly of old men and, of course, Helen, a woman still young. Homer emphasizes the matter of age throughout, beginning before the *teichoskopia* itself, when he has Menelaos insist that Priam, because he is an old man, certify the oaths to be taken before the duel that will be fought between Paris and himself for the possession of Helen (3.108–10). Within the *teichoskopia,* Homer explicitly identifies Priam and the seven men sitting at the gate with him as 'elders of the people' (δημογέροντες, 3.149) and repeatedly refers to Priam as an old man (γεραιός, 3.191, 225). My claim is that Homer crafts the scene to present a double view of the old men, one positive, one negative. In this paper, I will show the two views and then try to suggest why Homer joined them in the *teichoskopia.*

The coexistence of contrasting perspectives is indicated in the comparison to cicadas that Homer makes immediately upon introducing the elders. We read:

> γήραϊ δὴ πολέμοιο πεπαυμένοι, ἀλλ' ἀγορηταὶ
> ἐσθλοί, τεττίγεσσιν ἐοικότες, οἵ τε καθ' ὕλην
> δενδρέῳ ἐφεζόμενοι ὄπα λειριόεσσαν ἱεῖσι·
> τοῖοι ἄρα Τρώων ἡγήτορες ἧντ' ἐπὶ πύργῳ.

> Because of their old age they had ceased from battle, but
> they were excellent talkers – like cicadas, who send forth
> a lily-like voice sitting on a tree in the wood. Such were the men
> who were sitting on the tower, the leaders of the Trojans.
>
> (3.150–3)

The passage gives prominence to the old men's speaking ability, but presents it ambiguously. On the one hand, the comparison of the old men's voices to the 'lily-like' voice of cicadas sitting on a tree in the forest is suggestive of a special beauty and delicacy. The LSJ notes that the chirping of the cicada was thought to be particularly sweet.[6] Along with the description of the men as 'excellent talkers', it points up their speaking ability and makes it a worthy quality of old age, of no less value than the fighting ability that, as the lines note, the old men no longer have. This view is supported by the description of Antenor and Oukalegon as 'men of good counsel' (πεπνυμένω ἄμφω, 3.148).

On the other hand, through its association with the myth of Tithonos, the cicada is a symbol of old age, with all of its deficiencies.[7] According to the myth, Tithonos or the goddess Eos (depending on the source), who was enamored of him, requested his immortality for him but forgot to ask for agelessness as well. Eustathius, writing on *Iliad* 11.1(Hieronymus fr. 15 We = Erbse III p. 123), describes Tithonos as the one who makes the request and adds that when Tithonos (whom the Homeric muse depicts in that line as a haughty young man) becomes old, he prays for death, but Eos cannot grant it. Tithonos then asks to become an *alogon* (*aloga*, 825.60), literally a thing without speech or reason, and Eos transforms him into a *tettix*, a cicada, so she can continue to listen to his sweet voice.[8] Coming in place of speech and reason, the sweetness of the cricket's voice here seems to be associated with the intellectual deficiencies of old age, and in a way portrayed almost as a recompense for the failing physical prowess.[9] It is pleasing, even beautiful, but without reason.[10]

Contrasting perspectives of old age, similar to those that I will show in the *teichoskopia*, can be found in later writings. A positive image is found in the depiction of a three-generational household by a speaker in the corpus of Demosthenes' speeches (Dem. 25.87–9). In this depiction, the elders, described as fathers of grown sons and possibly grandfathers, ensure the harmony and proper management of the home and community by playing their part in maintaining what the speaker calls the bond of 'mutual kindliness' (ἡ πρὸς ἀλλήλους φιλανθρωπία, 25.87), through their forbearance toward the less-than-desirable conduct of the young. As the speaker states: 'The elders…if they see any spending or drinking or entertainment beyond due measure, manage to see these things without revealing that they have seen them. The result is that everything their natures [that is, the different natures of the young and the old] suggest is done, and done well' (25.88).[11] Although the speaker groups fathers and grandfathers, what is relevant to the purpose here is that the image of the observant yet tactful and tolerant older man applies to the elderly.

Negative images, on the other hand, are found in Aristotle and Theophrastus. Aristotle describes how old men live in their memories and how this relates to their loquacity. We read (*Rhet.* 1390a12–13):[12]

καὶ ζῶσι τῇ μνήμῃ μᾶλλον ἢ τῇ ἐλπίδι· τοῦ γὰρ βίου τὸ μὲν λοιπὸν ὀλίγον τὸ δὲ παρεληλυθὸς πολύ, ἔστι δὲ ἡ μὲν ἐλπὶς τοῦ μέλλοντος ἡ δὲ μνήμη τῶν παροιχομένων. ὅπερ αἴτιον καὶ τῆς ἀδολεσχίας αὐτοῖς· διατελοῦσι γὰρ τὰ γενόμενα λέγοντες· ἀναμιμνησκόμενοι γὰρ ἥδονται.

They live in their memory rather than in hope; for the part of life remaining to them is short, but that which is gone past is long, and hope belongs to the future, memory to what is done. This is the reason for their loquacity; for they are continually talking of the past, because they enjoy remembering.[13]

Theophrastus, in his *Characters*, depicts men of sixty plus as making fools of themselves in their efforts to act young. Among the ridiculous behaviors he describes are the old man's infatuation with a prostitute, which leads him to try to break down the door to her room with a battering ram, and 'when young women are nearby, he practices a chorus-dance and whistles to himself' (καὶ ὅταν ὦσιν ἐγγὺς γυναῖκες, μελετᾶν ὀρχεῖσθαι αὐτὸς αὑτῷ τερετίζων, 27).

The old men in the *teichoskopia* may be seen at one and the same time as kind, tolerant and forbearing, and as exhibiting the loquacity of the elderly in the negative sense with which Aristotle invested it, as well as a rather unseemly interest in the ever youthful and beautiful Helen. The first view would be consistent with the sweetness of the cicada's song, the second with its lack of reason and endlessness.

This double perspective may be applied to the content of the old men's 'murmuring' among themselves as they see Helen approaching. We read:

> οὐ νέμεσις Τρῶας καὶ ἐϋκνήμιδας Ἀχαιοὺς
> τοιῇδ' ἀμφὶ γυναικὶ πολὺν χρόνον ἄλγεα πάσχειν·
> αἰνῶς ἀθανάτῃσι θεῇς εἰς ὦπα ἔοικεν·
> ἀλλὰ καὶ ὣς τοίη περ ἐοῦσ' ἐν νηυσὶ νεέσθω,
> μηδ' ἡμῖν τεκέεσσί τ'ὀπίσσω πῆμα λίποιτο. (3.156–60)

> There is no blame for the Trojans and the well-greaved Akhaians
> that they suffered woes so long for such a woman. Terribly she
> resembles in her face immortal goddesses. But, in spite of
> her being such a woman, let her go back in the ships, so
> she may be not be left here, a bane to us and our children.

These lines express the old men's appreciation of Helen's beauty and their understanding of how it drove the parties in the conflict to fight for her, at the same time as it expresses their war-weariness and desire for Helen to return to her homeland rather than endanger them and their children in Troy. According to one reading, the lines show the old men's generosity of spirit, understanding of the passions that drive those younger than themselves, and balanced and sensible assessment of the situation. According to the other and equally plausible reading, their talk smacks of the fatuous attraction that old men may feel for beautiful young women. Their praise of Helen's beauty as comparable to that of the immortal goddesses may be seen as excessive, or allusive to the judgment of Paris. That they clear her and the warring parties of responsibility may be seen as an act of moral laxity which, moreover, ignores Helen's wilful betrayal of her husband.

Both Hektor and Helen herself, it may be noted, were much less forgiving. Earlier, Hektor had called his brother 'woman-crazy' and 'cajoling' (γυναιμανές, ἠπεροπευτά, 3.39), wished that he had never been born or had been killed unwed (ἄγονός…ἄγαμός, 3.40, cf. also 6.282–5), pointed out the sorrow that he had caused his father and his people by bringing Helen to Troy (πατρί τε σῷ μέγα πῆμα πόληΐ τε παντί τε δήμῳ, 3.50, cf. 6.282–3). Helen tells Priam that she wishes she had died rather than eloped with his son and admits to having 'forsaken' (λιποῦσα) her marital bed, her grown child, and her kin to that end (3.173–5). Most harshly, she describes herself as κυνῶπις, 'dog-faced' (3.180, cf. κυνὸς κακομηχάνου ὀκρυοέσσης, 6.344) – a strong term of opprobrium applied to persons who have committed an unacceptable act.[14] Seen against these criticisms, the old men's charitable interpretation seems to reflect a rather lax morality.

A similar double perspective informs Priam's conversation with Helen, beginning with his invitation that she sit next to him and continuing through the three identifications that he asks her to make. The reason he gives for the invitation – that sitting next to him she will be able to see Menelaos, her relatives by marriage, and her near and dear ones – looks very much like a pretext, and an awkward one at that. For why would a father-in-law want his daughter-in-law to get a good look at her former husband and his relatives?[15] And why would he think that she would want to see them after having run away with another man? The pretext can be understood in two ways. On the one hand, it can be seen as a gallant act aimed at making his daughter-in-law, who is not very popular among the Trojans, feel welcome. This reading would be consistent with the appreciation that Helen expresses at Hektor's funeral for Priam's constant kindness (24.770). On the other hand, it can also be seen as a convenient excuse for striking up a conversation with the beautiful woman his companions were whispering about and of showing off his relation to her – which is what allows him, but not them, to call her to his side.

Priam follows the invitation by repeating his companions' seeming exculpation of Helen. 'You are not culpable in my eyes; the gods, I think, are to blame | who stirred up against me this wretched war with the Achaeans' (οὔ τί μοι αἰτίη ἐσσί, θεοί νύ μοι αἴτιοί εἰσιν, | οἵ μοι ἐφώρμησαν πόλεμον πολύδακρυν Ἀχαιῶν, 3.164–5). Again, we can read these lines as either a generous effort to put Helen at ease along with a demonstration of the admirable forbearance of the elderly toward the passions of youth, or, conversely, as a self-serving exculpation of someone who is indeed blameworthy. With respect to the second reading, it is of note that while his companions had expressed their understanding of those falling for Helen, among themselves and out of Helen's earshot, Priam does so directly to her. It thus strikes one as being an old man's ploy to ingratiate himself with a beautiful young woman.[16]

With regard to Priam's three requests for identification, which follow his exculpation, I will begin by pointing out that the text provides indications that he did know who the warriors were whom he asked Helen to identify. The clearest is perhaps Antenor's saying that he had hosted Odysseus and Menelaos when they were in Troy to negotiate Helen's return (3.203–24). It is hard to believe that Antenor would have met with Odysseus while Priam did not, especially given the importance of the matter under negotiation both to Troy in general and to the royal house in particular. Hinting at this unlikelihood, Homer has Antenor make a special point of saying that he had 'learned the shape/form of both of them' (ἀμφοτέρων δὲ φυὴν ἐδάην, 3.208). In addition, we may note that Priam does not ask Helen to identify Menelaos. Obviously, there may be any number of reasons for this. The simplest reason would be that Menelaos' appearance did not arouse Priam's curiosity, as he claims the appearance of the warriors about whom he asked did. But it may also be that Priam sensed he could not get away with pretending that he did not recognize her ex-husband. My sense is that if he knew who Menelaos was, he would have known who Agamemnon, Menelaos' brother, was too.

Assuming that Priam does know who Agamemnon is, his request for identification would appear to be an intentional act aimed at allowing him to praise Agamemnon for Helen's benefit. He praises Agamemnon lavishly, once, before Helen identifies him, as the most handsome man he has ever seen (καλὸν δ᾽ οὕτω ἐγὼν οὔ πω ἴδον ὀφθαλμοῖσιν, 3.169), and then again, after she identifies him as the commander of the Greek army, as a 'child of fortune, favored by heaven' (μοιρηγενές ὀλβιόδαιμον, 3.182). In our first reading, these praises may be seen as yet another effort to make Helen feel good (under the assumption that she would be pleased to hear her kinsman commended), as well as a generous acknowledgement of the stature and worth of his enemy.

At the same time, his praise may be seen as the effusive and hyperbolic comments of an old man, aimed at ingratiating himself with his beautiful daughter-in-law and keeping the conversation going. In this reading, one might wonder whether Helen would want to hear her ex-brother-in-law praised so highly, especially for his looks, and whether it would not make her feel a bit cornered and imposed on – whether because she senses its ulterior motive or because she is in no position either to agree or disagree with it.

In either view, Priam's praise of the enemy commander in the midst of a siege comes across as rather bizarre, as does the fact that it is couched in the form of a direct address to someone who is too far away to hear:

ὦ μάκαρ Ἀτρεΐδη, μοιρηγενές, ὀλβιόδαιμον,
ἦ ῥά νύ τοι πολλοὶ δεδμήατο κοῦροι Ἀχαιῶν. (3.182–3)

Blessed son of Atreus, child of fortune, favored by heaven,
many youths of the Akhaians are subject to your command.

The direct address shows Priam absorbed in his own thoughts, detached from a conversation he had initiated, and enthusing to himself in the presence of his interlocutor and others, as though they weren't there or couldn't hear him. His detachment from the reality at hand is highlighted by the fact that the term μοιρηγενές (child of fortune), which he applies to Agamemnon, is a *hapax legomenon* in the Homeric epic, as well as by its redundancy with ὀλβιόδαιμον – 'favored by heaven'.

His praise is followed by six lines of reminiscences about his visit to the Phrygians as an *epikouros*, a helper or an ally, when they were at war with the Amazons. Their ostensible purpose seems to be to allow Priam to augment further his praise of Agamemnon by comparing the splendor and vast number of soldiers in the Phrygian encampment with the even greater splendor and larger number of those under Agamemnon's command (3.190). These recollections of distant places and times gone by, however, are typical of Greek portrayals of old men, as is his reference – somewhat boastful – to his former military activities.[17]

Priam's request for identification of Odysseus may be similarly approached from two perspectives: as indicative of the courtesy and generosity of the old or as an old man's ploy to keep a beautiful women engaged with him for another seven lines. By the time Priam gets to asking about Aias, the Homeric muse has made her point, so the third exchange is rather short. I will not say anything more about it for the time being.

Of greater interest is Antenor's interjection between Priam's second and third questions, with his assertion that he agrees with the observations that Helen has just made about Odysseus's character (3.204–5).[18] Antenor's intervention can be seen to be bidding for a bit of Helen's attention for himself. He directs his statement solely to Helen and speaks for 21 consecutive lines, double the number of lines of any of Priam's statements, or of Helen's replies, for that matter. His agreement with Helen's observation that Odysseus 'knows all manner of trickery and cunning plans' (εἰδὼς παντοίους τε δόλους καὶ μήδεα πυκνά; 3.202) coincides with the common view of Odysseus, but it also contains an element of flattery, as it implicitly commends Helen for her perspicacity and powers of observation. Like Priam's earlier assurance that he did not consider Helen to blame for the war, Antenor's ready agreement with her assessment can be read as an old man's effort to ingratiate himself with a beautiful young woman, while his elaboration on how he played host to Odysseus and Menelaos when they came to negotiate Helen's return has much the same quality of an old man's recollection of his former deeds as Priam's mention of his role in the war against the Amazons.[19]

Moreover, it is difficult to see the relevance of his excursus on Menelaos' and Odysseus' manner of speaking, so it comes across as idle talk aimed at keeping Helen's attention. This view may be supported by a certain awkwardness in his speaking style, as noted by Kirk and others. As

Kirk points out, Antenor's term μήδεα πυκνά to refer to Odysseus' and Menelaos' 'cunning devices' (3.208): 'is somewhat prosaic, especially since the earlier application [by Helen, 3.202] to Odysseus was connected with his δόλοι and a development of his character as πολύμητις; Menelaos did not possess these traits' (to line 3.208). Antenor's statement that Menelaos and Odysseus wove their speeches or stories (μύθοι) and counsels (μήδεα) (3.212) joins words that are used together nowhere else in the Homeric text; and his use of the word γένος to denote 'age' is also a one-time occurrence (Kirk, to line 215). There is nothing wrong with these terms; but the singularity of so many terms suggests a certain strain in Antenor's diction, as if he were speaking to impress. Monro observes that line 3.224 – οὐ τότε γ' ὧδ' 'Οδυσῆος ἀγασσάμεθ' εἶδος ἰδόντες – 'then we thus did not marvel at having seen the appearance of Odysseus' is 'weak and awkward'; Leaf comments that it is awkward and tautological. The line is generally thought to be spurious, in particular because of the neglect of the digamma in two words ϝεῖδος and ϝιδόντες. In addition, I would suggest that Antenor's comparison of Odysseus' words to snowflakes (3.221–2) is somewhat flowery. All in all, his style suggests that he is having difficulty relating his thoughts, whether because he is old or because he is busy trying to keep Helen's attention and to impress her.[20]

Helen responds to Priam without calling his bluff, telling him that he must have seen the key Greek warriors before. As a woman, and an understandably unpopular one in Troy (cf. 24.767–72), she is not in a position to tell him that she sees through his ploys. But there are indications in the text that she is aware of the old men's game and not entirely pleased by it. Priam addresses her warmly as 'dear child' (φίλον τέκος, 3.162), but in her first words to him she replies with a certain distancing: αἰδοῖός τέ μοί ἐσσι, φίλε ἑκυρέ, δεινός τε. (3.172) – 'Dear father-in-law, you arouse both respect and dread in me.' The warmth inherent in the word φίλε is cooled somewhat by her reference to her dread (δεινός) of Priam.[21] Then, instead of expressing gratitude for Priam's offer of a better view of her former husband and her relatives by marriage (πηούς, 3.163), she replies that she wishes she had died before following Paris to Troy and that she misses persons who are not present, and cannot be: namely, her daughter, her women friends, and her own kinsmen, who are included in the term γνωτοί that she uses for relatives. This reply plays on Priam's compassion and is aimed at retaining and augmenting it. But it also conveys the sense that her thoughts are not with her former husband and his family, and that she is less than enthusiastic about seeing them.

Finally, her short four-line reply to Priam's transparent query about Odysseus and her terse one-line identification of Aias convey the sense that she is running out of patience with Priam's efforts to make talk and that she would like to bring the conversation to an end. So does her brief, unsolicited identification of Idomeneus, as if she both anticipated Priam's next query and wished to put an end to his questions – which she, in fact, does, by changing the subject to her brothers, whose absence she notices. It is of note, too, that she doesn't respond at all to Antenor's long speech.[22]

Why would Homer present the old men at the wall from this double perspective? Why does he make it possible for the audience to see them as excellent speakers and as kind, tolerant, and forbearing – that is, as wise – on the one hand, and, on the other as foolish babblers, recalling their former glory, and over-eager for the company of a young woman who certainly has no interest in them?

I think that the answer has to do with the role Priam will play in certifying the oaths that precede the upcoming duel between Paris and Menelaos to determine the disposition of Helen and end the war. The *teichoskopia* follows shortly upon the agreement reached by Menelaos and Hektor that Priam will be asked to certify the oaths to be taken by the dueling parties to the effect that Helen and her possessions will go to whoever wins the duel and that the other side will drop its claim. Menelaos insists that Priam certify them on the grounds that, as an old man, he is particularly well suited to the task. As Menelaos puts it: 'The minds of younger men are ever flighty, but in whatever an old man takes part, he looks both before and after, so it will be by far the best for both sides' (3.108–10).[23]

The rationale contains two related ideas. The first is that old men are more reliable and cautious than young, that their minds are more stable or ready, and that their age enables and inclines them to base their actions on prior experience and to give thought to their consequences. The second is that the old men will use their mental capacities to attain the optimal outcome for the warring parties.

The expectation that the old men will act wisely probably reflects a commonplace association between age and wisdom.[24] We hear it, for example, in Nestor's demand in Book 1 that Agamemnon and Akhilles heed his advice on how to resolve their conflict because they are younger than he (1.259–61) and again in Book 4, where Homer describes Nestor as 'wise in fighting from of old' (4.310) and Nestor develops the idea to propose that he command the younger horsemen in word and counsel while they do the fighting, because 'this is the privilege of old men' (4.318–25).

The depiction of the old men in the *teichoskopia* as kind, tolerant and forbearing seems designed to accord with Menelaos' expectations. Homer depicts the men as above the fray and beyond the fierce passions (whether of desire or possession) and the powerful competitiveness that drive the younger men in the epic, forces that had given rise both to the ten-year war between the Greeks and the Trojans and to the shorter, but also calamitous, conflict between Agamemnon and Akhilles. The positive qualities of old age depicted in the elders on the wall would justify the hope that Menelaos places in them and the promise that the impending duel will put an end to the exhausting conflict.

However, as we know, the duel does not end the war. Aphrodite spirits Paris away just as Menelaos is about to kill him, and, even though Paris himself acknowledges defeat and Agamemnon claims an Akhaian victory, that soon becomes a dead letter and the fighting resumes when Pandaros, an ally of Troy, is prompted by Athena to shoot an arrow at Menelaos and wounds him (4.104–82). The depiction of Priam and his companions as foolish and garrulous highlights the ineffectuality of the old men. It tells us that for all their fine qualities and for all the hope that is placed in them, they have little weight in the scheme of things. There is certainly no way that they will be able to put an end to the war until the gods are good and ready and one side is trounced.

The old men in the *Iliad* are those who express the desire for peace and who suffer the most from the war. In his speech to Helen, Antenor alludes to the failure of earlier negotiations to return her, and in Book Seven, we see him in yet another failed attempt to attain a truce, as Paris totally rejects his advice that Helen be returned to the Greeks and Priam capitulates to his son's refusal (7.345–78).[25] The suffering of the old men is conveyed in the record the Homeric muse presents throughout the *Iliad* of the death in battle of one after another of Antenor's brave sons (11.240, 260) and is finally epitomized in Homer's depiction in Book 24 of Priam as the bereaved father, begging Akhilles to stop dragging his son's corpse and allow his burial. The failure of the truce attempts that they oversee and the descriptions of their suffering convey the old men's helplessness – the human helplessness – before the forces of passion and the power of the gods.

The dual perspective the Homeric muse gives old men on the wall brings together their wisdom and their powerlessness and embodies the tragedy of the human condition.

Notes

1 Kirk 1987, on lines.
2 For the awareness of the Trojans of the identity of the various Akhaian heroes who

are trying to storm the city, see Andromakhe's comment to Hektor about the Aiantes and Idomeneus, *Iliad* 6.435–8.

³ Sheppard 1933, 34–5, maintains that of course Priam knows who the heroes are: 'Homer's old men often seem, like Nestor, artless, vague, inconsequent'. Bergren 1979/80, maintains that the violation of chronology is not an epic mistake, but a convention used by the poet to create a sense of timelessness and to stress the universality of his subject. Stanley 1993, 63–4, suggests that the anachronism is no major issue since the scene 'functions less to identify the Greeks leaders for Priam during a "respite not otherwise possible" – than to introduce the audience to Helen and to Agamemnon's counterpart [Priam].'

⁴ Bowra 1958, 112–13 says: 'The third case of the τειχοσκοπία is a scene of such beauty that it might almost stand on its own merits and transcend criticism'. He explains Priam's lack of knowledge by the expectation of the audience to hear traditional stories, and the concern of the Homeric narrative 'with the moment and its immediate future.' He points out that the episode presents to us the 'chief personalities on the Achaean side at close view.' Seaford 1964, 9, maintains that Homer 'may not have cared about time; but if Helen surveys the Greek forces in the tenth year of the war, it is because the absence of Akhilles permits a respite not otherwise possible.' For a summary of the different views addressing the suspension of temporal verisimilitude in the scene see Bergren 1979/80, 19–20. Bergren sees the *teichoskopia*'s suspension of temporal realism as analogous to that of traditional epithets. These too are at times used in a way that contradicts their actual contextual moment, e.g., ' "starry sky" in daytime' (21–3).

⁵ Tsagarakis 1982, 69–71; cf. Sheppard 1933, 34–5. Tsagarakis also rejects the idea that the episode must belong to an earlier stage of the war (69). Edwards 1987, 56–7 maintains that the *teichoskopia* 'superbly characterizes Helen,' and emphasizes her isolation.

⁶ For references and further discussion see Cressey 1979. For λειριόεσσαν as referring to sweet voice see Hes. *Th.* 40.

⁷ In *Iliad* 20.237–8, Tithonos is also a name of one of the brothers of Priam. Out of the three brothers Tithonos, Clytius, and Hicetaeon, only Tithonos seems absent from the company above the Scaean Gates. One can only wonder whether the reference to the cicada serves as a substitute. For the cicada as associated with 'the weakness and impotence of old age', see Falkner 1995, 16, 115, 119,who sees in the ever-aging Tithonos and Priam's brother one and the same. For later association of the tettix with garrulity, see Cressey 1979, 38. For the overall pessimistic view of old age in Greek literature see Miller 1955.

⁸ The transformation into a cicada is found also in the scholion to Lykophron *Alexandra* 18, and the song of the cicada is given as the reason for its choice. See also King 1986, 21–7, for the idea that, because of their diet of nothing, air, and dew, cicadas were also considered agelessly immortal.

⁹ A similarly negative view of the image is suggested by the version of the myth told in the *Homeric Hymn to Aphrodite*: when Tithonos becomes very old, Eos shuts him for eternity in an inner room, where his voice 'flows endlessly'(ῥεῖ ἄσπεστος, 237) and his limbs lack their former strength. The endless, undifferentiated 'flow' of sound has nothing sweet about it, but suggests rather the senseless prattle and loquacity of impotent old age. Cf. Smith 1981, 81: 'Having heard that he could not move any of

his limbs, we take his unending speech as a reaction to that helplessness.'

[10] It is therefore misguided to think that the old men are in the same league as Odysseus, who, not many lines later, is described as an excellent speaker. But see Moulton 1977, 92.

[11] See Thuc. 2.37, where Pericles asserts that discretion and overlooking lapses helps to ease tensions of living together, as well as Cohen 1991, 93. For elders' tact, cf. Bailey 1991, 33.

[12] For the entire description see *Rhet.* 2.13 1389b13–1390a21.

[13] Cf. Horace *Ars Poetica* 169–74:

> multa senem circumveniunt incommoda, vel quod
> quaerit et inventis miser abstinet ac timet uti,
> vel quod res omnis timide gelideque ministrat,
> dilator spe longus, iners avidusque futuri,
> difficilis, querulus, laudator temporis acti
> se puero, castigator censorque minorum.

> Many ills surround an old man, either because he
> seeks wealth and then miserably holds on to it and fears to use it,
> or because he manages everything timidly and without enthusiasm,
> delays long in hope, is inactive and greedy
> for the future, is surly, complains, and boasts of his former life
> when he was a boy, and castigates and reproaches the young.

[14] The only other person of whom the term is used in the *Iliad* is Hera, to whom Hephaistos applies it in his criticism of her for hurling him from Olympos (18.396). In the *Odyssey* it is used by Helen of herself (4.145), Agamemnon of Klytaimnestra (11.424), and Hephaistos uses of Aphrodite in Demodokos' song (8.319). For Helen's self-blame see Ebbott 1999.

[15] Unless of course he would like to invoke in her feelings for her former husband and thus encourage her to go back to Argos. However, everywhere else, he sides with Paris and does not support those of the Trojans who would prefer her to go home (7.372–4).

[16] For calculation as part of old men's manner of life, see Aristotle, *Rhet.* 1390a14–15: καὶ μᾶλλον ζῶσι κατὰ λογισμὸν ἢ κατὰ δ᾽ ἦθος – 'And they live more by calculation than by moral character'.

[17] For the structural function of such paradeigmata in establishing the speaker's claim to be heard and his advice taken into account, see Austin 1966, Edwards 1983. The peculiar thing is that in our instance there is no advice given, or claim to be heard. The past achievements are a boast and no more.

[18] Espermann's claim 1980, 116–18, that the speech is devoid of function is unconvincing. It is strange that neither here nor when Priam goes to the plain to certify the oaths and Antenor joins him (3.262), is there any indication by the Homeric muse that he is being invited to participate in any of these interactions.

[19] Sheppard 1933, who maintains that both Priam and Antenor wish to help Helen 'to relieve her heart by leading her to speak of her husband' (34), thinks that Antenor talks about Odysseus, but contrives to give the wife a picture of her husband' (35).

[20] For the claim that the passage is a part of a late addition and that Antenor's language is heavily Odyssean, see Espermann 1980, 108–18.

[21] For the use of the distancing δεινός, cf. also 18.394, Hephaistos to Thetis.

[22] Sheppard 1933, 36–7, suggests that Helen's mention of Idomeneus comes out of Antenor's mention of Menelaos: 'Is it fanciful to suggest that, when she hears about the entertainment of the embassy, her mind goes back to the old days in Sparta, when, as Menelaus' wife, she entertained his friends?'.

[23] In the Homeric epics youth is regularly associated with recklessness and impetuosity: *Il.* 23.589–90, *Od.* 2.324.

[24] Old age is almost always associated with wisdom both in the *Iliad* and the *Odyssey*: *Il.* 4.322–3, 13.355, 19.217–19, 21.440; *Od.* 2.16.

[25] Seaford 1964, 11, claims that the lack of detail in Book 7 about Antenor's proposal to return Helen, and the remarkable influence that Paris still wields, in spite of his notorious failure in the duel, point to the antiquity of the theme of the embassy on behalf of Helen's return, of which the above are mere variations.

Bibliography

Austin, N.
   1966   'The function of digression in the *Iliad*,' *GRBS* 7, 296–312.
Bailey, F.G.
   1991   *The Relevance of Deceit*, Ithaca.
Bergren, A.
   1979/80   'Helen's web: time and tableau in the *Iliad*,' *Helios* 7, 19–34.
Bowra, C.M.
   1958   *Tradition and Design in the* Iliad, Oxford.
Cohen, D.
   1991   *Law, Sexuality, and Society: The enforcement of morals in classical Athens*, Cambridge.
Cressey, J.
   1979   'The grasshopper of the Greeks and Romans', *LCM* 4, 37–40.
Ebbott, E.
   1999   'The wrath of Helen: self-blame and nemesis in the *Iliad*,' in M. Carlisle and O. Levaniouk (eds.) *Nine Essays on Homer*, Lanham, Boulder, New York, Oxford. 3–20.
Edwards, M.W.
   1987   '*Topos* and transformation,' in J.M. Bremer et al. (eds.) *Homer Beyond Oral Poetry*, Amsterdam, 47–60.
Espermann, I.
   1980   *Antenor, Theano, Antenoriden*, Beiträge zur Klassischen Philologie, 120, Meisenheim am Glan.
Falkner, T.M.
   1995   *The Poetics of Old Age in Greek Epic, Lyric, and Tragedy*, Norman and London.
King, H.
   1986   'Tithonos and the *Tettix*', *Arethusa* 19.1, 15–35.
Kirk, G.S.
   1987   *The* Iliad: *A commentary*, vol. 1, Books 1–4, Cambridge.

Miller, P.S.
   1955   'Old age in the Greek poets', *CW* 48, 177–182.

Reckford, K.J.
   1964   'Helen in the *Iliad*', *GRBS* 5, 5–20.

Sheppard, J.T.
   1933   'Helen with Priam', *G&R* 7, 31–7.

Smith, P.
   1981   *Nursing of Mortality: A study of the Homeric hymn to Aphrodite*, Frankfurt.

Stanley, K.
   1993   *The Shield of Homer: Narrative structure in the* Iliad, Princeton, New Jersey.

Tsagarakis, O.
   1982   'The *Teichoskopia* cannot belong in the beginning of the Trojan War', *QUCC* 42, 61–72.

7

THE DEATH OF ACHILLES BY RHAPSODES

Jonathan S. Burgess

Neo-analysts have demonstrated that there are reflections of non-Homeric material in Homeric poetry. In particular they have focused on scenes in the *Iliad* that suggest the death and funeral of Achilles. In the first part of this article, it will be shown that reflections of myth about Achilles are much more organized than previously suspected. In the second part, it will be argued that the patterning of Homeric allusion is comparable to techniques of rhapsode performance. The similarity is more than coincidental, I propose; it is indicative of the influence of performance on Homeric narrative. That does not mean that rhapsodes composed the *Iliad*. But reference to performance techniques can explain much about narrative strategy in the *Iliad* and also suggest something about the historical context of the poem's genesis.

A. The death of Achilles

To pursue this argument, it will first be necessary to provide a summary reconstruction of myth about the end of Achilles' life. Traditionally Achilles kills Memnon in battle shortly before his own death in front of the Trojan walls, which is followed by a magnificent funeral for the hero. The most complete surviving accounts of these episodes are the summary of the *Aethiopis* by Proclus, a similar summary by Apollodorus (*Epit.* 5.3–5), and Quintus of Smyrna (Books 2–4). Pindar often provides further testimony, and artistic representations portray many images of this narrative. With these sources a series of motifs that constitute the tale can be established. What is offered below is not *the* myth of the death of Achilles, but rather a composite of evidence from art and literature that will serve to suggest the narrative as it would have been commonly understood in the archaic age. In narratological terms I am outlining a *fabula*, the essential yet notional sequence of a narrative, not a specific poem's version of that *fabula*.[1]

Reconstruction of Achilles' death

A. *Memnon arrives to defend Troy, and before battle Thetis predicts to Achilles that he will die shortly after Memnon's death.*
Main sources: The *Aethiopis* (Proclus), Apollodorus *Epit.* 5.3, Quintus of Smyrna 2.26–242.

B. *Achilles duels with Memnon, who has killed Antilochus, and kills him; divine scales are used to signify the outcome.*
Main sources: *Od.* 4.187–8; the *Aethiopis* (Proclus); Pindar *Ol.* 2.83, *Nem.* 3.61–3, 6.49–53, *Isthm.* 5.39–41, 8.54; Apollodorus *Epit.* 5.3; Quintus of Smyrna 2.243–548. The duel was popular with artists from at least the sixth century onward;[2] sometimes Antilochus appears as a corpse on the ground between Achilles and Memnon.[3]

C. *Eos requests a special afterlife for Memnon; his corpse is removed from the field by divine intervention and buried.*
Main sources: The *Aethiopis* (Proclus); Quintus of Smyrna 2.550–655. In art, Memnon's corpse is depicted being handled by Aethiopians, Eos, or Sleep and Death.[4]

D. *Immediately after killing Memnon, Achilles routs the Trojans and attacks Troy.*
Main sources: The *Aethiopis* (Proclus); Apollodorus *Epit.* 5.3; Quintus of Smyrna 3.1–29.

E. *Achilles is killed by Apollo and Paris by bow at the Scaean gates.*
Main Sources: *Il.* 19.416–7, 21.277–8, 23.80–1; the *Aethiopis* (Proclus); Pindar *Paean* 6.78–86; Apollodorus *Epit.* 5.3; Quintos of Smyrna 3.30–185. The rare artistic representations depict Paris and occasionally Apollo at the death scene.[5]

F. *There is a battle over the corpse of Achilles (in which Glaucus is killed by Ajax), and Ajax carries the body to safety as Odysseus defends.*
Main Sources: *Od.* 5.308–10, 24.36–42; the *Aethiopis* (Proclus); Apollodorus *Epit.* 5.4; Quintus of Smyrna 3.204–387. A well-known image on a lost Chalcidian vase pictures Ajax wounding Glaucus at the very moment Glaucus is attempting to attach a cord to Achilles' ankle.[6] Some representations depict Ajax about to lift the corpse;[7] from an early date numerous images show him carrying the corpse.[8]

G. *There is an elaborate funeral ceremony for Achilles which Thetis, the Nereids, and the Muses attend; Thetis takes Achilles from the pyre to a paradisiacal location;[9] the Greeks build a conspicuous funeral mound at Troy.*
Main Sources: *Od.* 24.43–84; the *Aethiopis* (Proclus); Pindar *Pyth.* 3.100–3,

Isth. 8.56–60; Apollodorus *Epit.* 5.5; Quintus of Smyrna 3.525–787.

H. *Games are held in honor of Achilles.*
Main Sources: *Od.* 24.85–92; the *Aethiopis* (Proclus); Apollodorus *Epit.* 5.5–6; Quintus of Smyrna 4.88–595.

B. THE DEATH OF ACHILLES IN THE *ILIAD*

By using the letters identifying motifs in my reconstruction, it is possible to summarize concisely how Achilles' death is reflected within the *Iliad*. By 'reflection' I do not mean direct and explicit allusion to future events, but rather implicit foreshadowing or 'mirroring' of extra-Iliadic material. This occurs when certain motifs or actions within the *Iliad* correspond to non-Homeric traditional narrative. Neo-analysis is the main methodology employed to identify motif reflection in the argument below, but it is modified by an oralist perspective, particularly in regard to textualization and typology.

In earlier manifestations of neo-analysis, its practitioners spoke of the influences on Homer as written texts that Homer had 'before his eyes' (e.g. Kullmann 1960, 349). Sometimes neo-analysts even argued that the poems of the epic cycle were pre-Homeric,[10] or it was assumed that hypothetical poems like a 'Memnonis' existed in written form. But few today would follow this line of thought.[11] The change results from the influence of oral theory, which scholars have increasingly recognized as compatible with neo-analysis (Kullmann 1984). Acceptance of an oral Cyclic tradition removes the need to regard specific texts (real or imagined) as the sources for the *Iliad* or *Odyssey*.[12] Interconnections between Cyclic and Homeric traditions can be attributed to common traditions that they share, not to self-conscious interaction and rivalry between poetic traditions.[13] The pre-Homeric tradition was a web of different media which expressed fluid yet coherent traditional narratives. There is not necessarily any need to privilege the Epic Cycle, or even epic at all, though it undoubtedly had a prominent role in the development of mythological traditions.

A second major issue for neo-analysis is typology. A number of the elements identified above in the death of Achilles are specific; that is, they belong to this *fabula* and not to others. But many of these elements are typical motifs; for example, a battle over a corpse. The presence of typological elements in my reconstruction challenges the validity of the neo-analytical view that motifs were 'transferred' from this *fabula* to the *Iliad*.[14]

The definition of a motif as 'typical' or 'specific' often depends on the scope of focus. Kullmann acknowledges that typical motifs exist, but argues that there are also 'more specific motifs or specific nuances in general motifs' whose adoption by the Homeric poems can be recognized (1984, 312). And neo-analysts have pointed out that the transference of specific motifs is not so much a contradiction of oral typology as an extension of it.[15] Most recurrent elements are largely generic, and they cannot be labeled primary or derivative. But recurrent elements in Homer do not always function in an automatic, insignificant manner.[16] Typology can be limited, as when one variant may serve as an 'anticipatory doublet' that foreshadows a second one. An example is the flame that burns around Diomedes' head at 5.4–8. that seems to anticipate the flame that burns around Achilles' head at 18.205–27. Reflection of post-Iliadic myth within the *Iliad* might be considered a type of anticipatory doublet; what is anticipated lies outside the poem. The transference of specific motifs from an extra-Iliadic context into the context of the *Iliad* is therefore compatible with the typology in oral poetics. In addition, the same collocation of a number of typical motifs in two different narratives would seem more than coincidence and suggest transference.

Though my analysis of motif reflection below follows the previous work of neo-analysts, I disagree with the common acceptance of a correspondence between Patroclus and Antilochus. This assumption lies at the heart of what I have called the 'vengeance theory'. In the vengeance theory, Achilles' revenge on Hector for his slaying of Patroclus is thought to be modeled on Achilles' supposed vengeance on Memnon for the slaying of Antilochus. But there is little evidence that Antilochus was central to myth about Achilles and Memnon, or that Patroclus is modeled on Antilochus.[17] Once the vengeance theory is rejected, and the strained association between Antilochus and Patroclus is dropped, then it becomes apparent that motifs in the *Iliad* concerning Achilles' death have a certain organization. The motifs, as identified by commonly accepted arguments of neo-analysts, seem to exist within certain extended narrative patterns. Most of these motifs can be organized into two groups, or 'sequences,' that revolve around the characters Patroclus (reflecting the death of Achilles) and Achilles (foreshadowing his coming death).[18] Below I graph the two motif sequences side by side, using the letters employed above in my reconstruction of Achilles' death.

In the Patroclus sequence, the actions of Patroclus reflect the actions of Achilles in myth about his death. Here Patroclus is an Achilles figure and Sarpedon is a Memnon figure. Most of the possible motifs in the reconstruction are evoked, and they occur in the chronological order of the narrative of the death of Achilles. In the 'Achilles sequence' Achilles prefigures himself and Hector represents Memnon. The Achilles sequence

The Patroclus sequence and the Achilles sequence

Patroclus Sequence (A, B, C, D, E, F, G, H) *Patroclus–Achilles, Sarpedon–Memnon*	Achilles sequence (G, A, B, D) *Achilles prefigures his own death, Hector –Memnon*
Bk. 16 A. Achilles warns Patroclus before battle (cf. the warning of Achilles by Thetis)[19]	
B. Patroclus kills Sarpedon (cf. the slaying of Memnon by Achilles)[20]	
C. The corpse of Sarpedon is removed by divine intervention (cf. the removal of the corpse of Memnon by divine intervention)[21]	
D. Patroclus attacks Troy (cf. Achilles' attack on Troy)[22]	
E. Patroclus is killed by Apollo and Euphorbus by the walls of Troy (cf. the slaying of Achilles by Apollo and Paris)[23]	
Bk. 17 F. A battle rages over the corpse of Patroclus (cf. the battle over the corpse of Achilles)[24]	
Bk. 18	G. Thetis and the Nereids mourn a prostrate Achilles (cf. their mourning of him at his funeral)[25]
	A. Thetis warns Achilles he will die after Hector's death (cf. her warning that he will die after Memnon's death)[26]
Bk. 22	B. Achilles kills Hector after the use of divine scales (cf. his killing of Memnon)[27]
	D. Achilles considers attacking Troy (cf. his attack on Troy)[28]
Bk. 23 G. A funeral ceremony is given for Patroclus (cf. the funeral for Achilles)[29]	
H. Games are held for Patroclus (cf. the games for Achilles)[30]	

cannot reflect the final elements of Achilles' story, for Achilles does not actually die in the *Iliad*. Some motifs are specific to myth about Achilles, even when considered alone (e.g. death through Apollo).[31] Other motifs are typical (e.g. the battle over a corpse), and do not certainly reflect the Achilles *fabula* when considered by themselves. But the order of typical motifs in the Patroclus sequence and the Achilles sequence separately corresponds to the order of typical motifs in the narrative of Achilles' death.

It may seem confusing that both Patroclus and Achilles reflect later events in the life of Achilles, but the two 'sequences' actually do this in a cooperative manner. The Patroclus sequence is interrupted when Patroclus dies and his corpse is recovered. Then the *Iliad* jumps from the tracks of the Patroclus sequence to the Achilles sequence. This sequence begins with motif G, exactly the motif that follows the last motif in the Patroclus sequence (motif F) before it is interrupted. Just after the corpse of Patroclus has been recovered, representing the recovery of the corpse of Achilles, Thetis and the Nereids mourn Achilles, who prefigures his own corpse at his funeral. We move from the corpse of Patroclus as a symbolic corpse of Achilles to Achilles appearing like the corpse he will later be.

The Achilles sequence then starts at the beginning of the Achilles *fabula* with motif A and proceeds through those motifs that Achilles can appropriately foreshadow. The Achilles sequence must stop when an attack on Troy is considered (motif D), for Achilles does not die in the *Iliad*. At this point the *Iliad* jumps tracks again back onto the Patroclus sequence. With the funeral of Patroclus (motif G) it picks up where it had left off at the end of Book 17. The Patroclus sequence proceeds to finish the story, though reference to the immortality of Achilles is not explicit. The two sequences effectively interlock to foreshadow the whole of the Achilles-Memnon episode. The Patroclus sequence contains most of the motifs, for Patroclus in his death can act out the death of Achilles. The Achilles sequence interrupts the Patroclus sequence so that the hero himself may evoke his oncoming fate in a striking and memorable manner. The run of the two sequences together thus proceeds in this manner: A, B, C, D, E, F [G, A, B, D] G, H.

C. RHAPSODE SEQUENCING IN THE *ILIAD*

If patterned sequences of allusive motif reflections exist in the *Iliad*, how did they get there? I propose that the narrative techniques demonstrated above reflect the practices of rhapsodes in performance. It has been recognized that techniques of rhapsode performance are reflected within the Homeric poems themselves.[32] In recent work Nagy has focussed on a performative technique that he calls 'sequencing'. This term designates the manner in which multiple performers perform passages in a sequential fashion.[33] My use of the term 'sequence' is independent of Nagy's argument, but I would like to suggest a connection between rhapsode 'sequencing' and motif 'sequences.'

Portions of the Trojan war seem to be embedded in narrative order over the course of several Books of the *Odyssey*. In Book 8 Demodocus sings of the quarrel between Achilles and Odysseus, an incident sometimes placed at the beginning of the war, and later sings of the Trojan horse, which is followed by a simile evoking the fall of Troy. Then Odysseus gives an account of his homecoming.[34] It is notable that this 'sequence' of secondary narrative in the *Odyssey* is not continuous. Large gaps of time separate the embedded Trojan war episodes, which nonetheless adhere to the order of events in the narrative of the Trojan war.[35] This organization of the embedded secondary episodes is probably not dissimilar to the practice of rhapsodes in real competition. Multiple performers who were presenting a large narrative in a limited time could have performed different episodes in chronological sequence, with gaps left between the episodes. This technique for approximating a large narrative in performance may underlie the so-called 'Panathenaic rule'.[36] This is a conventional phrase used by Classicists on the basis of ancient testimony about regulation of rhapsode competition at the Panathenaic festival (Diog. Laert. 1.57, [Plato] *Hipparch.* 228b–c). It appears that one rhapsode was required to pick up a narrative from where another left off. The sequence of Trojan war episodes within the *Odyssey* can be compared to a sequence of passages performed by rhapsodes.

Also relevant is the reflection of extra-Iliadic events within the *Iliad*. There is much Trojan war material in the *Iliad* that does not belong to the dramatic time of the poem.[37] Especially notable are scenes in early Books of the *Iliad* that seem more appropriate for the beginning of the war. The catalogue of ships reflects the situation at Aulis, the marshaling of troops seems to be in preparation for the first battle, the duel between Paris and Menelaus would more sensibly occur at the beginning of the war, and the inability of Priam to recognize the Greek leaders from the wall of the city suggests that he is seeing them for the first time.[38] Early stages of the Trojan war are suggested in the early Books of the *Iliad*, and later stages of the war increasingly become the focus of the later Books. Often these allusions and reflections seem to occur in chronological order. Arguably this organization reflects the way that rhapsodes would have suggested the outlines of a large mythological *fabula* by performing select performance segments in narrative order.

Rhapsode technique may also underlie the Patroclus sequence and the Achilles sequence demonstrated above. These together serve to evoke an extra-Iliadic narrative, the death of Achilles. What is more, the two sequences interact in significant ways. The manner in which the two sequences start and stop the run of motifs is particularly comparable to rhapsode technique. In rhapsode sequencing one rhapsode leaves off a narrative and another picks it up; within the *Iliad* Achilles picks up the motif-reflection from the point where Patroclus left off; later Patroclus picks it up from Achilles. In other words, the characters are agents in this type of secondary narration, just as rhapsodes are performers of epic narrative.[39] Patroclus and Achilles 'play a part,' in a sense, and their actions serve to narrate the death and funeral of Achilles. The series of motif-reflections revolving around them are comparable to a series of epic passages that together suggest a narrative, and the cooperative nature in which the two characters effect a *fabula* is comparable to the participatory nature of rhapsode sequencing.

D. Conclusion

Above it was shown that reflections of various motifs in the story of the death of Achilles occur in certain narrative sequences. Purposeful organization also seems to occur with other secondary narrative within the Homeric poems, whether allusion, reflection, or narration by characters. This phenomenon was compared to the performance of passages in accordance with the chronology of a narrative. Motif series revolving around the characters Patroclus and Achilles effect the narrative of the death of Achilles in a co-operative manner, just as multiple rhapsodes performed a long narrative together. The analogy focuses both on the sequence of narrative parts (motifs/performance units) and on the participation of multiple agents (Patroclus and Achilles/rhapsodes) in achieving the narrative.

The comparison of motif sequences to rhapsode sequencing is not an idle one. Internally to the *Iliad*, it helps to explain the existence of certain patterns within the poem. Externally, it suggests that the poem developed within the historical context of performance culture. If techniques of performance influenced a narrative technique within the *Iliad*, the poem was not simply a composition that happened to be performed; its very composition resulted from performance. We need not conclude that rhapsodes composed the *Iliad* and *Odyssey*, or that the Homeric poems were created within the context of the Panathenaic festival in sixth-century Athens. Some would not find that conclusion disagreeable, it is true, and it is plausible enough to suppose that the important Panathenaic phase of the Homeric performance traditions left some mark on the poems.[40] But the motif sequences that I have identified are too central to the poem to be a relatively late development.

It must be, then, that rhapsode techniques go far enough back in time to influence central compositional aspects of the Homeric poems. Rhapsode performance techniques, including 'sequencing,' did not originate at the Panathenaic festival.[41] Other festivals, such as the Panionia or the festival at Delos, might have provided an early venue for performance by multiple contestants,[42] and there is no reason to discount more informal circumstances. The performance of Achilles in the *Iliad* Book 9 suggests one possibility. As Nagy has argued, this scene depicts not only non-professional performance but also the potentiality of shared performance through 'sequencing'.[43] Amateur performance in an informal setting might have often involved more than one performer participating in the narration of a large narrative.

My thesis will be found difficult by those who sharply distinguish between the creative bard and the performing rhapsode, but the distinction has been effectively challenged.[44] Whatever terminology one prefers to use, it is most likely that techniques employed by rhapsodes also existed in earlier 'bardic' performance. Demodocus and other bards in Homeric poetry are portrayed in accordance with an imagined distant world of the heroic past, and cannot be assumed to be an exact reflection of contemporaneous performance. More instructive are the indirect indications of performance techniques that are observable in the poems. Performance techniques, including 'sequencing,' must have been part and parcel of the oral epic tradition.

In a long performance tradition of the *Iliad*, the poem would remain fluid for some time.[45] Gradually it would incorporate the circumstances of its performance. It is entirely conceivable that as the *Iliad* tradition developed, it was performed by different performers presenting different episodes in sequential order in a participatory manner. Performance sequencing would have provided a model for organizing motif sequences. Patterning of extra-Iliadic reflection may have been suggested by the way in which performers took turns presenting performance units. Motif reflection would be organized around certain characters within the story, as if they were performing the tale to which allusion was being made. Motif *sequences*, in this way, may result from rhapsode *sequencing*.

Acknowledgements

I thank the other panel presenters and the audience members at the CAMWS meeting in Lexington for their interest and helpful comments, and Bob Rabel for his energetic editorial efforts. I am also grateful to the Social Sciences and Humanities Research Council of Canada for financial support and Michal Dziong for proofreading.

Notes

[1] See de Jong 1987, x–xii, xiv on this terminology.

[2] Cf. *LIMC*, 'Achilleus', nos. 807–47; 'Achle', nos. 122–4; 'Memnon', nos. 14–60 (see also no. 98); 'Eos', nos. 300–16; 'Eos/Thesan', no. 35; 'Thetis', pp. 12–13. On the psychostasia motif in early Greek art, including possible images of Achilles and Memnon in the seventh century, see Burgess 2004a.

[3] See *LIMC*, 'Antilochos I', nos. 27–32.

[4] Cf. *LIMC*, 'Memnon', no. 61–92; 'Eos', nos. 317–33; 'Eos/Thesan', nos. 36–45.

[5] *LIMC*, 'Achilleus', nos. 848–59. See Burgess 1995.

[6] *LIMC*, 'Achilleus', no. 850.

[7] Cf. *LIMC*, 'Achilleus', nos. 849, 853c, 854 and 854a, 859; 'Achle', nos. 134, 135.

[8] Cf. *LIMC*, 'Achilleus', 860–96; 'Achle', 136–46.

[9] On the supposition that translation and a tumulus are incompatible, it has often been supposed that a cenotaph was raised. An alternative view from antiquity onward is that only an immortal, corporeal part of the semi-divine hero was translated, with his mortal part remaining behind to be burned and buried (*pace* S. West 2003, 162 n. 41, this view does not involve translation of the hero's *psyche*). For an analysis see Burgess 2001b.

[10] For an overview of this line of argument, see Jouan 1980, 96; Kullmann 1991, 428–30.

[11] But see Dowden 1996; West 2003; both a step backwards in this regard.

[12] Dihle 1970, 149–50, A. Edwards 1985, 219–20, and Davies 1989, 5, intelligently discuss the possibilities of an oral pre-Homeric Cyclic tradition. I do not think there were single prototypes of each poem in the Epic Cycle, but rather fluid Cyclic performance traditions among many other epic traditions. One should not think that poets and performers necessarily had to feel constrained by a particular poetic tradition, however. The full scope of heroic myth would be known by all; thus the apparent intertextuality of any particular poem could result from a single composer's experience with different narratives. For this concept applied to Homer, cf. Woodhouse 1930, 242–3; Lord 1960, 151; Willcock 1976, 287; M. Edwards 1991, 17–18; West 2003, 6.

[13] On intertextuality and early epic, cf. Lang 1983; Pucci 1987; Usener 1990; Danek 1998, 2002; Rengakos 2002. I find the analysis of Danek especially attractive. For an application of this approach to the Cyclic traditions, see Nagy 1990b, 70–9. For skeptical discussion, see Beye 1993, 30–4, 262–5; Clay 1997, 241–6.

[14] See Page 1963, 23; Fenik 1964 (esp. 32–3), 1968, 231–40; Nagler 1974, 25–6; Nagy 1990a, 130–1.

[15] Heubeck 1978, 8–9; Kullmann 1981, 14–18, 1984, 311–16, 1991, 426. Cf. Slatkin 1991, 3–6.

[16] M. Edwards 1987, 47–60, 1991, 11–23 extensively discusses significant use of repeated elements, often in reference to neo-analysis. See also Andersen 1987 on the phenomenon of 'mirroring' in repeated elements, Lowenstam 1993 on the significance

of repetition within Homeric poetry, and Nickel 2002, 221–5 on doublets.

[17] Burgess 1997. See also now West 2003, 10–11.

[18] I do not mean to suggest that all motif transference occurs in a sequential pattern. Two commonly accepted examples do not occur in any sequential pattern: the rescue of Nestor in Book 8 (comparable to his rescue from Memnon by Antilochus) and the wounding of Diomedes in the foot in Book 11 (comparable to the wounding of Achilles in the ankle). But I am inclined to believe that purposeful allusion is especially effected when there is a collocation of related transferred motifs that follow a recognizable sequence. Cf. discussion of the 'script' in Minchin 2001, whereby narrative sequences are said to mirror sequences of events in the real world, as comprehended by cognitive processes.

[19] See Pestalozzi 1945, 45; Schadewaldt 1965, 195; Schoeck 1961, 85–91; Janko 1992, 313, 315–17.

[20] Pestalozzi 1945, 13–15, 44–5; Schadewaldt 1965, 169; Kullmann 1960, 318; Schoeck 1961, 15–16, 23–6, 58–61; Janko 1992, 313.

[21] Pestalozzi 1945, 13–15; Schadewaldt 1965, 160, 165; Kullmann 1960, 318–20; Schoeck 1961, 8, 16, 23–5; Janko 1992, 313 and ad 16.666–83; M. Edwards 1991, 18. On the evidence of vases, see Clark and Coulson 1978, with reply by Bothmer 1981. In the *LIMC*, Weiss 1986 (the 'Eos' article) tends to favor identification of Memnon on uncertain vases, whereas Kossatz-Deissmann 1992 (the 'Memnon' article) is more skeptical.

[22] Pestalozzi 1945, 45; Schadewaldt 1965, 195; Schoeck 1961, 68–74; Janko 1992, 399.

[23] Kakridis 1949, 85–8; Pestalozzi 1945, 16, 45; Schadewaldt 1965, 169, 194–5; Kullmann 1960, 321; 1981, 9, 19; 1984, 310; 1991, 440; Schoeck 1961, 15–6, 68–74; Janko 1992 ad 16.777–867. On Euphorbos as a doublet of Paris, see Mühlestein 1987, 79–89, with the critique at Nickel 2002.

[24] Pestalozzi 1945, 17–22, 45; Schadewaldt 1965, 170; Kullmann 1960, 80–1, 328–330; 1981, 18–19; 1991, 441 n.65; Schoeck 1961 *passim*; Willcock 1987, 192–4; M. Edwards 1991, 62, 132.

[25] Kakridis 1949, 65–75; Pestalozzi 1945, 26, 32, 42; Schadewaldt 1965, 166; Kullmann 1960, 331–2; 1984, 310; 1991, 441; Schoeck 1961, 43–4; M. Edwards 1990, 312.

[26] Pestalozzi 1945, 9; Schadewaldt 1965, 167; Kullmann 1960, 311; 1981, 8–9; 1991, 440; Schoeck 1961, 38–45; Janko 1992, 313; M. Edwards 1991 ad 18.95–6.

[27] Kakridis 1949, 94; Pestalozzi 1945, 11–13, 42, 45; Schadewaldt 1965, 164; Kullmann 1960, 316–18 (cf. 31–4); 1984, 318; 1991, 441 n.65; Schoeck 1961, 25–31; M. Edwards 1991, 18; Janko 1992, 313; Richardson 1993 ad 22.208–13.

[28] Schadewaldt 1965, 168; Kullmann 1960, 325; 1991, 441 n.65; M. Edwards 1991, 18. Richardson 1993 ad 22.376–94 agrees but is more skeptical. There is a major difference between the timing of duel and rout in the *Iliad* and in myth about the death of Achilles. In the *Iliad* Achilles routs the enemy before he meets Hector, whereas he kills Memnon before he routs the Trojans. At West 1993, 8 this is explained in terms of the development of an ur-*Iliad* into the *Iliad*, but it is simpler to understand the influence of the Achilles *fabula* ceding here to immediate poetic needs of the *Iliad*, as is always the case. By preceding, the long rout makes the duel seem especially climactic, and the placement of the duel immediately before the city

walls allows the pathos of the addresses of Priam and Hecuba to Hector, and the later pathos of Andromache's reaction to the sight of her dead husband. Because Achilles does not die in the *Iliad*, he must desist from sacking the city, and this is most easily done if the duel follows the rout, allowing Achilles to retire with his main goal completed.

[29] Kakridis 1949, 75–83; Pestalozzi 1945, 29–33; Schadewaldt 1965, 170; Kullmann 1960, 331–3; 1984, 310–11; 1991, 441 n.65; Schoeck 1961, 104–8.

[30] Kakridis 1949, 88; Pestalozzi 1945, 29–33; Schadewaldt 1965, 173, 180, 195; Kullmann 1960, 110, 333–5; 1981, 42; 1984, 310–11; 1991, 441 n.65; Schoeck 1961, 15; M. Edwards 1991, 18.

[31] Though some think this is a typical motif, citing accounts of Meleager killed by Apollo (Paus. 10.31.3 reports that this version was in the Hesiodic *Catalogue* and in the *Minyas*; see Hesiod fr. 25, 12–13, 280 M-W; *Minyas* fr. 5 Bernabe = 3 Davies). But it is clear that the death of Patroclus has specific details that foreshadow the death of Achilles. See Burgess 2001a, 75.

[32] See Pagliaro 1951, esp. 39–46; Tarditi 1968, 140–1; Ford 1992, 110–18. This issue is discussed more thoroughly at Burgess 2004b.

[33] See Nagy 1996, 71–3; 2002; 2003, 43–4.

[34] Cf. Ford 1992, 111–14; Cook 1999, 159 n.29; Louden 1999, xvi.

[35] As Pellicia 2003 notes in his criticism of Cook's analysis.

[36] See Burgess 2004b. There would not have been enough time at the Panathenaic festival for continuous recitation of the Homeric poems, though this is commonly assumed. At Neils 1992 it is argued that the first day only of an eight-day festival was set aside for musical and rhapsode contests.

[37] As has been frequently noted. See esp. Else 1957, 585–6; Schein 1984, 19–25; Taplin 1992, 83–109, 257–84.

[38] See Roisman (this volume), where it is shown that reflection of extra-Iliadic material need not preclude a passage's ability to have effective and sophisticated poetic significance.

[39] Recent scholarship has seen Homeric characters as agents and performers of narrative. Cf. Martin 1989; Felson-Rubin 1994; Doherty 1995; Rabel 1997.

[40] For sixth-century Athenian influence on an ongoing, fluid tradition of the *Odyssey*, cf. Cook 1995; Seaford 1994. Panathenaic recension or dictation theories have been revived in recent years, most plausibly by Jensen 1980.

[41] Nagy 1990b, 23 n.27; Ford 1992, 115.

[42] Cf. Murray 1934, 191–2; Wade-Gery 1950, 14–17; Webster 1958, 267–75; Ford 1992, 115 n.33.

[43] See Nagy 2002, 16–19.

[44] Notably at Nagy 1990a, 42–3; 1990b, 21–8; 1996a, 60–74; 1996b, 82–9; 2003, 6–7.

[45] Here I follow Nagy's evolutionary hypothesis; see especially his analysis at 1996, 109–11. I favor a seventh-century date for the beginning of identifiably Homeric traditions, that is, in a state of some fixation yet not textualized. This position may seem vague (Kullmann 2002, 170 n.50), but anything more specific is bound to misrepresent the nature of early Greek epic. It is time to state that the old *communis opinio* for an eighth-century date has been overturned (see Burgess 2001a, 49–53), though great variance exists among the many theories involving a later date.

Bibliography

Andersen, Ø.
1987   'Myth, paradigm and "spatial form" in the *Iliad*', in J.M. Bremer, I.J.F. de Jong and J. Kalff (eds.) *Homer: Beyond oral poetry*, Amsterdam.

Beye, C.R.
1993   *Ancient Epic Poetry*, Ithaca, N.Y.

Bothmer, D. von
1981   'The death of Sarpedon', in S.L. Hyatt (ed.) *The Greek Vase*, Latham, N.Y.

Burgess, J.S.
1995   'Achilles' heel: the death of Achilles in ancient myth,' *CA* 14, 217–43.
1997   'Beyond neo-analysis: problems with the vengeance theory', *AJP* 118, 1–19.
2001a   *The Tradition of the Trojan War in Homer and the Epic Cycle*, Baltimore.
2001b   'Coronis aflame: the gender of mortality,' *CP* 96, 214–27.
2004a   'Early images of Achilles and Memnon?', *QUCC*. 76, 33–51.
2004b   'Performance and the epic cycle', *CJ* 100, 1–23.

Clark, M.E. and Coulson, W.D.E.
1978   'Memnon and Sarpedon,' *MH* 35, 65–73.

Clay, J.S.
1997   *The Wrath of Athena*, 2nd edn, Lanham, MD.

Cook, E.
1999   ' "Active" and "passive" heroics in the *Odyssey*', *CW* 93, 149–67.

Danek, G.
1998   *Epos und Zitat*, Vienna.
2002   'Traditional referentiality and Homeric intertextuality', in F. Montanari (ed.) *Omero tremila anni dopo*, Rome.

Davies, M.
1989   *The Epic Cycle*, Bristol.

de Jong, I.J.F.
1987   *Narrators and Focalizers*, Amsterdam.

Dihle, A.
1970   *Homer-Probleme*, Opladen.

Doherty, L.E.
1995   *Siren Songs*, Ann Arbor.

Dowden, K.
1996   'Homer's sense of text', *JHS* 116, 47–61.

Edwards, A.T.
1985   'Achilles in the underworld: *Iliad, Odyssey*, and *Aethiopis*,' *GRBS* 26, 215–28.

Edwards, M.W.
1987   'Topos and transformation in Homer,' in J.M. Bremer, I.J.F. de Jong and J. Kalff (eds.) *Homer: Beyond oral poetry*, Amsterdam.
1991   *The* Iliad: *A commentary*, vol. 5, Cambridge.

Else, G.F.
1957   *Aristotle's* Poetics: *The argument*, Cambridge, Mass.

Felson-Rubin, N.
  1994   *Regarding Penelope*, Princeton, N.J.
Fenik, B.C.
  1964   Iliad *X and the Rhesus*, Brussels.
  1968   *Typical battle scenes in the* Iliad, Hermes Einzelschriften 21, Wiesbaden.
Ford, A.
  1992   *Homer: The poetry of the past*, Ithaca.
Hainsworth, J.B.
  1993   *The* Iliad*: A commentary*, vol. 3, Cambridge.
Heubeck, A.
  1978   'Homeric studies today: results and prospects,' in B.C. Fenik (ed.) *Homer: Tradition and invention*, Leiden.
Janko, R.
  1992   *The* Iliad*: A commentary*, vol. 4, Cambridge.
Jensen, M.S.
  1980   *The Homeric Question and the Oral-Formulaic Theory*, Copenhagen.
Jouan, F.
  1980   'Le cycle épique: état des questions,' in *Association Guillaume Budé, Actes du Xe Congrès*, Paris.
Kakridis, J.T.
  1949   *Homeric Researches*, Lund.
Kossatz-Deissmann, A.
  1992   'Memnon', in *LIMC* 6.1, 448–61.
Kullmann, W.
  1960   *Die Quellen der* Ilias, Hermes Einzelschriften 14, Wiesbaden.
  1981   'Zur Methode der Neoanalyse in der Homerforschung', *WS* 15, 5–42.
  1984   'Oral poetry theory and neoanalysis in Homeric research,' *GRBS* 25, 307–24.
  1991   'Ergebnisse der motivgeschichtlichen Forschung zu Homer (Neoanalyse)', in J. Latacz (ed.) *Zweihundert Jahre Homer-Forschung*, Stuttgart.
  2002   'Nachlese zur Neoanalyse', in A. Rengakos (ed.) *Realität, Imagination und Theorie*, Stuttgart.
Lang, M.L.
  1983   'Reverberation and mythology in the *Iliad*,' in C.A. Rubino and C.W. Shelmerdine (eds.) *Approaches to Homer*, Austin, Tex.
Lord, A.B.
  1960   *The Singer of Tales*, Cambridge, Mass.
Louden, B.
  1999   *The* Odyssey. *Structure, narration, and meaning*, Baltimore.
Lowenstam, S.
  1993   *The Scepter and the Spear*, Lanham, Md.
Martin, R.
  1989   *The Language of Heroes*, Ithaca.
Minchin, E.
  2001   *Homer and the Resources of Memory*, Oxford.
Mühlestein, H.
  1987   *Homerische Namenstudien*, Frankfurt am Main.

Murray, G.
   1934   *The Rise of the Greek Epic*, 4th edn, Oxford.
Nagler, M.N.
   1974   *Spontaneity and Tradition*, Berkeley.
Nagy, G.
   1990a   *Greek Mythology and Poetics*, Ithaca, N.Y.
   1990b   *Pindar's Homer*, Baltimore.
   1996   *Poetry as Performance*, Cambridge.
   2002   *Plato's Rhapsody and Homer's Music*, Washington, D.C.
   2003   *Homeric Responses*, Austin, Tex.
Neils, J.
   1992   'The Panathenaia: an introduction,' in J. Neils (ed.) *Goddess and Polis. The Panathenaic festival in ancient Athens*, Princeton, N.J.
Nickel, R.
   2002   'Euphorbus and the death of Achilles', *Phoenix* 56, 215–33.
Page, D.L.
   1963   Review of Schoeck 1961, *CR* 13, 21–4.
Pagliaro, A.
   1951   'La terminologia poetica di Omero e l'origine dell'epica', *Ricerche Linguistiche* 2, 1–46.
Pellicia, H.
   2003   'Two points about rhapsodes', in M. Finkelberg, G.G. Stroumsa (eds.) *Homer, the Bible, and Beyond*, Leiden.
Pestalozzi, H.
   1945   *Die Achilleis als Quelle der Ilias*, Zurich.
Pucci, P.
   1987   *Odysseus Polutropos*, Ithaca, N.Y.
Rabel, R.J.
   1997   *Plot and Point of View in the* Iliad, Ann Arbor.
Rengakos, A.
   2002   'Narrativität, Intertextualität, Selbstreferentialität. Die neue Deutung der *Odyssee'*, in M. Reichel and A. Rengakos (eds.) *Epea Pteroenta*, Stuttgart.
Richardson, N.J.
   1993   *The* Iliad: *A commentary*, vol. 6, Cambridge.
Schadewaldt, W.
   1965   *Von Homers Welt und Werk*, 4th edn, Stuttgart.
Schein, S.L.
   1984   *The Mortal Hero*, Berkeley.
Schoeck, G.
   1961   *Ilias und Aithiopis*, Zurich.
Seaford, R.
   1994   *Reciprocity and Ritual*, Oxford.
Slatkin, L.M.
   1991   *The Power of Thetis*, Berkeley.
Taplin, O.
   1992   *Homeric Soundings*, Oxford.

Tarditi, G.

1968   'Sull' origine e sul significato della parola rapsodo', *Maia* 20, 137–45.

Usener, K.

1990   *Beobachtungen zum Verhältnis der Odyssee zur Ilias*, Tübingen.

Wade-Gery, H.T.

1950   *The Poet of the* Iliad, Cambridge.

Webster, T.B.L.

1958   *From Mycenae to Homer*, London.

Weiss, C.

1986   'Eos', in *LIMC* 3.1, 747–89.

West, M.L.

2003   '*Iliad* and *Aethiopis*', *CQ* 53, 1–14.

West, S.F.

2003   ' "The most marvellous of all seas"; the Greek encounter with the Euxine,' *G&R* 50, 151–67.

Willcock, M.M.

1976   *A Companion to the* Iliad, Chicago.

1987   'The final scenes of *Iliad* XVII', in J.M. Bremer, I.J.F. de Jong and J. Kalff (eds.) *Homer: Beyond oral poetry*, Amsterdam.

Woodhouse, W.J.

1930   *The Composition of Homer's* Odyssey, repr. Oxford, 1969.

8

THE CICONIANS, REVISITED
(HOMER, *ODYSSEY* 9.39–66)

Rick M. Newton

Odysseus' account of the raid on the Ciconians – the first of the adventures narrated in the Phaeacian apologue in *Odyssey* 9 to 12 – has been studied in different, but complementary, lights. It has been viewed as a 'transition piece', looking back to the Iliadic world of cattle raids and skirmishes in the areas outlying Troy. Set among an historical people living in Thrace, the *Ciconeia* serves as a bridge from the Iliadic world of warfare to the Odyssean realm of fantastic travel.[1] The episode has also been viewed as establishing a moral context for the sufferings of Odysseus and his men. In keeping with the declaration in the proem of the poem (1.1–9), according to which all the losses sustained on the homeward voyage are attributable to the recklessness of the crewmen and not to Odysseus, the disasters in this particular episode are undeniably attributable to the folly of the Ithacan sailors.[2] Indeed, their disobedience in this first adventure, as they continue slaughtering cattle and drinking wine, serves as prelude to the final disaster on Thrinacia, where the remaining crewmen will fatally disobey their leader's prohibition against the sacred cattle of Hyperion. For this reason, the *Ciconeia* has been described as an 'anticipatory doublet' of the Thrinacian episode.[3] Thus, while looking back to the *Iliad*, the episode is also paradigmatic in establishing a pattern of etiology for future disasters that Odysseus and his men will suffer.

But also at work in the *Ciconeia*, according to the narrating hero, is no small degree of divine enmity directed against him and his comrades. Odysseus specifically cites the ill will of Zeus. 'It was then that the grim fate of Zeus (κακὴ Διὸς αἶσα, 9.52) loomed over us in our doomed state (ἡμῖν αἰνομόροισιν, 9.53) to make us suffer great woes', he explains as the Ciconians' inland neighbors appear on the horizon the next dawn. Heubeck and Hoekstra (1989, 15) best summarize this expression of theodicy:

The grim αἶσα of Zeus which overshadows the travelers places the whole journey in a quite specific theological context; just as now, so throughout

135

the following nine years, the will of Zeus is fulfilled; the hero's sufferings are inflicted by fate.

Other commentators have likewise endorsed Odysseus' assessment of hostile gods in this and other adventures, without scrutinizing the hero's conclusions or assumptions.[4] De Jong explains, for example, that as a 'primary narrator' who can offer only a subjective account of his experiences, Odysseus does not know which particular god has afflicted him. His point of view is necessarily limited. For this reason, Odysseus cites Zeus – in an apparent instance of Jörgensen's law – in order to encompass any one or number of unnamed deities harassing him: 'The omniscient narrator would have identified the god.'[5]

But the theological question raised by Odysseus' allegation is not *who* among the gods is hounding him but, rather, *are indeed* the gods harassing him as he claims? Is the hero's perspective limited, or is it wrong? This is a pressing question. For if this first adventure is indeed paradigmatic of future adventures, it obliges us to balance Odysseus' condemnation of Zeus with the declaration of theodicy pronounced by the god himself in the opening of the poem. There, the supreme Olympian states explicitly and indignantly that not all human sufferings are fated or attributable to the divine since mortals bring troubles on themselves that are 'beyond fate' through their own acts of wanton folly (οἱ δὲ καὶ αὐτοὶ | σφῇσιν ἀτασθαλίῃσιν ὑπὲρ μόρον ἄλγε' ἔχουσιν, 1.33–4). With regard to the *Ciconeia*, the case is clearly made that the disobedient men are guilty of recklessness. But what of the behavior of Odysseus himself, and what of the role of the gods?[6] Are Odysseus and his men doomed by fate and malicious deities to suffer, as he claims, or could he himself as the commander responsible for the welfare of his men have behaved in a manner that might have prevented or mitigated the debacle?[7] If so, the loss of 72 comrades and the ensuing grief of the survivors might be construed as standing 'beyond fate' (ὑπὲρ μόρον) and not as constituting a manifestation of divine hostility.

The *Ciconeia* may thus be viewed as a test case, as it were, through which the poem's external audience is invited to evaluate the competing claims of Odysseus and Zeus. On the one hand, the narrating hero's condemnation of his comrades is consistent both with the pronouncement of the *Odyssey*-poet in 1.6–9 and with Zeus' tirade in 1.32–4. Odysseus' own report to the Phaeacians of the great foolishness of his crewmen (μέγα νήπιοι οὐκ ἐπίθοντο, 9.44) provides a specific-case endorsement of these earlier and more general verdicts. On the other hand, Odysseus' implication of Zeus stands in direct contradiction to the words of the god himself. The result is a narrative tension which the reader or listener of the poem must either resolve or attempt to balance.[8] Accompanying these competing voices, furthermore, are two audiences. The internal audience of Phaeacians, who have not heard the proem or the pronouncement of Zeus, may not be in a position to scrutinize their guest's allegations of divine ill will. Indeed, it appears from the enthusiastic response of Queen Arete in 11.336–40 and Alcinous' orders to the Phaeacian noblemen in 13.4–15 that Odysseus succeeds quite conspicuously in enlisting their full sympathy. Specifically, the king is so moved by the hero's sufferings (εἰ καὶ μάλα πέπονθας, 13.6) that he will tax the deme in order to lighten the financial burden incurred by the gift-giving noblemen. Odysseus' own narrative agenda is made explicit when, at the beginning of the apologue, he declares to his hosts that he will tell of the 'grievous homecoming inflicted' on him by Zeus (νόστον ἐμὸν πολυκηδέ' ἐνίσπω | ὅν μοι Ζεὺς ἐφέηκεν, 9.37–8). The external audience, by contrast, has been forewarned about blanket condemnations of the gods. When, therefore, the narrating hero concludes the story of his first disaster with an accusation of Zeus, we may well respond with the very question that Zeus has raised in Book 1: is this disaster divinely inflicted simply because Odysseus says it is?[9]

In terms of Iliadic echoes, the Ciconian episode may be read as a variant of a type-scene.[10] Specifically, the account of Odysseus attempting to muster his rioting troops back to the ships invites a comparison with *Iliad* 2.142–210, where the same hero halts the rush of the pan-Achaean army toward the ships. There is an inversion, of course, in that the Iliadic troops must be restrained *from* the ships, whereas in the *Odyssey* the troops are ordered, however unsuccessfully, to return *to* the ships. Underlining the parallels between the two scenes is a verbal echo. The Ciconians' neighbors who appear at dawn, after Odysseus fails to restrain the men, are described 'as countless as the leaves and flowers in springtime' (ἦλθον ἔπειθ' ὅσα φύλλα καὶ ἄνθεα γίγνεται ὥρῃ, 9.51). The same description appears in *Iliad* 2.468, referring to the number of Achaeans who are marshaled into battle formation after Odysseus has successfully quelled the riot. The question may therefore occur to the external audience: what does Odysseus do for the twelve or more hours that ensue after he loses control of the troops? He creates – or at least allows – the impression that he stands helplessly by, a victim of human disobedience and divine hostility. But this impression is inconsistent, first, with the Iliadic parallel, which shows the hero wielding his scepter and beating the common soldiers into submission (*Il.* 2.198–210).[11] It is also inconsistent with the response he registers to the crewmen's disobedience in the encounter with the Lotus Eaters, the very next of the narrated adventures. There, he personally drags the reluctant scouts back to the ships and chains them to the rowing benches (*Od.* 9.98–9). Within the

27 lines devoted to the *Ciconeia*, however, the hero is curiously silent about his own actions while the men remain slaughtering, eating, and drinking on the Thracian shore until the next morning.

It is only in the prologue to the *Cyclopeia* that we receive information that allows us to fill in the blanks. As he prepares to sail across the bay to visit Polyphemus, Odysseus takes a skin of Ismaric wine which is one of many valuable gifts he received from Maron, the Ismarian priest of Apollo. Odysseus received from this priest twelve jars of magically potent wine (perhaps one for each ship in his fleet), along with seven talents of gold, and a silver crater (9.201–3). This information is interesting for the light it sheds on both the *Ciconeia* and the *Cyclopeia*. Read retrospectively, this account portrays Odysseus as a pious man who, during the Ciconian raid, spared the life of a priest. It becomes all the more puzzling, therefore, that he should have been the target of the grim doom of Zeus while in Thrace. Read prospectively, the detail of the Ismaric wine contributes to the self-flattering portrait of Odysseus as a virtuous guest, a point with significant implications both for his upcoming story of Polyphemus and for its reception by the Phaeacian audience.

Note especially that Maron gives him the prizes not as ransom (ἄποινα) but as 'resplendent gifts' (ἀγλαὰ δῶρα, 9.201).[12] Odysseus makes it clear that he entered the wooded grove of Apollo in which Maron lived (9.200–1) and that he was entertained by the host whose family he had spared.[13] Not only was he taken into the house, but he was admitted into one of the family's most carefully guarded secrets. For the wine was kept in a room known only to Maron, his wife, and a single housekeeper who maintained the inventory. It is from personal experience, furthermore, that he describes this wine as not only overwhelmingly potent but also as irresistible: its very bouquet compelled one to imbibe freely (9.210–11). It is for this reason that Odysseus arms himself with a sack of the vintage as he prepares to meet the Cyclops: he himself drank from this wine.[14] Herein lies the point of his divulging this information at this time: the man who was a model guest in Maron's house and received impressively generous gifts will now encounter a Cyclops who devours those who seek his hospitality. This message is certainly not lost on the Phaeacians, from whom he hopes to receive generous parting gifts. But the poem's external audience may register a different response: it occurs to us that, at some point during the seaside raid after the men disregarded their commander's order to return to the ships, Odysseus left the shore area. Perhaps drawn by the sight of smoke rising from within Apollo's sacred grove, the location of Maron's house, he entered it. He thereupon spared the life of the priest and his family and was received as a guest, where he enjoyed lavish hospitality.[15]

What emerges from the scattered pieces of this narrative is consistent with the hero's behavior in other adventures. In this respect, the *Ciconeia* is paradigmatic of future episodes. What begins as a cattle raid in Thrace ends as an exercise in ξενεία in which Odysseus functions not so much as a leader of his men as a private citizen in search of prizes. He says twice that Maron gave the gifts to him alone (ὅν μοι δῶκε Μάρων, 9.197; ὁ δέ μοι πόρεν, 201).[16] This pattern will repeat in the *Cyclopeia*: tempted by the sounds of bleating sheep and goats and by the sight of smoke rising from hearths (9.166–7), Odysseus will venture across the water in hopes of finding 'hospitable' inhabitants (φιλόξεινοι, 9.176). After his men inside the cave beg to leave at once with the cattle and cheeses, he insists on remaining so that he can see the master of the house and collect gifts (9.229). The episode in the Cyclops' cave is not, therefore, the first instance of Odysseus leaving his men behind. The crewmen themselves comment on this pattern while their leader is asleep on the ship after leaving the island of Aeolus:

> This man becomes a dear and valued friend to anyone whose city or land he comes to…while we make our way homeward with empty hands. Even now Aeolus has given him gifts of friendship (10.38–44).

It is interesting to note that the only adventures preceding the stay with Aeolus are the encounter with Polyphemus, where Odysseus received no gifts, the brush with the Lotus Eaters, who also gave no gifts, and the raid on the Ciconians, during which Odysseus did precisely what his men complain of: he left them and returned with valuable gifts which he proceeded to load onto his own ship.

The fact that Maron shares his special wine with Odysseus is also telling. As a guest, Odysseus has a unique talent for quickly working his way into the innermost compartments of his host's home. When he finds himself at the entrance to the Cyclops' cave, for example, he does not wait for the owner of the property to return and invite him in, as protocol would dictate.[17] Instead he boldly makes his way into the inner recesses, the hearth itself (ἐς μυχὸν ἄντρου, 9.236), where he lights a fire and prepares a meal.[18] With Circe, he alone will enter the nymph's bedchamber while the men fend for themselves an entire year. On Scheria, furthermore, this nameless stranger who has literally rolled into the hearth of the palace from under the knees of Queen Arete has displaced the king's very son from his seat and been offered the princess' hand in marriage.[19] When Odysseus separates from his men, therefore, he does so in an impressively rapid and extreme manner, quickly leaving their company to enter deep within his host's domain. Once ensconced, furthermore, he exhibits no urgency to leave.

Finally, I would suggest that while Odysseus is drinking wine with his Thracian host, he regales him with accounts of his exploits at Troy. For, within the epic context of ξενεία, such tales are told after dinner has been served and while the wine is being poured by stewards.[20] Among the Phaeacians, Odysseus has dined and now, as the wine flows, he begins his four-book tale of woes, 'A wind wafted me from Ilium and brought me to the land of the Ciconians' (9.39). He will later announce to his hosts that, though eager to be on his way, he would gladly stay a full year if they would load him with 'resplendent gifts' (ἀγλαὰ δῶρα, 11.357). As a result of this suggestion, his Phaeacian escort is provided a day later than originally planned by Alcinous and as originally requested by Odysseus himself: it will take time for the Phaeacians to amass their gifts, and Odysseus will gladly wait. In Polyphemus' cave, after he has helped himself to a meal in the host's absence, he will introduce himself and offer wine as he declares, 'We are Achaeans who were driven off course over the broad stretch of sea by all sorts of winds' (9.259–60), an opening line that sounds like the beginning of an after-dinner entertainment. It is in this manner that Odysseus hopes to regale his hosts with lengthy tales of his exploits so that he can ingratiate himself more deeply and inspire them to give him a generous, if delayed, send-off.[21] The very length of the Phaeacian apologue may itself be read as an indication of Odysseus as a heroic-level performer of ξενεία.

Likewise, on Thrace, therefore, it is not only possible but probable that, after he was welcomed into Maron's house and served a meal, Odysseus regaled his host with an account of his exploits that ran well into the night. As he spoke, he and his company drank – and they drank a wine as remarkable for its irresistible sweetness as for its potency![22] It is interesting to note in this context that Odysseus' Ciconian narrative contains a hint of such over-consumption: in describing the riotous behavior of his men on the shore, he says – in the passive voice – 'and great quantities of wine were consumed' (ἔνθα δὲ πολλὸν μέθυ μὲν πίνετο, 9.45). As we listen to the narrative, we may assume that he means that only the men were drinking. But in the light of the information provided in the prologue to the *Cyclopeia*, it occurs to us that Odysseus himself may have been imbibing, at a different location. For Odysseus gives no clear account of his whereabouts after he orders the men to return to the ships. He simply says that the Ciconians' neighbors appeared on the horizon the next dawn 'as countless as the leaves and flowers in springtime.' It is possible, however, that it was Odysseus himself who appeared on the horizon the next dawn, returning gift-laden from Maron's house, either still inebriated or at least feeling the next-morning effects of having drunk to excess.[23] But in the

140

narrative proper, Odysseus bypasses all this detail and simply states, 'It was then that the grim fate of Zeus loomed over us in our doomed state to make us suffer many woes.'

The *Ciconeia*, therefore, is much more than a cattle raid gone awry, although that it is. It is also an episode which, like certain others of the hero's adventures, conflates aspects of a pirate raid (specifically a cattle raid) from the Iliadic past with elements of Odyssean hospitality. Both undertakings have the same goal, in a sense: the acquisition of property that will enhance the honor and status of the hero.[24] For this reason, I would suggest, Odysseus is not ashamed to declare openly to the Phaeacians or to Polyphemus or even to his crewmen in the cave that he is intent on amassing gifts. Like Iliadic warfare, Odyssean hospitality is a heroic enterprise, and Odysseus is a hero. Read with an eye to the Iliadic past, the *Ciconeia* presents a failed raid: 72 men are lost and the homecoming expedition is delayed by a day. But read with an eye to the Odyssean future (or, rather, present), Odysseus' performance as a guest is, at best, a tainted success. On the one hand, he walks off from the Thracians laden with resplendent gifts, a consummate hero in this new world. But that heroic hospitality, like successful warfare in the *Iliad*, comes at a price, and a high one. From this perspective, the *Ciconeia* marks the beginning of the end: as a result of events in which Odysseus, along with his men, plays a causative role, he will reach Ithaca late and alone.[25]

It is for these reasons that, when Odysseus blames the malice of the gods as driving the disasters that engulf him both among the Ciconians and elsewhere throughout his νόστος, his accusation may not ring true, at least in the ears of the external audience. The hero certainly appears justified in blaming the 'great fools' of his unruly men. But he has not made the case against Zeus or any of the Olympians. Nowhere does his narrative or that of the *Odyssey*-poet convincingly implicate divine malice aimed against the Ithacans as they raid the Ismarians. No indications are provided that these sufferings are fated and predetermined. Indeed, as we reconstruct the events from the hero's own words, it becomes clear that he had choices to make and that he made them: he chose to leave his men on the shore, he chose to visit Maron, and he chose to spend the night there, leaving his comrades – whose penchant for falling into trouble is well-known – to fend for themselves. It is possible that, had Odysseus himself – and not only his men – made other choices, the disasters could have been avoided: the loss of these comrades cannot therefore fairly be attributed to destiny or divine enmity and may stand 'beyond fate'. The events in the *Ciconeia* can all be traced to the purely human motivations and actions of Odysseus and his men; the malice of Zeus is nowhere in evidence, despite the narrating hero's allegation. It lies beyond the scope of this paper to determine whether or not Odysseus' choices and actions constitute the sort of recklessness that Zeus decries in the opening of the poem. Indeed, it remains unclear whether any errors in Odysseus' judgment are to be attributed to his individual character or to the value system of the heroic culture to which he subscribes.[26] But in this first, and highly paradigmatic, adventure of the Phaeacian apologue, it appears as if the verdict of Zeus is upheld. Odysseus is to be included among those mortal men who blame the gods for sufferings that might have been avoided through more prudent behavior.

Notes

[1] Heubeck and Hoekstra 1989, 15, itemize the Iliadic references in the episode and conclude, 'The fighting is described in the language of the *Iliad*, thereby reinforcing the link with the events around Troy.' Cf. de Jong 2001, 29: 'This episode forms the transition to the fairy-tale world which follows.'

[2] See Heubeck and Hoekstra 1989, 16: 'By their folly men make themselves the victims of fate; men bring their appointed fate on themselves by their own deeds.' This comment raises, but does not answer, the question whether indeed the loss of the 72 men in this adventure, simply because it happened, was fated.

[3] This description is given by de Jong 2001, 229, who appears to build on the study of Homeric doublets in Fenik 1974, 144–71.

[4] For example, Clay 1983, 230, says of the Thrinacian disaster: 'The cards are inexorably stacked against them (i.e. the crewmen). They are obliged to eat, and thereby to commit a crime, or to perish.' For Clay 1983, 213–39, the poem presents a 'double theodicy,' according to which the gods, while punishing human recklessness, are also capricious in inflicting unwarranted sufferings on the innocent (among whom Odysseus is included). Cf. Pedrick 1992, 49, on the Thrinacian disaster: 'The sailors hardly seem guilty of ἀτασθαλίαι; if anything, Odysseus pitches his narrative to exculpate them on the grounds of necessity due to the gods' arbitrariness.' It is curious that Homeric critics have, for the most part, accepted Odysseus' complaints against Zeus and the gods as justified. Ahl and Roisman 1996, 150 express a view that is notably different: 'In the course of his self-exculpation, elements show through which cast doubt on his (Odysseus') pose of guiltlessness.'

[5] See de Jong 2001, 224. For Jörgensen's law – according to which a character cites Zeus by name or invokes a generic term for the divine (e.g., θεός, θεοί, δαίμων) when the particular Olympian is unknown to the speaker – see de Jong 2001, xv, and Jörgensen 1904.

[6] The clearest explanation of the term ἀτασθαλίαι is provided by de Jong 2001, 12: 'It indicates outrageous or reckless behavior, and which people pursue *despite specific warnings*.' The crewmen who defy their commander's orders to return to the ships engage, by this definition, in the reckless behavior of prolonged eating and drinking.

[7] Shay 2002, 270, for example, suggests that Odysseus' particular failure in the

episode lies 'in failing to pull out with the booty in time to evade the Ciconians' counter-attack'.

⁸ For a discussion of the proem of the poem as expressing the voice of the poet, as distinct from the voice of the Muse (which begins after the formal proem), see Rabel 1997, 9–11. Along similar lines, Clay 1983, 9–53 suggests that the proem of the *Odyssey* expresses a philodyssean bias which is not shared by the Muse who inspires the text after 1.10. See also Clay 1976. Scodel 2002, 21, by contrast, argues that the audience would hear a single voice while the poem is being performed and not necessarily distinguish between 'poet' and 'narrator'. For the purposes of this paper, it suffices only to recognize that the text of the *Odyssey* includes points of view which are at odds with one another and that this tension informs the audience's reception and experience of the poem.

⁹ The clearest example of tension between Zeus' declaration of human responsibility for unnecessary suffering and the propensity of mortals for blaming the gods is provided by the example of Aegisthus, whom Zeus names in 1.35–41. Zeus' account of the gods' sending Hermes to warn Aegisthus not to seduce Clytemnestra or kill Agamemnon makes it clear to the audience of the poem that the murder of Agamemnon was neither fated nor divinely willed. When Nestor, recounting the same event to Telemachus in 3.254–72, however, states that 'the fate of the gods' (μοῖρα θεῶν, 3.269) was the driving force behind Aegisthus' crime, the audience hears an explanation that contradicts Zeus' earlier account that the gods actively sought to avert the criminal deed. Nestor's statement appears to substantiate Zeus' complaint: mortals do indeed seem to blame the gods in routine fashion. See Schein 1984, 62–4, for a lucid account of how Homeric characters look retrospectively on things that have already happened as either destined by an impersonal fate or willed by individual gods: 'from the human point of view, only when something happens to someone does he realize (or Homer tell us) that it was his *moira*.' The *Odyssey* thus invites the audience to ponder this underlying assumption. Is it indeed the case that every grievous event that has happened in life occurs only because it is fated or divinely willed? Can human recklessness be such a powerful force that it can bring on sufferings that both the gods and fate have not initiated?

¹⁰ For accounts of type-scenes and the uses to which the epic tradition puts them, see Fenik 1968; Edwards 1992; Foley 1991, 1–60; and Foley 1995.

¹¹ The scholiast on *Od.* 9.44 observes the discrepancy between the Iliadic portrait of Odysseus as an effective commander of riotous troops and his inability to control his own men in the *Ciconeia* (ἐν μὲν γὰρ Ἰλιάδι παράγει τὸν Ὀδυσσέα τύπτοντα καὶ τοὺς μηδὲν αὐτῷ προσήκοντας τῶν στρατιωτῶν…ἐνταῦθα δὲ οὐδὲ τῶν ἰδίων ἄρχειν δύναται).

¹² For this distinction between ἀγλαὰ δῶρα ('resplendent gifts') and ἀγλαὰ ἄποινα ('resplendent ransom'), cf. *Il.* 1.23 and 1.213: in 1.23, priest Chryses brings 'resplendent ransom' to buy back his daughter from Agamemnon, while in 1.213 Athena promises Achilles that, if he restrains his anger for the present moment, he will later receive three times as many 'resplendent gifts' from Agamemnon.

¹³ Cf. Eur. *Cyc.* 141, where Odysseus tells Silenus that the wine was a gift from Maron (καὶ μὴν Μάρων μοι πῶμ' ἔδωκεν, παῖς θεοῦ). Similarly, in his summary of the plot of the *Odyssey*, Apollodorus notes that the Ismaric wine was a gift from Maron (ἀσκὸν οἴνου τὸν ὑπὸ Μάρωνος αὐτῷ δοθέντα, Apollod. *Epit.* 7.4). It appears that the

ancients understood that the wine was freely given by Maron and not seized during the raid.

[14] Ahl and Roisman 1996, 106–9, suggest that Maron uses his wine as a weapon to inebriate Odysseus and his men. In their reconstruction, the twelve jars were consumed by the Ithacans that day, and it was their ensuing drunkenness that enabled the Ciconians to buy time and summon their neighbors. They also suggest that Odysseus, after being thus duped into drunkenness by Maron, appropriates the priest's cleverness and directs the same treachery against Polyphemus. Odysseus does not, however, give any indication that Maron tricked him: because any such admission would compromise his reputation as the wiliest of men, Odysseus would understandably suppress this detail. But it is also unlikely that the *Odyssey*-poet would allow the possibility that anyone could outsmart this hero. If Odysseus and comrades had consumed the wine on the shore, furthermore, the question arises as to how any was left to intoxicate the Cyclops. Odysseus himself states that the wine is irresistible. Because we have only Odysseus' narrative, it remains impossible to delve with complete confidence into the details of the hero's whereabouts throughout the night. But what he does say indicates that he entered Maron's house and stayed long enough to be let in on a carefully guarded family secret and to leave heavily laden with costly gifts. We can be reasonably sure, therefore, that Odysseus was entertained as a guest in Maron's home: see especially the complaint of the crewmen in 10.38–45.

[15] A similar pattern marks the encounter with Circe in 10.133–574. In each case an initially hostile encounter (raid on the Ciconians by Ithacans; Circe's attempt to transform the sailors into swine and to weaken Odysseus himself) gives way to an offering of hospitality. Both Maron and Circe end up extending a warm welcome to Odysseus, whom they first viewed as an enemy.

[16] de Jong 2001, 229, comments on Odysseus' pattern in the *Ciconeia* of distinguishing his own actions from those of his men. His narrative indicates a tension between 'him' and 'them'.

[17] In 1.119–20 the disguised Athena waits at the entrance to Odysseus' palace until Telemachus takes note and moves to welcome her. Similarly in 3.36, Nestor's son Peisistratus arises to welcome Telemachus and Athena, leading them in by the hand. The same protocol is exhibited in Sparta (4.26–38): the newly-arrived guests wait until Eteoneus welcomes them, although Eteoneus must first consult with Menelaus. In considering the protocol of hospitality as exhibited in the *Cyclopeia*, it is important to note, of course, that Polyphemus is absent when Odysseus arrives. When Odysseus thus enters and ponders stealing the contents of the cave, he is functioning not so much as a guest as a pirate. Indeed, Polyphemus' first question when he returns and sees them is to ask if they are pirates (9.251–5). Had Odysseus taken the advice of his men and left with stolen goods before the Cyclops' return, he would have committed an act of piracy which would have been no breach of ξενεία. But in breaking into the cave and then waiting for the master to return so that he can demand gifts, the hero conflates the protocol of hospitality with piracy.

[18] The contents of this meal have been a topic of debate: does Odysseus light the fire merely to eat cheese, or is his description of performing a sacrifice (πῦρ κήαντες ἐθύσαμεν, 9.231) a euphemistic cover-up for his killing and eating of one or more of the Cyclops' lambs? If the latter is true, his violation of ξενεία is especially egregious. See Newton 1997, 13 and Fredrich 1991, 26.

[19] On Odysseus' tumbling into the Phaeacian hearth, see Newton 1984.

[20] For an insightful comparison of the symposium and the setting for epic narration see Ford 1999.

[21] The *Odyssey* establishes a direct correlation between the length of a guest's stay and the generosity of the gifts he receives. Note especially 15.80–91: Menelaus offers to escort Telemachus on a tour through Hellas, from which they can amass costly gifts from their hosts. Telemachus declines, however, since he wishes to hurry home and safeguard his Ithacan homestead. Compare also Telemachus' request of Peisistratus (15.195–214) to return directly to his ship on the shore at Pylos without stopping again to visit Nestor. The ξενεία ritual is time-consuming. Gifts come at the price of delays, which may be more costly in the end than the items collected.

[22] For an interesting study establishing a connection between Odysseus and the Ismaric wine celebrated by Archilochus, see Seidensticker 1978, 20–1.

[23] Austin 1983 presents an interesting discussion of 'mitosis' (the doubling of the one Cyclops into multiple Cyclopes, the doubling of one group of Ciconians into two). Since these doublings occur within contexts of heavy drinking, it is interesting to speculate if the 'double vision' implied therein may not be attributable to intoxication.

[24] Zeus' pronouncement in *Od.* 5.37–40 that Odysseus will return to Ithaca laden with more Phaeacian gifts than all the booty he could ever have amassed at Troy establishes an important analogy that bears an in-depth exploration. If guest-gifts are the equivalent of γέρας, then the Odyssey may present hospitality as a new forum for heroism: excellence in ξενεία displaces prowess on the battlefield.

[25] In *Od.* 4.90–9 Menelaus expresses regret for having delayed his own homecoming in order to amass riches. He feels that, had he come home in a more timely fashion, he might have prevented his brother's assassination.

[26] Cf. the famous characterization of Odysseus by Stanford 1965, 356: 'Note Odysseus' motives – inquisitiveness and acquisitiveness – very typical of himself and many later Greeks.'

Bibliography

Ahl, F. and Roisman, H.M.
    1996   *The* Odyssey *Re-Formed*, Ithaca.

Austin, N.O.
    1983   'Who is who', in C.A. Rubino and C.W. Shelmerdine (eds.) *Approaches to Homer*, Austin.

Clay, J.S.
    1976   'The beginning of the *Odyssey*', *American Journal of Philology* 97, 313–36.
    1983   *The Wrath of Athena: Gods and men in the* Odyssey, Princeton.

de Jong, I.J.F.
    2001   *A Narratological Commentary on the* Odyssey, Cambridge.

Edwards, M.W.
    1992   'Homer and oral tradition: the type-scene', *Oral Tradition* 7, 285–330.

Fenik, B.
    1968   *Typical Battle Scenes in the* Iliad: *Studies in the narrative techniques of Homeric battle descriptions*, Wiesbaden.

1974   *Studies in the* Odyssey, Wiesbaden.

Foley, J.M.

1991   *Immanent Art: From structure to meaning in traditional oral epic*, Bloomington.

1995   *The Singer of Tales in Performance*, Bloomington.

Ford, A.

1999   'Odysseus after dinner: *Odyssey* 9.2–11 and the traditions of sympotic song', in J.N. Kazazis and A. Rengakos (eds.) *Euphrosyne: Studies in ancient epic and its legacy in honor of Dimitris N. Maronitis*, Stuttgart.

Fredrich, R.

1991   'The *hybris* of Odysseus', *Journal of Hellenic Studies* 111, 121–33.

Heubeck A. and Hoekstra, A.

1989   *A Commentary on Homer's* Odyssey, volume II, Oxford.

Jörgensen, Ø.

1904   'Das Auftreten der Götter in den Büchern IX–XII der *Odyssee*', *Hermes* 39, 357–82.

Newton, R.M.

1984   'The rebirth of Odysseus', *Greek, Roman and Byzantine Studies* 25, 5–20.

1997   'Odysseus and Melanthius', *Greek, Roman and Byzantine Studies* 38, 5–18.

Pedrick, V.

1992   'The muse corrects: the opening of the *Odyssey*', *Yale Classical Studies* 29, 39–62.

Rabel, R.J.

1997   *Plot and Point of View in the* Iliad, Ann Arbor.

Schein, S.L.

1984   *The Mortal Hero: An introduction to Homer's* Iliad, Berkeley.

Scodel, R.

2002   *Listening to Homer: Tradition, narrative, and audience*, Ann Arbor.

Seidensticker, B.

1978   'Archilochus and Odysseus', *Greek, Roman and Byzantine Studies* 19, 5–22.

Shay, J.

2002   *Odysseus in America: Combat trauma and the trials of homecoming*, New York.

Stanford, W.B.

1965   *The* Odyssey *of Homer*, edited with general and grammatical introduction, commentary and notes, volume II, London.

9

ODYSSEUS' ETHNOGRAPHIC DIGRESSIONS

Ruth Scodel

The four passages in which Odysseus describes the land and customs of the Cyclopes (*Od.* 9.106–15), the family of Aeolus (*Od.* 10.1–13), the Laestrygonians (*Od.* 10.82–6), and the Cimmerians (*Od.* 11.13–19) have much in common, all of it perplexing. Much scholarship has looked for the sources of this material in travelers' tales, folklore, and earlier epic.[1] The considerable literature on the cultural implications of the Cyclopes naturally looks closely at the introductory descriptions.[2] However, although critics have certainly noticed the narrative peculiarities of these passages, their complexities have not received the attention they deserve from a narratological perspective.

First, they are all detached from the following narratives, both formally and in content. All use present tenses, for example (the introduction of Circe, similar in other ways, uses the imperfect at *Od.* 10.135). Not only are the facts they convey still true in the time of speaking; Odysseus presents them as current information, not as part of his lived experience.[3] However, he avoids mentioning the most dangerous characteristics of these peoples – Cyclopes and Laestrygonians are not said to eat people until the event occurs. Yet to say that Odysseus uses 'experiencing focalization', that is, that he says only what he knew when he arrived, leads to incoherence, since he simultaneously reveals and suppresses what he learned during his visits.[4] Even in the very brief introduction he offers when he reaches the Lotus-Eaters, he identifies them as 'those who eat a flowery food' (*Od.* 9.84), but does not mention its effects until his men consume it (*Od.* 9.94–7).[5]

The descriptions do not just suppress the most critical facts in the interests of narrative suspense: their details are more generally detached from the following narrative. The description of the Cyclopes is a notorious problem:

Κυκλώπων δ' ἐς γαῖαν ὑπερφιάλων ἀθεμίστων
ἱκόμεθ', οἵ ῥα θεοῖσι πεποιθότες ἀθανάτοισιν
οὔτε φυτεύουσιν χερσὶν φυτὸν οὔτ' ἀρόωσιν,
ἀλλὰ τά γ' ἄσπαρτα καὶ ἀνήροτα πάντα φύονται,

πυροὶ καὶ κριθαὶ ἠδ' ἄμπελοι, αἵ τε φέρουσιν
οἶνον ἐρισταφυλον, καί σφιν Διὸς ὄμβρος ἀέξει.
τοῖσιν δ' οὔτ' ἀγοραὶ βουληφόροι οὔτε θέμιστες,
ἀλλ' οἵ γ' ὑψηλῶν ὀρέων ναίουσι κάρηνα
ἐν σπέεσι γλαφυροῖσι, θεμιστεύει δὲ ἕκαστος
παίδων ἠδ' ἀλόχων, οὐδ' ἀλλήλων ἀλέγουσι.

We came to the land of the arrogant, lawless Cyclopes, who, trusting in the immortal gods, do not plant any plant with labor or plow, but the crops, all of them, grow without being sown and without plowing – wheat, barley, and vines, which bear wine in strong clusters of grapes, and rain from Zeus increases it for their benefit. Among them there are no meeting-places where people confer, nor customary rules, but they inhabit the peaks of high mountains in hollow caves, and each makes the rules for his children and wives, and they do not care about each other.   (*Od.* 9. 106–15)[6]

Here the Cyclopes live a Golden-Age existence, although Polyphemus is a hard-working shepherd.[7] The Cyclopes are said to 'trust in the immortal gods', although Polyphemus claims that the Cyclopes are so powerful that they do not care about Zeus and the other gods (*Od.* 9.275–6).[8] Formally, since immediately after this passage Odysseus and his companions arrive at the Goat Island and he describes that island, the introduction's separateness from the narrative is even more stressed by its separation within the narrative.

The description of Aeolus' island is formally distinguished by ring-composition.

Αἰολίην δ' ἐς νῆσον ἀφικόμεθ'· ἔνθα δ' ἔναιεν
Αἴολος Ἱπποτάδης, φίλος ἀθανάτοισι θεοῖσι,
πλωτῇ ἐνὶ νήσῳ· πᾶσαν δέ τέ μιν πέρι τεῖχος
χάλκεον ἄρρηκτον, λισσὴ δ' ἀναδέδρομε πέτρη.
τοῦ καὶ δώδεκα παῖδες ἐνὶ μεγάροις γεγάασιν,
ἓξ μὲν θυγατέρες, ἓξ δ' υἱέες ἡβώοντες.
ἔνθ' ὅ γε θυγατέρας πόρεν υἱάσιν εἶναι ἀκοίτις.
οἱ δ' αἰεὶ παρὰ πατρὶ φίλῳ καὶ μητέρι κεδνῇ
δαίνυνται· παρὰ δέ σφιν ὀνείατα μυρία κεῖται,
κνισῆεν δέ τε δῶμα περιστεναχίζεται αὐλῇ,
ἤματα· νύκτας δ' αὖτε παρ' αἰδοίης ἀλόχοισιν
εὕδουσ' ἔν τε τάπησι καὶ ἐν τρητοῖσι λέχεσσι.
καὶ μὲν τῶν ἱκόμεσθα πόλιν καὶ δώματα καλά.

We reached the island of Aeolus, son of Hippotes, dear to the immortal gods, on a floating island. All around it is a bronze, unbreakable wall, and a sheer cliff runs up. Twelve children were born to him in his halls, six daughters and six sons in the prime of youth. So he gave his daughters as wives to his sons. Always by their dear father and wise mother they feast. Innumerable good things are set beside them, and the fragrant house resounds in the

courtyard by day. At night, they sleep beside their honored wives in blankets
and on beds decorated with inlays. Their city and fine houses we reached.

(*Od.* 10.1–13)

Although this information does not contradict the function of the visit
in the story, it is completely irrelevant to it. That Zeus made Aeolus
steward of the winds, the critical fact, appears when it is needed within the
narrative itself, at 10.21, in accordance with Homeric style. The first verb
is an imperfect, ἔναιεν, and Odysseus tells how Aeolus married his sons to
his daughters in the aorist, πόρεν. So far, then, the description is within
Odysseus' experience, in the past. Then, however, like the passage on the
Cyclopes, it uses present tenses for the ongoing feasting of the family,
which thus goes from being a narrative of Odysseus' visit to a report on
a continuing state of affairs.

Similarly, the Laestrygonians are initially described by their peculiar
relation to the day and its economic results, again in present-tense verbs.

ἑξῆμαρ μὲν ὁμῶς πλέομεν νύκτας τε καὶ ἦμαρ·
ἑβδομάτῃ δ᾽ ἱκόμεσθα Λάμου αἰπὺ πτολίεθρον,
Τηλέπυλον Λαιστρυγονίην, ὅθι ποιμένα ποιμὴν
ἠπύει εἰσελάων, ὁ δέ τ᾽ ἐξελάων ὑπακούει.
ἔνθα κ᾽ ἄυπνος ἀνὴρ δοιοὺς ἐξήρατο μισθούς,
τὸν μὲν βουκολέων, τὸν δ᾽ ἄργυφα μῆλα νομεύων·
ἐγγὺς γὰρ νυκτός τε καὶ ἤματός εἰσι κέλευθοι.

(*Od.* 10.80–6)

We sailed six days, night and day alike, and on the seventh we reached
the steep city of Lamus, wide-gated Laestrygonia, where shepherd calls to
shepherd as he drives in, and the other as he drives out hears him. There
a man who did not sleep could get double wages, one herding cattle, one
pasturing white sheep. For the paths of Night and Day are near.

The meaning of these lines is an old puzzle.[9] Many scholars have suspected
that the spring Autarcie, where Odysseus' men meet the king's daughter,
indicates that this episode earlier belonged in the Argonautic tale.[10]
However, these lines seem to have no connection either with the probably
Argonautic source or with the cannibal behavior of the Laestrygonians
and their destruction of Odysseus' ships, the main topics of the actual
narrative.

The Cimmerians are in narrative terms perhaps the oddest of all:

ἔνθα δὲ Κιμμερίων ἀνδρῶν δῆμός τε πόλις τε,
ἠέρι καὶ νεφέλῃ κεκαλυμμένοι· οὐδέ ποτ᾽ αὐτοὺς
Ἠέλιος φαέθων καταδέρκεται ἀκτίνεσσιν,
οὔθ᾽ ὁπότ᾽ ἂν στείχῃσι πρὸς οὐρανὸν ἀστερόεντα,

οὔθ᾽ ὅτ᾽ ἂν ἂψ ἐπὶ γαῖαν ἀπ᾽ οὐρανόθεν προτράπηται,
ἀλλ᾽ ἐπὶ νὺξ ὀλοὴ τέταται δειλοῖσι βροτοῖσι.

There is the community and city of the Cimmerians, hidden in darkness and cloud. Never does the shining Sun look on them with his rays, neither when he goes into the starry sky, nor when he turns back to the earth from the heaven. But cruel Night is extended over miserable mortals.

(*Od.* 11.14–19)

The Cimmerians have no function at all in the following narrative. Their land of constant darkness provides an atmospheric introduction to the Underworld, but the inhabitants serve no further purpose and are not mentioned again. The passage is an introduction without a following story.

These passages also present a practical question of narrative authority. Odysseus can only learn from what he sees and what people tell him. Yet in these passages he speaks from full knowledge and tells more than even hindsight could provide. Aeolus is the exception. Having enjoyed Aeolus' hospitality for a month, and told him all about Troy, Odysseus surely had ample opportunity to learn about Aeolus' household. It would have been surprising if he had not questioned his host in return. Odysseus would indeed know that the Cyclopes are familiar with wine, because Polyphemus tells him that they are (*Od.* 9.357–8), but Odysseus reaches Polyphemus' cave 'quickly' – he does not examine what varieties of grain are in the fields, and there is no wheat or barley in the cave. There is no plausible way he could know that the Cyclopes lack political institutions. Odysseus did not see any civic buildings while in the Cyclopes' country, but he did not explore it, either. In the story, the Cyclopes respond to Polyphemus' screaming just as ordinary neighbors might do, so it would seem that they constitute some kind of community (*Od.* 9.399–406). Even though Polyphemus asserts that the Cyclopes do not care about Zeus or the gods (*Od.* 9.275–6), their response to his saying that 'nobody' is killing him is to say that it is not possible to escape a disease that comes from Zeus (*Od.* 9.410–12), and to recommend that he pray to Poseidon. The other Cyclopes, in fact, could be ordinary pious folk, insofar as Odysseus knows from his own experience, for he had no reason to think that Polyphemus is a reliable informant.

In Laestrygonia, whatever the oddities of day and night, Odysseus is not there long enough to find them out himself, since he is there only as long as it takes his scouts to reach the king's house, for the king to return and kill one of them, and for the surviving scouts to flee back to the harbor. The hearer can assume that Odysseus' companions reported to him, so there is no difficulty in his narrating what happened. However, nothing in that narrative clarifies the source of his information about the herdsmen. It is perhaps not naturalistically impossible that Odysseus' spies received their information from the king's daughter at the fountain (*Od.* 10.105–10), just as Nausicaa tells Odysseus about the Phaeacians' love of seafaring when she gives directions to her father's palace (*Od.* 6.270–2). One could object, however, that the Phaeacians, despite their isolation, are well-informed about the customs of the rest of the world, since they convey wanderers to their homes and listen to epic poetry. Nausicaa is thus fully aware of what makes her own city unusual. Where travelers are promptly eaten, the inhabitants would not be likely to realize that their own country is peculiar and so be ready to describe its oddities. There are apparently no ships belonging to the Laestrygonians themselves in their splendid harbor: certainly Odysseus does not mention any, and their eagerness to throw boulders over the cliffs surely means that they have no valuable property to be endangered. The introduction does not mention that the Laestrygonians do not practice agriculture, even though the narrative implies this, since Odysseus sees 'no works of men or oxen' when he looks out over the countryside (*Od.* 10.98).

Finally, Odysseus has no naturalistic way of knowing that there is always darkness over the Cimmerians, since dusk has already come when he arrives (*Od.* 11.12), and nothing in the narrative implies that he had any actual contact with them. He could, perhaps, infer that a people living at the edge of Ocean, so close to the other world, would be deprived of light. Nothing in the standard mythological pictures of the world, however, demands that Hades have a dim anteroom on earth.

The description of the Cimmerians is especially remarkable for its emotional coloration. Odysseus evidently sympathizes with these 'unfortunate mortals.' Yet there is also a more subtle personal voice in the other passages, too. The Homeric external narrator sometimes creates imaginary observers, but not imaginary participants; it is Odysseus who imagines that a man who could do without sleep could earn double wages. Nothing could be more Odyssean than the description of the place in terms of the extra wage one could get there. Even the idea of being able to do without sleep is closely linked to Odysseus himself, for the inability to go indefinitely without sleep is the cause of two of his worst misfortunes, when his companions open the bag of winds (*Od.* 10.31–3), and when they slaughter the cattle of Helius (*Od.* 12.338). Similarly, it is Odysseus who imagines what a fine settlement could be established on the Goat Island (*Od.* 9.130–41). Here Odysseus mentions explicitly that the Cyclopes have no ships or shipwrights:

οὐ γὰρ Κυκλώπεσσι νέες πάρα μιλτοπάρῃοι,
οὐδ' ἄνδρες νηῶν ἔνι τέκτονες, οἵ κε κάμοιεν
νῆας ἐϋσσέλμους, αἵ κεν τελέοιεν ἕκαστα
ἄστε' ἐπ' ἀνθρώπων ἱκνεύμεναι, οἷά τε πολλὰ
ἄνδρες ἐπ' ἀλλήλους νηυσὶν περόωσι θάλασσαν·

For there are no ships with red prows among the Cyclopes, nor men who are builders of ships, who could make ships with good benches, which would accomplish each thing, coming to people's towns, the various business that men do as they cross the sea with ships to one another.   (*Od.* 9.125–9)

The Cyclopes who, according to Odysseus' own account only a few lines earlier, live in a paradise that produces food spontaneously, would have no reason to want to settle the Goat Island, any more than Hesiod's Golden Age men need ships (*WD* 236–7). It is surely Odysseus who sees the place as desirable and so assumes that the Cyclopes would have settled it, had they had the means. Odysseus may also be flattering his nautical hosts with this reminder of the importance of seafaring to international development. Odysseus emphasizes the perpetual feasting of Aeolus' family both because he joined in it, and because it stands in such sharp contrast to his own home, which he has yet to reach. Odysseus also praises feasting at the beginning of the Apologos (*Od.* 9.5–11).

These introductions are thus quite distinct from the much shorter ones given the Lotus-Eaters, who are introduced simply as 'those who eat flowery food' (*Od.* 9.84), or Circe, who is introduced by her genealogy, as sister of Aeetes and daughter of Oceanus and Perse (*Od.* 10.135–9). In neither of these is there information that defies hindsight. The food of the Lotus-Eaters is central to this episode and Odysseus witnesses its effects. Odysseus has ample occasion, since he spends a year with Circe, to learn her genealogy, and her origins are surely directly relevant to her dangerous powers.

So what is the source of Odysseus' information, and why does he include these digressive introductions? I.J.F. de Jong suggests that the introductions represent traditional or 'mythological' knowledge that Odysseus has received through stories.[11] Yet if the characters within the story have such traditional knowledge, it is singularly useless. In the early adventures, Odysseus does not know what to expect, and makes many mistakes as a result. Perhaps he knew that the lotus was dangerous to eat, but not that the land where he had arrived was the land of the lotus; but if he had heard about the Cyclopes and Laestrygonians, he ought to have recognized the cave and the harbor. Odysseus, however, is surprised. Mythological knowledge could hardly include the peculiarities of the Laestrygonian climate without the information that they eat people.

Later, Circe's description of the perils yet to come (*Od.* 12.39–141) is clearly necessary. Odysseus has presumably heard an Argonautica, since the Argo is 'known to all' (*Od.* 12.70). However, he does not know about the Sirens, or Scylla and Charybdis, for these perils do not lie on the Argonauts' route. Circe informs Odysseus and the external audience at the same time, and she explains precisely what dangers each place presents. In the last adventures, the hearer can judge exactly how much of Circe's information Odysseus shares with his men, and how carefully he and his companions follow her instructions. This prior knowledge makes the last three adventures very different from the others.

Odysseus' introductions are odd partly because they keep the audience in the same condition as Odysseus, even though Odysseus tells them so much. We do not find out what is most important about these people until Odysseus does. The introductions do not offer a naïve, first view of a new land, one the narrative will correct, for they are synthetic, but neither do they summarize what is known. Instead, they misdirect by providing information that prepares only partially for the following events.[12] There is no way to decide whether Odysseus or the main narrator is responsible for the misdirection.

Similar geographic/ethnographic material seems to be a regular option in introductions for autobiographies. There are three such passages in the *Odyssey*: Odysseus' description of Ithaca at 9.21–7; Eumaeus' of Syrie at 15.403–14; the disguised Odysseus' description of Crete at 19.172–80. These are all formally-marked geographical expansion, marked by τις and ἔστι. These introductions include a mixture of information that is relevant to the tale and the situation of its telling and material that has no such obvious function in its context. So, when Odysseus identifies his home, he must explain where it is to the Phaeacians who are going to convey him there:

ναιετάω δ᾽ Ἰθάκην εὐδείελον· ἐν δ᾽ ὄρος αὐτῇ,
Νήριτον εἰνοσίφυλλον, ἀριπρεπές· ἀμφὶ δὲ νῆσοι
πολλαὶ ναιετάουσι μάλα σχεδὸν ἀλλήλῃσι,
Δουλίχιόν τε Σάμη τε καὶ ὑλήεσσα Ζάκυνθος.
αὐτὴ δὲ χθαμαλὴ πανυπερτάτη εἰν ἁλὶ κεῖται
πρὸς ζόφον, αἱ δέ τ᾽ ἄνευθε πρὸς ἠῶ τ᾽ ἠέλιόν τε
τρηχεῖ᾽, ἀλλ᾽ ἀγαθὴ κουροτρόφος· οὔ τι ἐγώ γε
ἧς γαίης δύναμαι γλυκερώτερον ἄλλο ἰδέσθαι.

I live in Ithaca, a distinct island. There is a mountain there, Neriton where the leaves shake, conspicuous. Around there are many islands quite near each other, Doulichium and Same and wooded Zacynthus. Ithaca itself is low, lying farthest in the sea to the west, and they are off towards the dawn and the sun. It is rough, but a good nurse. I am not at all able to see a land sweeter than one's own.   (*Od.* 9.21–8)

Odysseus emphasizes what a modest place Ithaca is in order to forestall questions about whether he would not prefer to remain in far more luxurious Scheria. He explains that everyone prefers his own native country. The passage is extremely difficult, both as Greek and in relation to realities, and it was a problem in antiquity (Strabo 10.451–8). The 'Ithaca Question' (whether the island of the text is the modern Thiaki) was largely based on it.[13] Within the poem, of course, there is no question whatever that Odysseus' description is accurate.

Eumaeus stresses the extraordinary blessedness of his native island:

νῆσός τις Συρίη κικλήσκεται, εἴ που ἀκούεις,
'Ορτυγίης καθύπερθεν, ὅθι τροπαὶ ἠελίοιο,
οὔ τι περιπληθὴς λίην τόσον, ἀλλ' ἀγαθὴ μέν,
εὔβοτος εὔμηλος, οἰνοπληθὴς πολύπυρος.
πείνη δ' οὔ ποτε δῆμον ἐσέρχεται, οὐδέ τις ἄλλη
νοῦσος ἐπὶ στυγερὴ πέλεται δειλοῖσι βροτοῖσιν·
ἀλλ' ὅτε γηράσκωσι πόλιν κάτα φῦλ' ἀνθρώπων,
ἐλθὼν ἀργυρότοξος Ἀπόλλων Ἀρτέμιδι ξύν,
οἷς ἀγανοῖσι βέλεσσιν ἐποιχόμενος κατέπεφνεν.
ἔνθα δύω πόλιες, δίχα δέ σφισι πάντα δέδασται·
τῇσιν δ' ἀμφοτέρῃσι πατὴρ ἐμὸς ἐμβασίλευε,
Κτήσιος 'Ορμενίδης, ἐπιείκελος ἀθανάτοισιν.

There is an island called 'Syrie' – maybe you've heard of it – north of Ortygia, where the sun turns. It is not excessively large, but it is good – rich in cattle and in sheep, full of wine, full of grain. Poverty never comes to the people, nor any other hateful plague is there to make people miserable. Rather, when the tribes of people grow old in the city, Apollo of the silver bow comes along with Artemis, and attacking them with his kind arrows he kills them. There are two cities, and everything is divided in two among them, but my father was king over both, Ktesius son of Ormen, like the immortals.

(*Od.* 15.403–14)

Eumaeus' conversation with the beggar is almost a competition in victimization. The more pleasant his home was, the more pathetic his change of fortune in being enslaved. Further, the story also serves to emphasize how much the good slaves need Odysseus. Eumaeus was unfortunate in being kidnapped, fortunate in coming to Ithaca, and unfortunate again because of Odysseus' absence and the suitors. Both good and bad fortune must be sharply defined.

On the other hand, the introductions, like those of the Apologos, go beyond such relevant information. The ships of the Phaeacians surely do not need Mt. Neriton to find Ithaca, or even the extended digression on its location. The happy life of Eumaeus' home is important, but probably not the fact that there are two cites. In his lie to Penelope, Odysseus gives a brief lecture on the inhabitants of Crete:

Κρήτη τις γαῖ' ἔστι μέσῳ ἐνὶ οἴνοπι πόντῳ,
καλὴ καὶ πίειρα, περίρρυτος· ἐν δ' ἄνθρωποι
πολλοὶ ἀπειρέσιοι, καὶ ἐννήκοντα πόληες·
ἄλλη δ' ἄλλων γλῶσσα μεμιγμένη· ἐν μὲν Ἀχαιοί,
ἐν δ' Ἐτεόκρητες μεγαλήτορες, ἐν δὲ Κύδωνες
Δωριέες τε τριχάϊκες δῖοί τε Πελασγοί·
τῇσι δ' ἐνὶ Κνωσός, μεγάλη πόλις, ἔνθα τε Μίνως
ἐννέωρος βασίλευε Διὸς μεγάλου ὀαριστής,
πατρὸς ἐμοῖο πατήρ, μεγαθύμου Δευκαλίωνος.
Δευκαλίων δ' ἐμὲ τίκτε καὶ Ἰδομενῆα ἄνακτα·

There is a certain land, 'Crete', in the wine-faced sea, lovely and rich, an island. There are many, boundless people there, and ninety cities. Different languages are mingled. There are Achaeans, great-hearted True-Cretans, there are Cydonians, Dorians, who live in three places, and splendid Pelasgians. Among the cities is Cnossos, a great city, where Minos ruled for nine cycles, he who conversed with great Zeus, the father of my father, great-minded Deucalion. Deucalion begat me and the lord Idomeneus.[14]

(*Od.* 19.172–81)

Only the speaker's immediate genealogy, and Cnossos, are obviously needed for the narrative. Certainly the variety of languages on Crete has little to do with Odysseus' visit there.

These passages should be understood as internally motivated by local pride and sentiment (or pseudo-pride in the case of the disguised Odysseus): people like to talk and to tell others about their homes. They display a basic repertory of rhetorical techniques for praising one's homeland. If it is large and important, like Crete, the speaker stresses its size (90 cities!). If it is small, but fertile and fortunate, the speaker catalogues its blessings. If it is neither great nor especially fertile, the speaker calls it a 'good nurse.' In speaking of Ithaca, Odysseus seems implicitly to anticipate the later ethnographic assumption that hard places breed strong men. These passages, in which the information comes from a native, confirm that Odysseus' authority in speaking of places he visited depends on autopsy. Indeed, it is striking that Odysseus does not offer such digressions on Thesprotia or Egypt in the lying tales. Whatever he may have done in other stories, in this poem he has not actually visited these places, and so is unable to describe their wonders or customs.

These three passages use the 'there is a place' formula. The formula conveys not affect, but authority; the epic poet uses it to mark stages in a narrative that are connected with significant locales. Outside the autobiographical introductions, it is used by the main narrator, by Nestor twice in the *Iliad* (knowledge from autopsy, 11.711, 722), and by Menelaus (from autopsy, *Od.* 4.354) and Nestor in the *Odyssey* (*Od.* 3.292–4, of Crete). Despite their affective qualities, these passages convey information. This information is not especially related to experience. Eumaeus left his home as a child, and would not naturalistically be likely to remember these facts about his home, or even to have known them. The knowledge of the number of cities and languages on Crete would not be confined to Cretans (Odysseus, of course, is not a real Cretan, though he has probably really been to Crete), and not perhaps universal among Cretans. The speaker's authority is that of the native, but this authority is conventional and artificial.

Surely an underlying assumption in all these ethnographic introductions is that such information is interesting to the audience. Part of the pleasure of hearing these stories lies in the opportunity to learn about the world. If those who deliver these introductions do so in order to convey information, some at least of what they say must be new. Eumaeus inserts εἴ που ἀκούεις. He regards it as possible, but not certain, that the beggar, whose story has shown him to be a much-travelled man, has heard of his home. In this case, at least, the ethnographic digression is meant to convey genuine information. When Odysseus describes Ithaca to the Phaeacians, he is again surely telling them facts they do not know. For them, after all, Euboea is remote (*Od.* 7.321–4). Furthermore, there is a fine contrast between the hero, with whose deeds they are well acquainted thanks to epic performance, and his modest home. It is harder to be certain about the other ethnographic digressions. The Phaeacians are only too well-acquainted with Cyclopes, who drove them away from their original home (*Od.* 6.4–6). Odysseus, however, has heard only Alcinous' assertion that his people are close to the gods, 'like the Cyclopes and the wild tribes of Giants' (*Od.* 7.205–6). Since Greek mythology included the very different Cyclopes who forged Zeus' thunderbolts, this reference would not be enough to prove that the Phaeacians are already familiar with these particular Cyclopes.

In the Apologos, Odysseus does not have the personal motivation for his introductions that speakers of autobiography do. Instead, he surely provides these introductions mostly because they are even more interesting than a description of Ithaca or Crete could be. All these adventures offer the opportunity to describe unusual human communities. There are no digressions for adventures that involve isolated individuals or places that would seem unremarkable to either Odysseus' internal audience or the poet's external one. Circe lives by herself. The Cicones are not described, because there is nothing special about them, and the Lotus-Eaters apparently have no defining characteristics other than their food. Even though we assume nobody lives on Aeolus' island except his own family (since otherwise the children would not need to marry each other), it is called a *polis*. Odysseus reaches the *demos* and *polis* of the Cimmerians. Typically, the poet combines special features of the place itself with the qualities of the inhabitants. It is presumably because grain and vines grow spontaneously in the Cyclopes' land that they are able to live in family units without complex social arrangements. Aeolus marries his daughters to his sons because the floating island does not permit regular contact with others. Evidently, it is some peculiar feature of the Laestrygonian climate that makes it possible for them to pasture different flocks at different times. They have adapted their economy to local conditions. These digressions, then, show features of later ethnographic thought in the implicit connection between places and the customs of the people who live in them.

The narrator sometimes provides such information in his own voice. Near the beginning of the *Odyssey*, he explains that Poseidon was away:

ἀλλ᾽ ὁ μὲν Αἰθίοπας μετεκίαθε τηλόθ᾽ ἐόντας,
Αἰθίοπας, τοὶ διχθὰ δεδαίαται, ἔσχατοι ἀνδρῶν,
οἱ μὲν δυσομένου Ὑπερίονος, οἱ δ᾽ ἀνιόντος,

But he had gone among the Ethiopians far away, the Ethiopians who are divided in two, remotest of men, some where Sun sets, others where he rises.

(*Od.* 1.22–4)

The mysterious two-fold division of the Aethiopians has nothing to do with Poseidon's absence; it is worth mentioning for its own sake. The poet presumably knows about it as he knows everything else he recounts, from the Muses. He makes no claim to personal acquaintance with the Aethiopians or naturalistic information about them. Odysseus famously compares Demodocus' knowledge of events at Troy, given him by the Muse or Apollo, to the knowledge of an eyewitness or someone who had heard directly from an eyewitness (*Od.* 8.491), at the very beginning of a naturalistic chain of transmission.[15]

What we have in the ethnographic introductions to Odysseus' adventures, then, is a distinct blurring of the distinction between the hero on one side and Circe or the omniscient narrator on the other.[16] For the poet, these ethnographies were traditional, part of the lore he learned as a singer. Some, at least, of this material must have been known to Homer's original audience. Certainly they must have known about Cyclopes, or Odysseus' failure to mention that Polyphemus has only one eye would be confusing. But insofar as the mimetic world imitates a real world, the poet

157

depicts an Odysseus whose knowledge is not based on tradition, but on autopsy, even when the narrative does not provide a likely opportunity for Odysseus to learn what he knows.

I would suggest, therefore, that Odysseus' unrealistic knowledge in these passages depends on their participation in an ethnographic subgenre. Odysseus is the main speaker of ethnographic material in the poem, not surprisingly, since the poet defines him as a potential source of ethnographic information in the proem: πολλῶν δ᾿ ἀνθρώπων ἴδεν ἄστεα καὶ νόον ἔγνω (*Od.* 1.3).[17] Since the poem has promised its hearers that they will learn about different parts of the world, the poet gives his own knowledge to the internal narrator, who has an authority that is internally motivated as autopsy but in practice belongs to the genre. It is the movement into and out of the subgenre that explains the disconnection between the introductions and the narratives. Aeolus' family arrangements have nothing to do with his treatment of Odysseus. In Laestrygonia, Odysseus sees no cultivated land when he looks from high ground (*Od.* 10.97–9), even though they have a built-up town (ἄστυ, 10.108), a good road, and their king is summoned from the ἀγορή (10.114). Does this indicate that the people do not practice agriculture, or only that the harbor is beyond the area of cultivation? Neither Odysseus nor the poet seems to think this matters; the detail of what Odysseus sees serves as an immediate motivation for his sending of the spies to the place where he sees smoke, and as a preparation for the companions' despair when they similarly see no signs of ordinary human life on Circe's island. Odysseus keeps ethnography in its place, which is the introductory digression.

To be sure, even outside the formal digressions, Odysseus can use his knowledge of the world for rhetorical purposes. So he compares Nausicaa to a palm tree he saw at Delos:

Δήλῳ δή ποτε τοῖον Ἀπόλλωνος παρὰ βωμῷ
φοίνικος νέον ἔρνος ἀνερχόμενον ἐνόησα·
ἦλθον γὰρ καὶ κεῖσε, πολὺς δέ μοι ἕσπετο λαός,
τὴν ὁδόν, ᾗ δὴ μέλλεν ἐμοὶ κακὰ κήδε᾿ ἔσεσθαι

Once at Delos I observed such a young shoot of a palm rising up beside the altar of Apollo. For I went there, too, and a great army followed me, on that journey on which many troubles were fated to happen to me.
(*Od.* 6.162–5)

Odysseus' purposes are evident enough. He wants to flatter Nausicaa and impress her. Here, however, the emphasis lies on Odysseus' personal experience of the palm tree.[18] He saw it, and he gives details of his situation at the time (many followers, a trip fated to have bad consequences). The style is utterly unlike that of the introductions.

One feature is similar, however. The remains of Greek epic do not confirm that Odysseus ever went to Delos (though in the *Cypria* the Greeks may have visited Anios there [F. 19 Davies]). Still, this young palm tree, within the fictional world, surely exists. The listener may fairly assume that Odysseus saw it, for a stop on Delos on the way to Troy is not unlikely in itself, and if he did not see it, it is hard to imagine why the image would have come to his mind.[19] When Odysseus introduces a place, he speaks as someone who has been there and knows. It does not matter if the subsequent narrative shows that his visit was actually very brief. Although the report is based on personal knowledge and may be emotionally colored, it claims a general validity and objectivity.

In the *Iliad*, in contrast, Achilles is the most significant ethnographic speaker, and he does not claim autopsy. In his great speech in response to Agamemnon's offer of compensation, he refers to the wealth of particular places:

οὐδ' ὅσ' ἐς 'Ορχομενὸν ποτινίσεται, οὐδ' ὅσα Θήβας
Αἰγυπτίας, ὅθι πλεῖστα δόμοις ἐν κτήματα κεῖται,
αἵ θ' ἑκατόμπυλοί εἰσι, διηκόσιοι δ' ἀν' ἑκάστας
ἀνέρες ἐξοιχνεῦσι σὺν ἵπποισιν καὶ ὄχεσφιν
(*Il.* 9.381–4)

Nor all that enters Orchomenos, nor Thebes in Egypt, where the greatest number of treasures are placed in the buildings, and there are a hundred gates, and two hundred men go out of each with chariots and horses.

A moment later, he recurs to the same style of comparison:

οὐ γὰρ ἐμοὶ ψυχῆς ἀντάξιον οὐδ' ὅσα φασὶν
'Ίλιον ἐκτῆσθαι εὖ ναιόμενον πτολίεθρον
τὸ πρὶν ἐπ' εἰρήνης, πρὶν ἐλθεῖν υἷας Ἀχαιῶν,
οὐδ' ὅσα λάϊνος οὐδὸς ἀφήτορος ἐντὸς ἐέργει
Φοίβου Ἀπόλλωνος Πυθοῖ ἔνι πετρηέσσῃ.

Not worth my life are not even all that they say Troy possessed, that populous city, formerly in peacetime, before the sons of the Achaeans came, nor all that the stone threshold of the archer Phoebus Apollo in rocky Pytho has within.
(*Il.* 9.401–5)

Achilles' use of present tenses is especially clear, since he refers to the wealth of Troy in the past. When he prays to Zeus, he refers specifically to the priests at Dodona:[20]

Ζεῦ ἄνα Δωδωναῖε Πελασγικὲ τηλόθι ναίων
Δωδώνης μεδέων δυσχειμέρου, ἀμφὶ δὲ Σελλοὶ
σοὶ ναίουσ' ὑποφῆται ἀνιπτόποδες χαμαιεῦναι.

Lord Zeus, of Dodona, Pelasgic, living far away, ruler of Dodona of harsh winters, and around live your Selloi, who speak for you, dirty-footed and lying on the ground. (*Il.* 16.233–5)

In his paradigm of Niobe, he digresses on Sipylus:

νῦν δέ που ἐν πέτρῃσιν ἐν οὔρεσιν οἰοπόλοισιν
ἐν Σιπύλῳ, ὅθι φασὶ θεάων ἔμμεναι εὐνὰς
νυμφάων, αἵ τ᾽ ἀμφ᾽ Ἀχελώϊον ἐρρώσαντο,[21]
ἔνθα λίθος περ ἐοῦσα θεῶν ἐκ κήδεα πέσσει.

But now in the rocks, in the sheep-lonely mountains, in Sipylus, where they say are the beds of the goddesses – the Nymphs, who dance around the Acheloos – there, though she is stone, she mulls over her griefs from the gods. (*Il.* 24.614–7)

Achilles may very well have been to Dodona, and perhaps to Delphi, but he has certainly not visited Egyptian Thebes, and he acknowledges that his knowledge of Sipylus comes from oral tradition, like his information about the former wealth of Troy. Indeed, in consoling Priam, he uses the φασί-form again, this time to refer to the previous happy condition of Priam:

ὅσσον Λέσβος ἄνω, Μάκαρος ἕδος, ἐντὸς ἐέργει
καὶ Φρυγίη καθύπερθε καὶ Ἑλλήσποντος ἀπείρων,
τῶν σε γέρον πλούτῳ τε καὶ υἱάσι φασὶ κεκάσθαι.

All that Lesbos to the north, seat of Makar, holds inside, and Phrygia up north and the boundless Hellespont, they say you excelled them all, old man, in wealth and sons. (*Il.* 24.544–6)

Achilles' ethnographic and geographical digressions are thus quite unlike those of the *Odyssey*, for they are distinctly independent of the speaker's personal experience. They are also distinct from those of the poet, since Achilles has no relationship to the Muses. These passages genuinely represent mythological, traditional, or realistic knowledge – information transmitted by being told. Achilles has heard these facts, and he uses them as material for rhetorical expansion just as the poet uses his own knowledge, whether this is realistic (φασί) or poetic. Achilles' ability to evoke famous places shows his imaginative power, but he depends for his knowledge on others.[22] Odysseus' knowledge is first-hand, Achilles' is not.

Even in the *Odyssey*, Odysseus and Eumaeus are not the only sources of information. Circe's advice to Odysseus describes places in the present tense (*Od.* 12.39–110); her information is strictly subordinated to Odysseus' needs. Indeed, only after he asks how to defend his men against Scylla does she mention Scylla's mother Krataiis, on whom he should call as he goes by (*Od.* 12.124–6). Since Circe is a goddess, her knowledge requires no explanation.

The narrator frequently provides descriptions of remarkable places. These are typically focalized in part by an arriving character (and use the past tense): Hermes' view of Calypso's cave (*Od.* 5.63–74), Odysseus' of Alcinous' palace and garden (*Od.* 7.84–132), and Odysseus' and Eumaeus' of the fountain in Ithaca (*Od.* 17.205–11). I call these semi-focalized, because they frequently include information the viewer does not have: that, for example, Hephaestus made the artificial watch-dogs of Alcinous (*Od.* 7.91–4). These regularly include details that are not of narrative importance in themselves but contribute to the narrative in a general way: it is important that we realize that Calypso's island is a very pleasant spot, that Alcinous is exceptionally fortunate. The poet mentions the three builders of the fountain because Melantheus abuses Odysseus there, prompting Eumaeus to pray for Odysseus' return to the Nymphs who have an altar there (*Od.* 17.240–6).

Wonder is the characteristic emotion of such descriptions. Here, as in Odysseus' introductions, there is significant blurring of the distinction between the narrator, who has access to limitless knowledge, and the internal focalizer, who would realistically not have this information but whose emotional response tells the hearer how to react. This is important, because the poet is very aware of the gap between himself and the characters. When Telemachus enters the palace of Menelaus, the narrator confines himself to two lines (*Od.* 4.45–6), identical, except in the name, to the beginning of his description of Alcinous' house (*Od.* 7.84–5). Telemachus expresses his astonishment to Pisistratus (*Od.* 4.71–5). The narrator is very restrained, because Telemachus' reaction, in which he compares the house to that of Zeus, is excessive and reveals his naiveté. More often, the internal and external observers merge. Descriptions of wonderful places, like ethnographies, call for a special voice that conveys simultaneously wonder and authority.

Finally, there is the implicit ethnography of the Phaeacians.[23] This is rich and complex. There is an authorial digression on the foundation of the city at *Od.* 6.3–12. Nausicaa gives a brief description of some of the civic monuments, and refers to the city's preference for seafaring over archery at 6.262–72. Athena gives Odysseus a full genealogy of Arete and a description of her role at 7.54–74. The narrator comments on the excellence of the weaving skills of Phaeacian women at 7.108–10, in the passage whose blurred focalization I have already mentioned. Alcinous describes their excellence in dancing at 8.246–9 (explicitly so that Odysseus may repeat this to his wife and children), and at *Od.* 8.556–63 he finally describes their wonderful ships – the feature about them that is most important to the story. The Phaeacians are simultaneously normal and marvelous. They are hospitable, yet there are suggestions that they might be unfriendly; they can go anywhere, yet seem to stay home except to help lost wanderers.[24] Their ambiguities make them perfect as ethnographic subject.

The author's digressions, like those of Achilles, but in contrast to the passages of blurred authority, convey the realistic side of how geographical/ethnographic knowledge is transmitted: those who travel convey information about their homes abroad, and about other places at home. Odysseus' visit to the Phaeacians would plausibly allow him to say quite a bit about their leadership, land, and customs. Alcinous expects Odysseus to talk about his experiences among the Phaeacians, just as he has described to the Phaeacians both the places he has visited and his home. People who are away from home spread information about their native places and about locations they have visited in a way that presupposes general curiosity about the world.

The narratological features of the *Odyssey*'s treatment of special locations show a heightened willingness to merge the poet's knowledge with the speaker's. The ethnographic introductions, though, occur in sequence, as if the poet decided that this was a genre he wished to include – almost as if he remembered the proem, and felt the need to fulfill the promise implied in πολλῶν δ' ἀνθρώπων ἴδεν ἄστεα καὶ νόον ἔγνω. He therefore groups together adventures he can treat under the heading 'strange foreign communities' and provides them with extended introductions.

Notes

[1] e.g. Page 1973, 23–48 (on Laestrygonians), 73–8 (on Aeolus and the winds), Stanford 1947, 382 (on 11.14, the Cimmerians).

[2] On the Cyclopes, see Dougherty 2001, especially 96–7, 123–7; Segal 1994, 202–15; Vidal-Naquet 1986, 21–2; Kirk 1970, 162–71.

[3] de Jong 2001, 225–6.

[4] On this see Suerbaum 1968, 150–77; Richardson 1990, 43–4.

[5] Race 1993, 102.

[6] Quotations from the *Iliad* follow West 1998–2000, except as noted; quotations from the *Odyssey* von der Mühll.

[7] Mondi 1993, 17–38.

[8] Heubeck 1989, 20–1 (on 9.106–15), insists that there is no contradiction, since the 'trust' is a general reliance on the good fortune the Cyclopes have always experienced. Yet Polyphemus realizes that the Cyclopes depend on Zeus for rain (9.358).

[9] For discussion and bibliography, see Heubeck 1989, 48. I myself suspect that the Laestrygonians live on the border between this world and another where day and night are reversed; see Scodel 2003.

[10] Most famously Meuli 1921, 89–91, followed by many in locating the story near Cyzicus.

[11] Note 3 above.

[12] For misdirection, see Morrison 1992.

[13] The best discussion is Stubbings 1962, 389–407. See also Simpson and Lazenby 1970, 103–6.

[14] Both τριχάϊκες and ἐννέωρος are extremely difficult. See Russo 1992, 84–5; Rutherford 1992, 159, 160–1.

[15] Ford 1992, 121–2, claims that the wanderer Odysseus has no authority in this passage; but he has said that he was at Troy at 8.220. Olson 1995, 1–23, discusses the movement of information in the world of the *Odyssey* and how speakers establish their authority. For the distinction between poetic and naturalistic knowledge, see Scodel 2002, 70–88.

[16] So Danek 1998, 173–4.

[17] Compare the complaint of Woodhouse 1930, 26: 'It is impossible to dodge the fact that in the experiences of Odysseus, as we have them, there is absolutely nothing corresponding to the phrase of the exordium in which reference is made to his wide experience of men and cities.' West in Heubeck et al. 1988, 68–9, argues that the proem was composed for a very different poem, in which Odysseus wandered through Crete, Thesprotia, and Egypt.

[18] Interpretations of the palm trees: Ahl and Roisman 1996, 54–5; Sourvinou-Inwood 1991, 127 n. 33.

[19] Garvie 1994, 124 (on *Od.* 6. 164–5).

[20] Achilles has connections with Epirus, where Neoptolemus goes after the war; Janko 1992, 348–9. His identification of Zeus Herkeios with the Zeus of Dodona is probably ancestral, but his expansive address is typical of his style, and his knowledge of the place reflects its broad fame.

[21] West 1998–2000 here reads Ἀχελήϊον, following an ancient reading cited in T and AD scholia. But the poet could have named any river he did not know 'Achelous'.

[22] Achilles is the most poetic speaker in the *Iliad*, as demonstrated by Martin 1989, esp. 146–205. He is not a good speaker, however, since he lacks prudence; see Thalmann 1984, 180–2. Achilles' rich use of geographical knowledge may be a symptom of his tendency to be intoxicated by his own rhetoric.

[23] Both Dougherty 2001, 96–7 and Segal 1994, 202–15, discuss parallels and contrasts between Phaeacians and Cyclopes.

[24] Reece 1993, 101–21.

Bibliography

Ahl, F. and Roisman, H.
   1996   *The* Odyssey *Re-formed,* Ithaca, N.Y.

Danek, G.
   1998   *Epos und Zitat. Studien zu den Quellen der* Odyssee, Wiener Studien Beiheft 22, Vienna.

de Jong, I.J.F.
   2001   *A Narratological Commentary on the* Odyssey, Cambridge.

Dougherty, C.
   2001   *The Raft of Odysseus*, Oxford.

Ford, A.
   1992   *Homer: The poetry of the past,* Ithaca, N.Y.
Garvie, A.F.
   1994   *Homer:* Odyssey VI–VIII, Cambridge.
Heubeck, A., West, S. and Hainsworth, J.B.
   1988   *A Commentary on Homer's* Odyssey, vol. I: Books i–viii, Oxford.
Heubeck, A. and Hoekstra, A.
   1989   *A Commentary on Homer's* Odyssey, vol. II: Books ix–xvi, Oxford.
Janko, R.
   1992   *The* Iliad*: A commentary,* vol. IV: Books 13–16, Cambridge.
Kirk, G.S.
   1970   *Myth: Its meaning and function in ancient and other cultures,* Berkeley.
Martin, R.
   1989   *The Language of Heroes,* Ithaca, N.Y.
Meuli, K.
   1921   *Odyssee und Argonautika,* Berlin.
Mondi, R.
   1993   'The Homeric Cyclopes: folktale, tradition, and theme', *TAPA* 113,
           17–38.
Morrison, J.
   1992   *Homeric Misdirection: False predictions in the* Iliad, Ann Arbor.
Mühll, P. von der
   1962   *Odyssea,* Basel, Melbing and Lichtenhahn.
Olson, S.D.
   1995   *Blood and Iron: Stories and storytelling in Homer's* Odyssey, *Mnemosyne
           Suppl.* 148, Leiden.
Page, D.L.
   1973   *Folktales in Homer's* Odyssey, Cambridge, Mass.
Race, W.
   1993   'First appearances in the *Odyssey*', *TAPA* 123, 79–107.
Reece, S.
   1993   *The Stranger's Welcome,* Ann Arbor.
Richardson, S.
   1990   *The Homeric Narrator,* Nashville.
Russo, J., Fernandez-Galliano, M. and Heubeck, A.
   1992   *A Commentary on Homer's* Odyssey, vol. III: Books xvii–xxiv, Oxford.
Rutherford, R.B.
   1992   *Homer:* Odyssey *Books XIX and XX,* Cambridge.
Scodel, R.
   2002   *Listening to Homer,* Ann Arbor.
   2003   'The paths of day and night', *Ordia Prima* 2, 83–6.
Segal, C.
   1994   *Singers, Heroes, and Gods in the* Odyssey, Ithaca, N.Y.
Simpson, R.H. and Lazenby, J.F.
   1970   *The Catalogue of Ships in Homer's* Iliad, Oxford.
Stanford, W.B.
   1947   *Homer:* Odyssey. *Books 1–12,* London.

Sourvinou-Inwood, C.
  1991   *Reading Greek Culture: Texts and images, rituals and myths*, Oxford.
Suerbaum, W.
  1968   'Die Ich-Erzählungen des Odysseus: Überlegungen zur epischen Technik der Odyssee', *Poetica* 2, 150–7.
Thalmann, W.G.
  1984   *Conventions of Form and Thought in Early Greek Epic Poetry*, Baltimore.
Vidal-Naquet, P.
  1986   *The Black Hunter*, trans. A. Szededy-Maszak, Baltimore.
Wace, A. and Stubbings, F.H. (ed.)
  1962   *A Companion to Homer*, London.
West, M.L.
  1998–2000   *Homerus:* Ilias, Munich and Leipzig.
Woodhouse, W.J.
  1930   *The Composition of Homer's* Odyssey, Oxford.

10

THE ART OF CREATIVE LISTENING IN THE *ODYSSEY*

Robert J. Rabel

But whatever the reason, the book of my life is a book of voices. When I ask myself how I arrived at where I am, the answer surprises me: 'Listening'.
Philip Roth

I think I will do nothing for a long time but listen,
And accrue what I hear into myself…and let sounds contribute
Toward it. Walt Whitman

In order to say good things, one's hearing must be good and one must hear good things.
Bertolt Brecht

Generally speaking, as Aristotle says in Book 1 of the *Metaphysics* (980a), people prefer sight to the other senses, for sight best helps them to know things by revealing the greatest number of distinctions.[1] Yet in the case of the art of oral storytelling, or indeed any form of storytelling, *listening* may perhaps be regarded as the more important sense.[2] Demodocus in the *Odyssey* was blind (*Od.* 8.64), as perhaps was Homer himself. The blind storyteller was not too disadvantaged in a society in which oral poetry flourished.[3] Indeed, listening may be privileged over sight even among literary artists. So Elledge says that (the blind) John Milton's creative artistry arose from the maintenance of 'a patient, receptive listening attitude', 'being alert…to the voice of the Muse' (1975, xiii). Bloom has characterized Shakespeare as probably 'the most preternaturally gifted of listeners' (2000, 146). Perhaps Roth's recognition of the creative power of listening – expressed above in the first epigraph to this paper – is not surprising after all. For at least in the case of third-person narrative, which Hamburger has identified as narrative's primary form (1973, 50), sight may even be dispensed with altogether. Omniscient narrators – unless they are gods – are prevented by the very conditions of their mode of storytelling from actually *seeing* the world they depict in their narratives. The omniscient narrator is not an *observer* of the world of the story in the sense of being visually privy to it. Narration is an act of representation, not perception, and the third-person narrator usually occupies an order of space and time different from that occupied by his or her characters.[4] Omniscience – at least for human storytellers – is purchased at the expense of sight. Hence Chatman prefers the word *slant* to the more traditional phrase *point of view* to describe the narrator's relationship to his or her story; for the third-person narrator literally *sees* nothing in that other world (1990, 142–4). The poet of the *Iliad* says much the same thing as Chatman: while the Muses know everything and are present everywhere, humans can only *hear* (ἀκούομεν) the events of the past recounted in epic song (*Il.* 2.486).[5]

The poet of the *Odyssey* openly acknowledges in the poem's prooemium that listening played a role in his own creative act. Using evidence garnered from the prooemium and from the poem itself, we can derive a conception of the good poet as a skilled listener, who both attends to others and – perhaps of equal importance – overhears *himself* in the process of composition. Furthermore, populating his poem with multiple audiences that react to and interpret what they hear, the poet invites the poem's external audience to reflect on the importance of their being good listeners also. Within the poem, he fashions contrasting exemplars of attentive and inattentive listeners, persons who succeed or fail at least partly because they possess or lack the characteristic poetic skill of good listening – both to self and to others. On the one hand, Odysseus, the poet's self-reflexive counterpart,[6] flourishes as both hero and storyteller at least partly because of an aptitude for attentive listening, which he harnesses in the interest of fashioning the material for his 'Song of Myself' in Books 9–12 of the *Odyssey* and elsewhere for various other purposes throughout the poem. The suitors, on the other hand, collectively represent the antithesis of the good listener: they constantly fall victim to dramatic irony – the common fate of characters who fail to overhear themselves – and eventually meet with destruction at least partly because of a failure to heed others and also to overhear what they themselves say. Listening being important in the creation and reception of the *Odyssey* and also in the successful living of life within the poem, let us look first at what the poet himself says about listening in his prooemium and then move on to consider how this theme is developed and expanded within the world of the story.

A set of striking similarities marks the prooemia of the *Iliad* and *Odyssey*. The themes of both are announced programmatically in the poems' first words: 'wrath' (μῆνιν, *Il.* 1.1) in the *Iliad* and 'man' (ἄνδρα, *Od.* 1.1) in the *Odyssey*. Invocations of the Muse ('goddess' [θεά, *Il.* 1.1]; 'Muse' [Μοῦσα, *Od.* 1.1]) come next, followed by four-syllable adjectives that characterize the poems' respective themes ('destructive' [οὐλομένην, *Il.* 1.2]; 'resourceful' [πολύτροπον, *Od.* 1.1]). Relative clauses follow (*Il.* 1. 2 ff.; *Od.* 1.1 f.), and these amplify and emphasize the magnitude of the stories about to be told (πολλάς, *Il.* 1.3; πολλά, *Od.* 1.1, πολλῶν, *Od.* 1.3, πολλά, *Od.* 1.4). Yet the prooemia differ in several respects. First of all, the poet of the *Iliad* presents himself as the mouthpiece of the Muse: he asks the goddess to do the singing (ἄειδε, *Il.* 1.1). As Redfield says, '[t]he bard in effect claims that his song is the authentic voice of the goddess' (1979, 98).[7] The poet of the *Odyssey*, on the other hand, uses the imperative ἔννεπε (*Od.* 1.1), usually translated as 'tell', in his invocation. Rüter sees no significance in whether the poet tells the Muse to sing or speak (1969, 29). Wilamowitz, however, saw in the change from 'sing' to 'tell' evidence of a shift from epic song to rhapsodic speech (1966, 354–5). Stewart raises the interesting possibility that the imperative ἔννεπε is a form of a very old verb that actually means something like 'to track down' or 'to search out' (1976, 185), so that on this interpretation the Muse is not being asked to become the narrator of the *Odyssey* but rather, as Stanford says, to guide the poet along the proper path of song (1959, 208). Regardless of the proper significance of the imperative 'tell' (ἔννεπε), a more telling point of contrast between the prooemia of the *Iliad* and the *Odyssey* seems not to have received much attention: the pronoun μοι ('tell *me*') in the *Odyssey* is strikingly absent from the corresponding invocation in the *Iliad*.[8] In effect, while the poet of the *Iliad* introduces himself as a kind of medium or channel for the voice of a goddess, the poet of the *Odyssey* presents himself to us as a *listener*; he is, he says, first of all a narratee.[9] He takes on the role of storyteller only after his prooemium is completed.[10] The poet may thus wish to signal an important aspect of the poetics implicit in the *Odyssey*: in a manner amplified in the course of the poem's narrative, he thus suggests that – at least in his case – listening precedes and somehow makes possible the process of poetic creation. (As we shall see below, Odysseus, his self-reflexive counterpart, also first engages in a process of creative listening before becoming a successful storyteller in his own right.) The poet then rounds off the prooemium in ring-compositional form by once again presenting himself as a listener, but he seems to say something in addition when he asks the goddess, in an enigmatic phrase, to '*speak also to us*' (εἰπὲ καὶ ἡμῖν, *Od.* 1.10). I suppose the plural ἡμῖν ('to us') could be taken as a kind of 'royal we' or alternatively used as evidence for pre-Homeric poems about Odysseus.[11] But as de Jong (2001, 5) and Lenz (1980, 49) have observed – and the point is worth development that, to my knowledge, it has not received – the poet by the use of the word 'us' seems to put himself as listener on an equal footing with his audience. For reasons we shall try to deduce from the poem as the narrative progresses, the poet's audience also seems to require the help and guidance of the Muse as they approach the tale of Odysseus.

By including himself in our number – and us in his – the poet perhaps means to signal that careful listening will play as important a role in his audience's *reception* of poetry as it does in the first place in his own initial act of *creation*. As regards poetic creation, Hyde has argued that at least two phases are involved in the composition of a verbal work of art: in one the will is suspended and in the other it is active. 'The suspension', he says, 'is primary. It is when the will is slack that we feel moved or we are struck by an event, intuition, or image'. The second phase is the working out of the material of the work itself. Hyde names Whitman, Kerouac, and Yeats as authors who place special emphasis on the first phase of artistic creation, the suspension of the will, which often takes the form of what Kerouac called 'open listening', keeping oneself highly receptive and aurally submissive to one's surroundings (Hyde 1979, 221–2). Open listening is as important for Whitman as for Kerouac, as is evidenced throughout the former's *Song of Myself*.[12] (In the *Odyssey*, I will claim, this suspension of the will also manifests itself as a phase of open listening.) Moreover, in the words εἰπὲ καὶ ἡμῖν, I think that the poet means to characterize himself as somehow our equal partner in the poetic enterprise. Booth distinguishes among novelists in a way that seems to me to have application also to ancient Greek poets:

> There is a sharp difference between authors who imply that we readers are essentially their equals in the imaginative enterprise, because we are embarked on the same quest, and those who suggest that we are either their inferiors or their superiors or that our path must be entirely different from theirs.[13]

In the first category, Booth places Dickens, Trollope, and others – authors who imply a relationship among equals. In the second grouping, falling just short of 'intolerable arrogance', he says, Booth places Milton, Joyce, Tolstoy, and others (1988, 185). Following this rough dichotomy, I would be minded on the evidence of the prooemium to place the poet of the *Iliad* within the second group, for he seems to regard himself as our superior or as one whose path is different from ours – at least insofar as he has privileged access to divine song, accessible to the rest of us only through his activity as a kind of medium.[14] However, there is no evidence to support a charge of arrogance on his part. On the other hand, the poet of the *Odyssey* seems to fit comfortably into Booth's first category. He wants to be our friend, much like Whitman, who wrote:

> The messages of great poets to each man and woman are, Come to us on

equal terms, Only then can you understand us, We are no better than you, What we enclose, you enclose, What you enjoy we may enjoy. Did you suppose there could be only one Supreme?[15]

Unlike the poet of the *Iliad,* the poet of the *Odyssey* invites us to come to his work on equal terms. He emphasizes that his poem does not directly express the word of a god, to which he alone has privileged access, but is rather a product of human craft and ingenuity. For this reason perhaps, he seems to take great pleasure in emphasizing the various 'seams and joints' of his work, the places in the text where the 'toolmarks' of his craft most visibly show.[16]

Booth has further argued that the implied authors of *all* stories purport to offer their audiences one or another kind of friendship, based on pleasure, utility, or shared aspirations and loves (1988, 174). Certainty about the kind of friendship the poet of the *Odyssey* offers his audience can probably never be reached, for, as Nagy, has pointed out, the *Odyssey* 'makes no overt reference to its own social context, the occasions of its own potential performability' (1996, 137). Moreover, the poet *of* the *Odyssey* differs from the poets *within* the *Odyssey* (Phemius and Demodocus) at least insofar as he has established an ascendancy over his audience, allowing him to produce a poem of monumental length without fear of the kind of interruption that constantly plagues his counterparts within the text.[17] Nonetheless, because the poem seems to exhibit a high coefficient of reflexivity – the processes at work in the production *of* the poem sometimes closely mirrored in the processes at work in the production of stories *within* the poem – we are invited to make some conjectures about the kind of friendship the poet offers us. In this regard, Louden has shown that within the *Odyssey* telling and listening to narratives are both parts of a reciprocal process of guest-reception. 'Most characters who function as hosts', Louden says, 'serve as audiences. Those characters not functioning as hosts, such as Eurykleia, may not serve as audiences' (1999, 50). The narrative exchange between the poet of the *Odyssey* and his authorial audience may perhaps also be taken to be a kind of guest-friendship, the poet being our guest and we his hosts. (Indeed, Booth himself resorts to a metaphor to which the poet gives concrete life within the text of the *Odyssey*. Booth speaks of books knocking on our doors and either being received or denied entry [1988, 179].) Such a relationship of guest-friendship seems to be modeled within the *Odyssey*, among other passages, in Book 8. The singer Demodocus, the guest of King Alcinous, must remain attentive and responsive throughout to his audience, singing the song for which they call. (In a later age, the rhapsode Ion bears witness to the performing poet's need to pay close attention to his audience in this way

[Plato *Ion* 535e4]).[18] On the other hand, the audience of the *Odyssey* assumes the subject position of Alcinous, his Phaeacian host, and the king's various guests, including Odysseus himself.

Alcinous and Odysseus perhaps model the proper responsive and critical behavior the poet expects from us in the act of reciprocity that constitutes the form of (guest-)friendship attending the creation and reception of his poem. As members of the audience to poetry *within* the *Odyssey*, they react to what they hear in very different ways, in the process providing two of the earliest examples of literary criticism to be found in Western literature.[19] Odysseus weeps during Demodocus' song about an early quarrel between Odysseus and Achilles (*Od.* 8.72–92). Explaining the hero's active engagement in the story, Segal plausibly claims that Odysseus is so moved because his long wanderings have changed some of his perspectives on the past (1994, 58). It is equally possible, however, that *hearing* the story of the quarrel in the song of the poet provides part of the catalyst for his change in perspective. Later in the book Odysseus politely ignores the poet's intervening song about the love affair between Ares and Aphrodite (*Od.* 8.266–366) as he reflects on the song about his quarrel with Achilles:

Δημόδοκ', ἔξοχα δή σε βροτῶν αἰνίζομ' ἁπάντων·
ἢ σέ γε Μοῦσ' ἐδίδαξε, Διὸς πάϊς, ἢ σέ γ' Ἀπόλλων.
λίην γὰρ κατὰ κόσμον Ἀχαιῶν οἶτον ἀείδεις,
ὅσσ' ἔρξαν τ' ἔπαθόν τε καὶ ὅσσ' ἐμόγησαν Ἀχαιοί,
ὥς τέ που ἢ αὐτὸς παρεὼν ἢ ἄλλου ἀκούσας.

Demodokos, above all mortals beside I prize you.
Surely the Muse, Zeus' daughter, or else Apollo has taught you,
for all too right (κατὰ κόσμον) following the tale you sing the Achaians'
venture, all they did and had done to them, all the sufferings
of these Achaians, as if you had been there yourself or heard it
from one who was.   (*Od.* 8.487–91)

Odysseus' comment, taken in conjunction with his tears, indicates that he is moved not so much by the truth and accuracy of Demodocus' song as by the vividness with which the poet is able to conjure up the events recounted.[20] In the same critical spirit, Plato much later in the *Ion* remarks upon poetry's strange and uncanny power to present an illusion that the emotions of the listener easily mistake for the reality being represented (*Ion* 531b1–e6). Also like Plato (*Ion* 533e), Odysseus attributes this power of poetry to divine agency. Later still, in response to Odysseus' narrative of his adventures, Alcinous reflects in a different way upon the nature and effects of poetry:

ὦ 'Οδυσεῦ, τὸ μὲν οὔ τί σ' ἐΐσκομεν εἰσορόωντες
ἠπεροπῆά τ' ἔμεν καὶ ἐπίκλοπον, οἷά τε πολλοὺς
βόσκει γαῖα μέλαινα πολυσπερέας ἀνθρώπους
ψεύδεά τ' ἀρτύνοντας, ὅθεν κέ τις οὐδὲ ἴδοιτο·
σοὶ δ' ἔπι μὲν μορφὴ ἐπέων, ἔνι δὲ φρένες ἐσθλαί,
μῦθον δ' ὡς ὅτ' ἀοιδὸς ἐπισταμένως κατέλεξας,
πάντων Ἀργείων σέο τ' αὐτοῦ κήδεα λυγρά.

Odysseus, we as we look upon you do not imagine
that you are a deceptive or thievish man, the sort that the black earth
breeds in great numbers, people who wander widely, making up
lying stories, from which no one could learn anything. You have
a grace upon your words, and there is sound sense within them,
and expertly, as a singer would do, you have told the story
of the dismal sorrows befallen yourself and all of the Argives.

(*Od.* 11.363–9)[21]

For his part, Alcinous takes the 'grace' (μορφή) of a song as an independent guarantee of its truth, contradicting Odysseus' earlier observation that only a god can guarantee poetic truth.[22] Which of the two listeners and interpreters of poetry may be correct is not relevant to the thesis of this paper. I am concerned only with the fact that *within* the *Odyssey* audiences seem to bear responsibility for the understanding and active interpretation of what they hear.[23] Good audiences within the poem do not, like the suitors of Penelope, sit dumbly by, entranced by what they hear (*Od.* 1.325–7). The behavior of the good audiences perhaps offers us a mirror in which we can glimpse our responsibilities as listeners to the song of the *Odyssey*. [24]

The poem's reflexivity thus allows for some conjecture about the kind of friendship the poet offers and also tells us something about the kind of attentive and critically aware reception he expects from his own host audience, partners in the reciprocal guest-host act involved in the creation and reception of poetry. Now, as we have just seen, the role of listening as reflected in the audience's *reception* of poetry is made evident through the reflexive example of the interpretive activity of audiences within the poem. This element of reflexivity may also help us come to terms with what it means when the poet includes both himself and the audience of poetry as narratees of the Muse.

Problems arise in understanding the relationship between poet and Muse (and Muse, poet, and audience) because, as Barmeyer has pointed out, the early poets never systematically explain the nature of their connection to the goddess. They simply announce their participation in some sort of uncanny experience that results in their becoming mediators between the world of the supernatural and the world of living men and women. At most, as Barmeyer says, we can say that the poet who invokes the Muse feels himself in need, and he looks to the Muse for some kind of help in the completion of the work at hand (1967, 97–101). Nevertheless, internal evidence, once again garnered from the poem, allows us to infer that the poet's invocation of the Muse, a prayer for inspiration and guidance on the road to 'tracking down' Odysseus, serves as prelude and perhaps a necessary condition for what Hyde, following Kerouac, has described as the process of open listening, or what Pound, speaking condescendingly of Yeats' spiritualism, once described as listening to 'spooks' (Hyde 1979, 223).[25]

Atwood has claimed that *all* narrative art 'is motivated, deep down, by a fear of and a fascination with mortality – by a desire to make the risky leap to the Underworld, and to bring something or someone back from the dead' (2002, 156). The great poet, Whitman says, 'drags the dead out of their coffins and stands them again on their feet…he says to the past, Rise and walk before me that I may realize you' (1959, 12). In the *Odyssey*, the poet makes concrete the metaphor of the poet as one who gives new life to the dead by way of depicting Odysseus' trip to the Underworld. In Book 10, Odysseus is directed by the goddess Circe to visit the land of the dead, where in Book 11 he literally sits among *his* 'spooks', listens to their stories, and collects information to be carried back to the world of the living and there transformed into epic song. In the process of narrating these events through the mouth of the hero, the poet perhaps means to provide a reflexive description or model of his own process of open listening, which resulted in the creation of the *Odyssey*. At the risk of straying too far off course into the realm of allegorical interpretation, I suggest that Circe, who ushers Odysseus into the realm of the Underworld, serves as a reflexive counterpart of the Muse of the *Odyssey*, whose mediation is necessary in order to provide the poet with access to the stories of the heroes of the past, while the Sirens, for their part, reflexively represent the Muse or Muses of the *Iliad* and instantiate a different view of the nature and source of poetry. Odysseus' very different experiences with Circe and the Sirens furnishes us with a fleeting glimpse of the 'intertextual debate' between the *Iliad* and the *Odyssey* on the question of the nature of poetry as a finished product of divine wisdom (the *Iliad*) or else as an artifact of human craft only assisted in the making by divine direction or inspiration (the *Odyssey*).[26]

In this regard, we should first note that the metaphorical connection between making art and sailing the sea has been prevalent in literature from Homer's *Odyssey* to Derek Walcott's *Omeros* (Dougherty 2001, 19–37) so that Odysseus' sea voyage to the realm of the dead provides a ready metaphor for the craft of poetic composition. Circe, for her part, directs Odysseus to set sail to the Underworld, and she aids him on his way with a favorable wind (*Od.* 11.6–8). She is responsible for the successful beginning of this journey: that is, the trip to the Underworld is made possible, as Reucher says, only through her 'mediating agency' (*Vermittlung*).[27] The hero, however, while given proper direction, must accomplish the 'risky leap' into the Underworld on his own. Only later will he transform the stories he hears there into epic song. Indeed, in the matter of the voyage to the Underworld and in their association in general, Odysseus and Circe 'relate to each other not so much by the intensity of their erotic connection as by the subtle variation in holding or sharing power' (Brilliant 1995, 172). Circe's cooperative role in directing Odysseus to the world of the epic past seems to me almost a perfect allegory for a process neatly described by Barmeyer, citing Garcia Lorca: while inspiration (the Muse of the *Odyssey* and the fair wind of Circe?) may offer the writer an idea, the artist himself must labor to produce the work itself (Barmeyer 1968, 12–13).[28]

Circe serves as Odysseus' 'staunch ally' against the Sirens (Doherty 1995, 136), who instantiate a different view of the nature of poetry and the responsibility of the artist for its creation. The Sirens promise the hero direct, unmediated access to their own divinely composed song about the epic past; he need only give up sailing and listen to them. Thereafter, or so at least they claim, he will go forth knowing a wealth of things (*Od.* 12.184–91). Now the connection of the Sirens with Muses has been well documented (Buschor 1944 and Doherty 1995a, 81–92). They not only resemble Muses, but they even sing using the diction of the *Iliad* (Pucci 1979, 126), and, as Ford says, their eerie art 'shows the dangers of an unmediated contact with the heroic tradition' (1992, 84), just such contact, I think, as the poet of the *Iliad* seems to offer when he claims that his poem, in Redfield's words, 'is the authentic voice of the goddess' (1979, 98). Odysseus manages to swerve away from the Sirens and avoid the fate of becoming an uncritical listener to their song. Thus he escapes the fate of the poet (and the audience?) of the *Iliad*.[29] Eventually then he makes his way to the land of the Phaeacians, where he becomes fully the self-reflexive counterpart of the poet of the *Odyssey* by turning into story what he has garnered through his adventures and especially through the process of open listening to his 'spooks'.

As regards the journey to the Underworld itself, the centerpiece and supreme achievement of his adventures, Reinhardt says that Odysseus' trip should be viewed as a conjuration of spirits rather than an actual journey after the manner of an Orpheus or Heracles (1996, 119). Griffin sees both aspects of the journey equally present: a trip to the Underworld is combined with the idea of a conjuration of spirits (1987, 28). According to Vernant, by exercising a ritual of evocation that brings the dead for a moment into the world of the living Odysseus accomplishes the same task as the bard (1996, 60). Vernant's insight is important, but I think that he conflates phases of the creative process that the poet keeps separate in the creation *of* the poem and that he carefully distinguishes in the experience of Odysseus, his self-reflexive counterpart, *within* the poem. For both poet and hero, listening precedes and makes possible poetic composition. When Odysseus performs a ritual evoking the dead in the Underworld, he experiences a phase preliminary to the actual composition of his story, open listening or 'listening to spooks'. Only when he brings their stories back into the world of the living, however, does Odysseus fully come to resemble the poet of the *Odyssey* in the actual composition and performance of his story.

'There is no hero', Prince says, 'who is above all a narratee' (1980, 8). Yet Odysseus approximates the condition of an ideal hero-narratee in the Underworld – if only we view him as an active and engaged listener, not like Walt Whitman, who merely 'leans and loafes [*sic*]' at his ease in the summer grass.[30] (Page wrongly criticizes the adventure in the Underworld on the grounds that Odysseus has very little of interest to *say* to the spirits.[31] However, since human existence is a dialogue with the world, as Eagleton says, speaking of Heidegger's philosophy, 'the more reverent activity is to listen rather than to speak' [1983, 62]. Moreover, as we will see below, like existence, thought – at least for Odysseus – consists of just such a dialogue of talking and listening, though in the case of the hero's manner of thought the dialogue, so to speak, is carried out within his own self.) Experiencing the slackening of the will that Hyde sees as preliminary to artistic creation, Odysseus, just like Whitman, first sits (ἥμην, *Od.* 11. 49), and Elpenor speaks to him (*Od.* 11.83). The two question and answer one another (*Od.* 11.81–2). The hero-narratee holds sway over the ghosts, not allowing them to approach the blood until he is ready to give them a hearing (*Od.* 11. 88–9). As Teiresias informs him, he has the power to determine which of the ghosts will be allowed to speak and in what order (*Od.* 11.146–9). He thus possesses and exercises both in the Underworld and in his later relating of the adventure before the Phaeacians the formal power of a poet to divide his story into sections of narrative and direct speech.

Odysseus' experience with Circe, his subsequent sojourn among the dead, and, finally, his performance before the Phaeacians may thus provide a mirror in which we may see reflected not Hyde's two phases of artistic creation discussed above but rather *three* seemingly discrete stages involved in the composition of the *Odyssey*. As Odysseus is given direction by Circe to the land of the dead, just so the poet receives direction, inspiration or enlightenment (*Erleuchtung* in Barmeyer's terms [1968, 105]) from his own helping female deity, the Muse.[32] (If, as West suggests, Circe gives the hero essential advice on how to *continue* his narrative [1997, 409], the Muse gives the poet essential advice on how to *begin* his.) However, unlike the poet of the *Iliad* and Demodocus, both of whom are directly provided with 'sweet song' (*Od.* 8.64) by the Muse, Odysseus and his poet must, in Atwood's phrase quoted above, 'make the risky leap to the Underworld' on their own.[33] That Odysseus quite literally descends to the shades and conducts with them a dialogue that we have termed 'open listening' is made visible to the audience of the poem within the text itself. Exactly how the hero's experience of open listening might reflexively mirror or provide an analogue to the poet's experience is subject to various possible interpretations. Some see Odysseus, voyager to the Underworld, as a kind of shaman taking an ecstatic journey into the world of the supernatural.[34] If so, the hero's experience among the shades might reflect the experience of the poet in a very direct manner, both Odysseus and the poet quite literally waiting upon and listening to their respective 'spooks', Odysseus communing with the ghosts of his heroic and mythological past and the poet with the spirits of the long-dead characters like Odysseus himself, who inhabit the world of *his* story. On the other hand, Odysseus' journey to the Underworld might be taken less literally as an analogue to the poet's coming to learn the traditional stories of the epic past by listening to the performances of other epic poets.[35] What Atwood says about writers would apply also to Homer and the performing poets of ancient Greece:

> All writers learn from the dead. As long as you continue to write, you continue to explore the work of writers who have preceded you; you also feel judged and held to account by them.[36]

In this regard it might be significant that Odysseus first listens to three songs performed by Demodocus (*Od.* 8.72–96, 266–369, 499–522) before he undertakes to tell the story of his own adventures. In any event, the hero's attendance upon the dead as narratee may be taken to reflect the poet's own practice of 'open listening', which puts him in touch one way or another with the stories he draws upon in the composition of his own work. Finally, following direction from their respective goddesses and experience in open listening, both hero and poet prove themselves accomplished composers in performance. Therefore, when the hero is praised for his manner of storytelling, the poet is praising himself at the same time.[37]

Perhaps the poet asks the Muse to 'speak also to us' (εἰπὲ καὶ ἡμῖν, *Od.* 1.10) – thus grouping himself together with his audience – because of the congruence of experience we share with him as listeners to his poem. Being an audience of the *Odyssey* requires that in the interpretation of the poem we employ just those qualities of intelligence, versatility, patience, and – last but not least – creative listening that the poet celebrates in his hero and reflexively attributes to himself.[38] Moreover, as soon as the audience begins to listen to the narrative of the *Odyssey* after the completion of the prooemium, we ourselves, like the poet and his hero, enter a kind of Underworld. What Atwood says about the experience of readers of books seems also to apply to audiences of epic poems: books and epic poems are metaphorical Underworlds; the living may enter, but then they must leave; they cannot live there.[39] Therefore, audiences perhaps also require the assistance of a protecting goddess to usher them into the world of the epic past.

In addition to highlighting the importance of listening to others, the poet of the *Odyssey* calls our attention to a further kind of creative listening, what we might, following Bloom, call 'self-overhearing', the listening of the self to the self. Bloom argues that the deepening or internalization of the self in literature can often best be understood in terms of an antithesis between what he views as two quite different kinds of listening, represented for him by the works of Cervantes and Shakespeare. In *Don Quixote*, Bloom says, what matters most are the ongoing conversations between Don Quixote and Sancho, who listen to each other and in the process develop richer egos. On the other hand, Bloom says, the great characters of Shakespearean drama, Falstaff and Hamlet in particular, actually have a lot of trouble listening to others, but they undergo a process of development by overhearing *themselves*.[40] 'When characters like Hamlet, Lear, Antony and Cleopatra change', Bloom says, 'more often than not it is because they overhear themselves, almost as if someone else had spoken' (2000, 194). Bloom is certainly correct in calling attention to the importance in life and literature of listening not only to others but also to the self. He may be mistaken, however, in seeing these two modes of conversation as in some basic way antithetical, for, as Arendt has argued, when thinking and deliberating, people in fact reveal themselves to be actually 'two in one', conductors of an inner dialogue of speaking and listening to the self (1971, 185). Yet while Arendt attributes to Socrates the discovery of thought – as opposed to consciousness – as internal dialogue, speaking and listening to the self represent a mode of thought often found in the *Odyssey* – and the *Iliad* too. Odysseus' aptitude for creative listening to others is exactly matched and complemented by his penchant for careful self-overhearing.

As Montiglio has shown, Odysseus characteristically puts a high value on silence. I suggest that he is so often silent in order to engage in the sort of dialogue Bloom describes as listening to the self, almost as if someone else has spoken. Such self-overhearing is often expressed in the *Odyssey* in scenes marked by use of the verb μερμηρίζειν ('to ponder' or 'to deliberate'), which, as Montiglio has shown, most often characterizes the thought of Odysseus or Penelope, whom I judge to be the two great self-overhearers of the *Odyssey*. Of the poem's twenty-five instances of μερμηρίζειν, she points out, fourteen refer to Odysseus and four to Penelope (Montiglio 2000, 257–63). The poet of the *Odyssey* seems to disregard or collapse what Bloom sees as a radical antithesis between listening to the self and listening to others by often depicting Odysseus' mental activity in the same terms as the operation of his public speech, so that conversations with his *self* are presented on the model of his conversations with others. Typically, when Odysseus ponders alternatives in a scene of deliberation characterized by the verb μερμηρίζειν, he rejects his first impulse and adopts an alternative course of action, just as if he has heard someone else speaking and giving what he regards as better advice.[41] Thus, for example, when Leucothea gives the shipwrecked Odysseus her veil and tells him to swim, the hero, fearing deception, addresses his 'great-hearted *thumos*' and proposes to it another course of action, which is then adopted: he stays with the raft. In effect, he listens to himself rather than to the goddess (*Od.* 5.354–64). An especially noteworthy example of thought as internal dialogue occurs when the disguised Odysseus' heart 'barks' in response to the actions of the insolent suitors of his wife. He practices restraint by addressing his heart and prompting it to endure. His heart listens and obeys (*Od.* 20.10–24). (Novelist Tom Holt makes witty satire against the background of Odysseus' habit of inner debate and self-overhearing, generalizing it as a practice typical of Greeks. The Phoenician trader-narrator of his novel *Olympiad* marvels constantly at the strange Greek practice of speaking with, listening to, and accepting or rejecting the promptings of the heart, as if Greeks, unlike Phoenicians, lacked a unified personality [Holt 2000].) Perhaps because of his habit of self-overhearing, Odysseus seldom falls victim to dramatic irony.[42] Unlike the suitors, he is able to control the meaning of his words because he listens to what he says. Hence, what Bloom says of Hamlet seems also true to a large extent of Odysseus: we are given little opportunity and virtually no authority to regard him in an ironic light.[43]

The suitors collectively represent the antithesis of the careful listener. They fail to develop richer egos because they fail to listen to others: the warnings of Odysseus (*Od.* 18.124–50, for example) and the culmi-nating and vivid dramatic prophecies of imminent destruction voiced by Theoclymenus (*Od.* 20.350–70) go unheeded. Perhaps just as importantly, however, the suitors are constantly victimized by dramatic irony because they typically fail to listen to what they themselves say. Throughout the poem they enjoy no moments of internal debate or dialogue characterized by the verb μερμηρίζειν, and they repeatedly *say* much more than they *mean*, so that perspectives on their actions and words of which they themselves are unaware constantly open up. To take a particularly rich example of this fault, Antinous proves himself a spectacular failure as a storyteller when he relates the tale of the Centaur Eurytion, intended as a 'dissuasive paradigm' for the beggar Odysseus in disguise. Eurytion, Antinous says, got drunk with wine at the palace of the 'great-hearted' hero Pirithous. (Antinous leaves out the detail that the Centaur was there attending Pirithous' wedding, where he tried to rape the bride Hippodamia.) The Centaur went mad as a result of his drinking, and so Pirithous and the Lapiths dragged him from the palace and cut off his nose and ears. Thus began the feud (νεῖκος) between the Lapiths and the Centaurs (*Od.* 21.291–306). Of course, Odysseus and the audience of the poem are in a position to appreciate the irony attending the telling of this story, for it is the suitors who have gone mad and are making unwanted advances toward the wife of another man. They also behave disgracefully at table, and they will soon receive punishment. Moreover, their deaths will give rise to a feud (νεῖκος, *Od.* 24.543) between Odysseus and their families. Dramatic irony here, I suggest, arises from Antinous' failure to overhear what he himself is saying.

Antinous' lack of success as a storyteller brings us to a consideration of a further and final type of self-overhearing that I wish to consider in conclusion. Does self-overhearing in any way manifest itself in the telling of a story within the *Odyssey*? What I mean can be seen with particular clarity in the stories told by Joseph Conrad's protagonist Marlow, perhaps Odysseus' greatest rival among literary characters (and sailors) as a teller of tales. In *Heart of Darkness*, Marlow relates the story of his journey along the Congo River to find a rogue company agent named Kurtz. The expedition itself teaches Marlow nothing, for as he says,

> I had no time. I had to mess about with white-lead and strips of woolen blanket helping to put bandages on those leaky steam-pipes – I tell you... There was surface truth enough in those things to save a wiser man.[44]

Nor does Marlow seem to discern through later acts of contemplation any deeper significance in events and things encountered during the expedition. Rather it is in the *telling* of the tale of his adventure that meaning begins to surface for him, however dimly he perceives it, as he listens to what he himself is saying. Thus, at one point he tells of how he first found his steamer at the bottom of the river before beginning the expedition from the company station:

I did not see the real significance of that wreck at once. I fancy I see it now, but I am not sure – not at all. Certainly the affair was too stupid – when I think of it – to be altogether natural. Still… But at that moment it presented itself simply as a confounded nuisance. The steamer was sunk.[45]

The telling of the tale leads Marlow to consider a possibility that never occurred to him at the time of the adventure: the sinking of the ship provides a marvelous metaphor for the journey that was about to take him into the heart of darkness.

While a *failure* to overhear the self in the act of narration can be clearly discerned in such stories as Antinous' pathetic little tale about the feud between the Lapiths and the Centaurs, the *presence* of self-overhearing in narration is nowhere so evident in the telling of the tale *of* the *Odyssey* by the poet, nor, as far as I can see, in the telling of tales *within* the *Odyssey*. In the stories told by Odysseus and others within the *Odyssey*, I can see no such obvious 'come-to-think-of-it' moments as Marlow experiences. Nonetheless, in the case of the poet himself, what cannot be directly deduced from the evidence at hand within the poem may possibly be at least inferred, if Lattimore is correct regarding ancient methods of literary composition. According to Lattimore's study of the structure of Herodotus' *History*, the ancients in general – including Homer, Hesiod, the elegiac poets, and even the philosophers – likely started at the beginning of a work and composed straight through to the end, employing a 'point-to-point' or progressive style that necessitated self-correction as the work progressed. Such a method of composition would not allow a literary artist – nor an oral poet – the opportunity to correct or revise a misstatement; he would have to correct himself later in the work (Lattimore 1953, 9–21). Lattimore provides abundant evidence of such 'correction-in-stride' in the work of Herodotus, and more recently Flory in an unpublished paper has argued that traces of such a method of composition can be discerned in the *Iliad* and *Odyssey* (1998). Though neither Lattimore nor Flory considers the implication I wish to draw from their work, such a practice would require a poet like the poet of the *Odyssey* to listen very carefully to what he himself was saying as the plot of his tale unfolded in order that he might be able later to correct misstatements as the work progressed. The evidence for such a method is by no means as conclusive for Homer as it seems to be for Herodotus, and the subject of self-overhearing in the act of narration obviously would require further study. Nonetheless, the possibility at least exists that when the poet of the *Odyssey* introduces himself as a narratee in line 1 of his poem he is cryptically referring to a practice of listening to *himself*.

Notes

[1] Gadamer would disagree. According to him, while the other senses afford only keys to their own specific fields, hearing is the only sense that has an 'immediate share in the universality of the linguistic experience of the world' (1975, 420). For Gadamer and other phenomenologists, hearing has priority over sight. Theophrastus, cited by Plutarch, offers the view that hearing is the most emotional of the senses, while Plutarch himself calls hearing more rational than emotional: see *De audiendo* (38a).

[2] As M. Parry pointed out in a discussion of the art of oral verse-making, 'there is no real memory without sound' (1971, 321).

[3] Garvie 1994, 250–1.

[4] Chatman 1990, 142.

[5] Throughout this paper I distinguish the poet of the *Iliad* from the poet of the *Odyssey* in the belief that the two works are the products of different artists or artistic traditions: see Pucci 1987, 17–18, especially n. 3.

[6] Or perhaps it is more correct to say that Odysseus is likened to a poet: see Rose 1992, 114–16, for Odysseus' likeness to a poet and for bibliography on his status as a self-reflexive counterpart of the poet of the *Odyssey*.

[7] On the other hand, Ledbetter argues that the voice of the Muses merges with the poet's voice (2003, 25). I would prefer, however, to take the poet at his word: the song of the *Iliad* is the song of the Muse. This is what the poet unambiguously asserts in the first line.

[8] Stewart sees the pronoun *moi* as a marker of the identity of the poet (1976, 187). I see it in addition as a designator of his role as narratee.

[9] Otto rightly says that, before singing, the human poet must first become a listener (*Hörender*): see Otto 1955, 71. While the poet of the *Iliad* describes himself as an audience of the Muses before the catalogue of ships (*Il.* 2.484), the poet of the *Odyssey* is concerned to emphasize his role as a listener in programmatic fashion in his prooemium.

[10] See Calame: 'Because of its syntactical form, the *I* is in the narratee's place and everything occurs as though the Muse-narrator were addressing her song to the *I*' (1995, 63). Of course, the idea of the poet as narratee may also be found in scattered, formulaic invocations to the Muses in the *Iliad* (*Il.* 2.484, 11.218, 14.508, 16.112), yet these isolated occurrences of the idea of a poet-narratee lack larger programmatic significance for the poem as a whole. The poet of the *Odyssey*, on the other hand, emphasizes the idea of the poet as narratee through contrast with the opening of the *Iliad*, emphatic repetition later in the prooemium, which we will discuss below, and elaboration throughout the poem of the theme of the power of creative listening.

[11] For the latter interpretation, see Stanford 1959, 208–9 and Latacz 1996, 135.

[12] For the importance of listening for Kerouac and Whitman, see Hyde 1979, 222. The second epigraph of this paper is taken from Whitman 1959, 51.

[13] Booth 1988, 184.

[14] Of course, the poet of the *Iliad* also groups himself with his audience in the invocation of the Muses in the catalogue of ships (*Il.* 2.485–6, cited above). But there the issue is the simple one of divine omniscience vs. human ignorance and, as I said above, lacks programmatic significance for the poem as a whole.

[15] Whitman 1959, 13.

[16] Quotation in this sentence is from Stewart 1976, 151. See also Crotty: 'In the

Odyssey song is a form of human speaking, and a good song naturally elicits an audience's praise' (1994, 123).

¹⁷ On this point, see Griffin 1987, 13 and Rabel 2002, 87.

¹⁸ For the performing poet's need to be attentive to his audience, see also Nagy 1996, 62.

¹⁹ Poet and critic James Fenton says that the first question he asks himself upon reading a poem is, 'How did it do that?' (2001, 101–2). This is precisely the question Odysseus and Alcinous ask. Goldhill takes Odysseus' and Alcinous' very different responses to Demodocus' song as testimony of 'the active work of the reader in the construction of meaning' (1991, 54).

²⁰ On this point, see Crotty 1994, 126 and Walsh 1985, 4.

²¹ It is not surprising that the *Odyssey* should place such a strong emphasis on the response of the audience: see Tompkins: 'When poetry takes its place parallel and in reciprocal relationship with other kinds of human activity, and when the author's relation to his audience is direct and intimate, audience response so crucially determines the nature and direction of literary activity that its importance is simply assumed' (1980, 213). The *Iliad*, on the other hand, which views itself as a product of divine knowledge and not human craft, places no emphasis on the importance of an interpretive act provided by the audience and even, as Ledbetter says, 'discourages interpretation' (2003, 39). I disagree, however, with Ledbetter's further contention that *both* the *Iliad and Odyssey* discourage the interpretation of the audience, for I see the *Odyssey* implying an aesthetic of poetic reception radically different from that of the *Iliad*.

²² So Walsh maintains that Odysseus and Alcinous manifest two distinct forms of poetics (1985, 5).

²³ See Pucci 1987, 231 *et passim* for a good account of the responsibilities of the audience as listeners and creators of meaning. For Alcinous and Odysseus as literary critics, see Rabel 2002.

²⁴ So Slatkin 1996, 229.

²⁵ So Pound spoke of Yeats in a conversation with Moore (1954, 225).

²⁶ The phrase 'intertextual debate' is taken from Dougherty (2001, 72–3). The polemical relationship between the *Iliad* and the *Odyssey* has been well documented by Pucci (1987). Cook claims that the *Odyssey* asserts its views and claims to greatness at the expense of the *Iliad* (1995, 10).

²⁷ Reucher 1989, 51; also see Frame: 'Circe's role in the *Odyssey* is to usher the hero into the underworld and to receive him back again from it' (1978, 48). According to Horkheimer and Adorno, Circe's foresight with regard to coming nautical difficulties 'lives on in the caricature of feminine wisdom' (2002, 57), just such wisdom, I suggest, as the Muse instantiates for the poet.

²⁸ In similar fashion, the Calypso episode might be taken as a complementary metaphor for poetic composition. As Dougherty points out, while Calypso provides the raw material for the hero's craft, Odysseus' skill transforms the cloth into sails, just as he creates a raft out of timber with the use of tools she provides (2001, 34).

²⁹ For the interpretation of Odysseus' 'swerve' away from the Sirens as a mark of the differences between the *Iliad* and *Odyssey*, see the remarks of Bloom on what he calls a 'strong poet's' *clinamen* or 'swerve' away from the work of his strong predecessors: 'A poet swerves away from his precursor by so reading his precursor's poem as to execute

a *clinamen* in relation to it' (1997, 14).

³⁰ Whitman 1959, 25. Interestingly enough, however, Whitman's phase of creative listening also takes place in the context of a scene redolent with images of the Underworld: for him, the grass in which he lies represents 'the beautiful uncut hair of graves' (1959, 30). In his poems, he sometimes felt surrounded by the spirits of dear friends, whether dead or alive: see Reynolds 1995, 263.

³¹ Page 1955, 36. Page also expresses surprise that the spirits seem so intent on reciting their pedigrees to Odysseus. But this is to ignore an important point made by Atwood: 'Hell is – presumably – the place where you are stuck in your own personal narrative forever' (2002, 174).

³² Hyde says that few literary artists have not had the sense that at least some element of their work comes to them from a source they do not control (1979, 144). For hero and poet, Circe and the Muse of the *Odyssey* seem to represent just this indeterminate element of outside control.

³³ So Dougherty says, speaking of the hero, 'Odysseus' poetic authority, after all, comes not from the Muses; rather, it is located in his own experiences and adventures overseas' (2001, 70).

³⁴ So Thornton 1970, 16–37 and Reucher 1989, 52. Burkert, speaking of the theory that shamanism may be the guiding principle, even the origin of storytelling, describes the ritual of the shaman in these terms: 'The shaman, in a state of ecstatic performance, acts out a quest of supernatural dimensions; he can ascend to heaven or go down to the netherworld; he meets with spirits, demons, and gods' (1996, 67). Burkert notes elsewhere what many scholars overlook: shamanism is a product of hunting societies and intimately bound up with animals (1979, 88). Circe's identification as mistress of animals may allow us then to identify her with the guardian spirit of the shaman, who often took the form of a woman: see Eliade 1964, 106–9.

³⁵ So M. Parry: 'Homer could only have learned his formulas by hearing them spoken in the full voice of those poets to whom he listened from his childhood' (1971, 322).

³⁶ Atwood 2002, 178.

³⁷ So Burckhardt 1998, 151.

³⁸ For the poem's celebration of intelligence, versatility, and patience see Clay 1983, 7.

³⁹ See Atwood 2002, 173. Also, see Murnaghan: '[l]istening to song involves a suspension of activity and a suspension of consciousness that makes those who do it resemble the dead' (1987, 151).

⁴⁰ See Bloom 2000, 145–8 and 1998, xvii.

⁴¹ For the normal operation of scenes of deliberation characterized by the verb μερμηρίζειν, see Russo 1992, 30. At *Od.* 17.235–8, however, Odysseus rejects two courses of action in regard to the reckless behavior of Melanthius in favor of a third alternative, simple endurance.

⁴² When Odysseus becomes the victim of dramatic irony, he tends to indulge in such irony at his own expense. Thus he tells the Phaeacians that, upon landing at Circe's island, he encouraged his men by telling them that they would not go down to the House of Hades before their time (*Od.* 10.174–5). Of course, as he well knew at the time of telling the tale, they would in fact descend to Hades immediately upon leaving Circe's island.

[43] See Bloom 2003, 144. In the case of Odysseus, Reucher rightly points out that, though the poet shows him operating in many situations, his being is essentially unknowable to us (1989, 7).

[44] Conrad 1983, 69–70.

[45] Conrad 1983, 49.

Bibliography

Arendt, H.
   1971   *The Life of the Mind: Thinking*, New York and London.
Atwood, M.
   2002   *Negotiating with the Dead: A writer on writing*, Cambridge.
Barmeyer, E.
   1968   *Die Musen: Ein Beitrag zur Inspirationstheorie*, Munich.
Bloom, H.
   1997   *The Anxiety of Influence: A theory of poetry*, 2nd edn, New York.
   1998   *Shakespeare: The invention of the human*, New York.
   2000   *How to Read and Why*, New York and London.
   2003   *Hamlet: Poem unlimited*, New York.
Booth, W.
   1988   *The Company We Keep: An ethics of fiction*, Berkeley, Los Angeles, and
           London.
Brilliant, R.
   1995   'Kirke's men: swine and sweethearts', in B. Cohen (ed.) *The Distaff Side:
           Representing the female in Homer's* Odyssey, New York and Oxford.
Burckhardt, J.
   1998   *The Greeks and Greek Civilization*, O. Murray (ed.), New York.
Burkert, W.
   1979   *Structure and History in Greek Mythology and Religion*, Berkeley.
   1996   *Creation of the Sacred: Tracks of biology in early religions*, Cambridge,
           Mass.
Buschor, E.
   1944   *Die Musen des Jenseits*, Munich.
Calame, C.
   1995   *The Craft of Poetic Speech in Ancient Greece*, trans. J. Orion, Ithaca and
           London.
Chatman, S.
   1990   *Coming to Terms: The rhetoric of narrative in fiction and film*, Ithaca and
           London.
Clay, J.S.
   1983   *The Wrath of Athena: Gods and men in the* Odyssey, Princeton.
Conrad, J.
   1983   *Heart of Darkness*, London.
Cook, E.F.
   1995   *The* Odyssey *in Athens*, Ithaca and London.
Crotty, K.
   1994   *The Poetics of Supplication: Homer's* Iliad *and* Odyssey, Ithaca.

de Jong, I.J.F.
2001   *A Narratological Commentary on the* Odyssey, Cambridge.
Doherty, L.E.
1995   *Siren Songs: Gender, audiences, and narrators in the* Odyssey, Ann Arbor.
1995a   'Sirens, muses, and female narrators in the *Odyssey*', in B.Cohen (ed.) *The Distaff Side: Representing the female in Homer's* Odyssey, New York and Oxford.
Dougherty, C.
2001   *The Raft of Odysseus: The ethnographic imagination of Homer's* Odyssey, Oxford.
Eagleton, T.
1983   *Literary Theory: An introduction*, Minneapolis and London.
Eliade, M.
1964   *Shamanism: Archaic techniques of ecstasy*, trans. W.R. Trask, New York.
Elledge, S. (ed.)
1975   *Paradise Lost*, New York and London.
Fenton, J.
2001   *The Strength of Poetry*, New York.
Flory, S.
1998   'Have we Homer's only draft?', Classical Association of the Middle West and South Annual Meeting, Charlottesville, Virginia.
Ford, A.
1992   *Homer: The poetry of the past,* Ithaca and London.
Frame, D.
1978   *The Myth of Return in Early Greek Epic*, New Haven and London.
Gadamer, H.-G.
1975   *Truth and Method*, New York.
Garvie, A.F.
1994   *Homer. Odyssey: Books vi–viii*, Cambridge.
Goldhill, S.
1991   *The Poet's Voice: Essays on poetics and Greek literature*, Cambridge.
Griffin, J.
1987   *Homer: The* Odyssey, Cambridge.
Hamburger, K.
1973   *The Logic of Literature*, 2nd, revised edn, Bloomington and London.
Holt, T.
1999   *Olympiad*, London.
Horkheimer, M. and Adorno, T.W.
2002   *Dialectic of Enlightenment: Philosophical fragments*, trans. E. Jephcott, Stanford.
Hyde, L.
1979   *The Gift: Imagination and the erotic life of property*, New York.
Latacz, J.
1996   *Homer: His art and his world*, trans. J.P. Holoka, Ann Arbor.
Lattimore, R.
1953   'The composition of the *History* of Herodotus', *Classical Philology* 53, 9–21.

Ledbetter, G. M.
    2003   *Poetics Before Plato: Interpretation and authority in early Greek theories of poetry*, Princeton and Oxford.
Lenz, A.
    1980   *Das Prooöm des frühen griechischen Epos*, Bonn.
Louden, B.
    1999   *The* Odyssey: *Structure, narration, and meaning*, Baltimore and London.
Montiglio, S.
    2000   *Silence in the Land of Logos*, Princeton.
Moore, V.
    1954   *The Unicorn: William Butler Yeats' search for reality*, New York.
Murnaghan, S.
    1987   *Disguise and Recognition in the* Odyssey, Princeton.
Nagy, G.
    1996   *Homeric Questions*, Austin.
Otto, W.F.
    1955   *Die Musen und der göttlische Ursprung des Singens und Sagens*, Düsseldorf and Cologne.
Page, D.
    1955   *The Homeric* Odyssey, Oxford.
Parry, M.
    1971   'Studies in the epic technique of oral verse-making. I. Homer and Homeric style', in A. Parry (ed.) *The Collected Papers of Milman Parry*, New York.
Prince, G.
    1980   'Introduction to the study of the narratee', in J.P. Tompkins (ed.) *Reader-Response Criticism: From formalism to post-structuralism*, Baltimore and London.
Pucci, P.
    1979   'The song of the sirens', *Arethusa* 12, 121–32.
    1987   *Odysseus Polutropos: Intertextual readings in the* Odyssey *and the* Iliad, Ithaca and London.
Rabel, R.J.
    2002   'Interruption in the *Odyssey*', *Colby Quarterly* 38, 77–93.
Redfield, J.
    1979   'The proem of the *Iliad:* Homer's art', *Classical Philology* 74, 95–110.
Reinhardt, K.
    1996   'The adventures in the *Odyssey*', in S.L. Schein (ed.) *Reading the Odyssey: Selected interpretive essays*, Princeton.
Reucher, T.
    1989   *Der unbekannte Odysseus: Eine Interpretation der* Odyssee, Bern and Stuttgart.
Reynolds, D.S.
    1995   *Walt Whitman's America: A cultural biography*, New York
Rose, P.W.
    1992   *Sons of the Gods, Children of Earth: Ideology and literary form in Ancient Greece*, Ithaca and London.

Russo, J., Fernández-Galiano, M. and A. Heubeck (eds.)
  1992   *A Commentary on Homer's* Odyssey. *Volume III: Books XVII–XXIV*, Oxford.
Rüter, K.
  1969   *Odysseeinterpretationen: Untersuchungen zum ersten Buch und zur Phaiakis*, Göttingen.
Segal, C.
  1994   *Singers, Heroes, and Gods in the* Odyssey, Ithaca and London.
Slatkin, L.
  1996   'Composition by theme and the mētis of the *Odyssey*', in S.L. Schein (ed.) *Reading the* Odyssey: *Selected interpretive essays*, Princeton.
Stanford, W.B.
  1959   *The* Odyssey *of Homer*, vol. I (Books I–XII), 2nd edn, London.
Stewart, D.J.
  1976   *The Disguised Guest: Rank, role, and identity in the* Odyssey, Lewisburg.
Thornton, A.
  1970   *People and Themes in Homer's* Odyssey, London.
Tompkins, J.P.
  1980   'The reader in history: the changing shape of literary response', in J.P. Tompkins (ed.) *Reader-Response Criticism: From formalism to post-structuralism*, Baltimore and London.
Vernant, J.-P.
  1996   'Death with two faces', in S.L. Schein (ed.) *Reading the* Odyssey: *Selected interpretive essays*, Princeton.
Walsh, G.B.
  1985   *Varieties of Enchantment: Early Greek views of the nature and function of poetry*, Chapel Hill.
West, M.L.
  1997   *The East Face of Helicon: West Asiatic elements in Greek poetry and myth*, Oxford.
Whitman, W.
  1959   *Leaves of Grass*, ed. M. Cowley, New York. First edn 1855.
Wilamowitz-Moellendorf, U. von
  1966   *Die* Ilias *und Homer*, 3rd edn, Berlin.

INDEX

Wikander, S. 16
Wilamowitz-Moellendorf, U. vii, x 169
Willcock, M. 67, 128
wind 6, 21, 23–9, 36–7, 39–40, 48, 74, 79,
   140, 149, 151, 162, 174–5
Wolf, F.A. vii
wrath, *see* anger
Wyatt, W. 86

Xanthus (river), 42

Xenophon 99

yawn 91

Zeus xiv, 13–16, 24–5, 28, 33–4, 36, 38–9,
   41–2, 47–8, 50, 58, 64, 95, 97, 99, 102,
   135–8, 141–3, 145, 148–50, 155–6,
   159–63, 172
   plan of 2–3, 40, 42, 50, 136

INDEX LOCORUM